Catho...
Ecumenical

Catholic and Ecumenical

History and Hope

Why the Catholic Church Is
Ecumenical and What She Is
Doing About It

Frederick M. Bliss, S.M.

SHEED & WARD
Franklin, Wisconsin

1999

Sheed & Ward
7373 South Lovers Lane Road
Franklin, Wisconsin 53132
1-800-558-0580

Printed in the United States of America

Cover and interior design: Scott Wannemuehler, GrafixStudio, Inc.

Cover and chapter opener art used with permission of the Orthodox Centre of the Oecumenical Patriarchate, Geneva, Switzerland and E. Tzaferis S. A., Athens, Greece

Library of Congress Cataloging-in-Publication Data

Bliss, Frederick M.
    Catholic and ecumenical: history and hope/Frederick M. Bliss,
        p. cm.
    ISBN 1-58051-056-6
    1. Christian union—Catholic Church—History. 2. Catholic
Church—Relations. I. Title.
BX1785.B57   1999
282—dc21   99–12580
                                          CIP

1 2 3 4 5 / 02 01 00 99

Contents

List of Abbreviations viii

Foreword ix

Introduction xv

Chapter 1: A Church to Change 1
  Church and Churches 3
  Families of Churches 5
    Provincial and Patriarchal Families of Churches 5;
    Arrival of East and West 7; Ecumenical Viewing of
    East-West Ecclesial Understandings 9
  Emergence of the Papacy 11
    Primacy Claim 12; Changing Role for Bishops 14;
    Changing Role for the Laity 15; Implications for
    Ecumenism 16; Ecclesiastical Writing and
    Liturgical Texts 17
  "No Salvation Outside the Church" 19
    Some Explanations from the Fathers 19; Teachings
    from Church Councils and the Papacy 21; The
    Teaching of Pius XII in Mystici Corporis Christi *22*
  The Catholic Culture 24
    The Catholic Subculture 24; Catholic Isolationism
    and Negativity 25

Chapter 2: A Changing Church 31
  Prophetic People and Movements 31
    Catholic Prophets of Unity 32; Prophetic
    Theologians at the Service of the Church 36;
    Movements Reaching into the Church 40
  Vatican II in Response 44

Chapter 3: Uniform No Longer 53
  Ecumenical Documents 53
  This Thing Called "Dialogue" 55
  Unity in Diversity: Scriptural Evidence 57
    Koinonia 58; Christ's Plan and Paul's
    Interpretation of It 59

Unity in Diversity: Patristic Evidence 60
Churches in Communion in Patristic Times 61;
Empire-wide Threats to the Communion 65

Chapter 4: Estranged Sisters 73
The Importance of Symbols 74
Catholic Arrival at a New Self-understanding 75
Document of the Preparatory Theological
Commission 75; Development in the
Commission's Thinking 76
Development of Contrasting Ecclesiologies 78
The "Universalism" of the East 78; The
"Universalism" of the West 79; Impact of
Contrasting Doctrinal and Nontheological Items 80
Attempts at Reconciliation: Eastern Catholic Churches . . 84
The Two Councils 84; Regional Reconciliations
and the Arrival of "Uniatism" 86; Eastern Catholic
Churches Today 87
The Orthodox Church 89
Orthodox-Catholic Dialogue Today 91
Two Churches Approaching Unity 91; The
Dialogue of Charity 93; Sister Churches 94;
The Dialogue of Doctrine 95

Chapter 5: Reform to Reformation 99
The Marks of the Church 99
Unitatis Redintegratio: The Church's Text on
Unity 100
Calls for Reform Before the Reformation 102
Individuals Calling for Reform 102; Groups
Calling for Reform 104; Theories about the
Nature and Mission of the Church 108; Reform
Calls Continue 109
The First Phase of the Reformation 111
Luther and the Birth of Lutheranism 111;
Lutheranism Today 114; International
Lutheran–Roman Catholic Dialogue 115
The Second Phase of the Reformation 119
Huldreich Zwingli and Martin Bucer 119;
Jean Calvin and John Knox 120;

Reformed/Presbyterianism Today 123;
Reformed–Roman Catholic Dialogue 124
The Third Phase of the Reformation 126
Beginnings of the Radical Reformation 126
The Fourth Phase: The Catholic Reformation 138
The Council of Trent 138; Robert Bellarmine 139

Chapter 6: Reformation in England 143
Which "Model of Church" Should Suit the Future? . . . 143
What Is the "Hierarchy of Truths"? 146
The Story of English Reform 148
First Stage: Designing a Change 149;
Second Stage: European Contributions 150;
Third Stage: Real Beginnings of the English
Reformation 151; Fourth Stage: Anglican Identity 153
The Anglican Communion Today 154
Anglican–Roman Catholic Dialogue 156
The Birth of Methodism 160
Work of the Wesley Brothers 161; Methodist
Churches Today 163; Methodist–Roman Catholic
Dialogue 164
The Arrival of Other Significant Churches 167
The Salvation Army 167; Evangelicals 169;
Evangelical–Roman Catholic Conversations 171;
Pentecostals 173; Pentecostal–Roman Catholic
Dialogue 174; Old Catholics 175

Chapter 7: Leaning Toward the Future 179
Strategies for the Future 180
United and Uniting Churches 181
Some Contemporary Problems 185
Agencies Working for Unity 187
Interreligious Dialogue 190
The Aim of Interreligious Dialogue 191; The
Catholic Understanding of Interreligious Dialogue
191; The Content of Interreligious Dialogue 192;
Some of the "Formal" Interreligious Dialogues 194

Endnotes 199

Index 231

List of Abbreviations

AAS	*Acta Apostolicae Sedis*
ARCIC	Anglican–Roman Catholic International Commission
BEM	Baptism, Eucharist, and Ministry (Lima Document)
BWA	Baptist World Alliance
CDF	Congregation for the Doctrine of the Faith
DH	*Dignitatis Humanae*
DS	Denzinger and Schönmetzer
DV	*Dei Verbum*
F&O	Faith and Order
GS	*Gaudium et Spes*
ILC	International Liaison Committee
IMC	International Missionary Council
JWG	Joint Working Group
LG	*Lumen Gentium*
L&W	Life and Works
LWF	Lutheran World Federation
NA	*Nostra Aetate*
OE	*Orientalium Ecclesiarum*
OR	*L'Osservatore Romano*
PCID	Pontifical Council for Inter-Religious Dialogue
PCPCU	Pontifical Council for Promoting Christian Unity
SPCU	Secretariat for Promoting Christian Unity
UR	*Unitatis Redintegratio*
UUS	*Ut Unum Sint*
WARC	World Alliance of Reformed Churches
WCC	World Council of Churches
WEF	World Evangelical Fellowship

Foreword

It is rare in the age of super specialization that we can find a work that has a wide range of accurate and useful information concerning the modern-day ecumenical movement. Father Fred Bliss presents us with a commanding *tour de force* of the whole ecumenical landscape in his *Catholic and Ecumenical: History and Hope*. Professor of ecumenism and ecclesiology in the ecumenical section of the Pontifical University of St. Thomas Aquinas known as "the Angelicum," the author demonstrates a maturity and depth of knowledge from his many years of teaching experience and introduces us to the complexities of the modern ecumenical movement and especially to the Catholic Church's engagement in this movement.

It becomes clear early on in the work that the author's balanced and impartial evaluation of the key moments in the history of the ecumenical movement comes from a broad knowledge of the sources and documents produced by the churches engaged in the search for Christian unity. But the book is no pure history book! Rather it is a theological history of ecumenism. The reader may ask why make such a distinction? For the simple reason that the book is constructed from the vantage of a theologian's point of view, namely from the theological starting point of koinonia or communion.

Many[1] have acknowledged that one of Vatican II's principal contributions to the ecclesial scene at the end of this century has been the re-employment of a theology of communion as the starting point for the evaluation of the structure and nature of the Church of Christ. Hence Bliss begins his analysis of the search for unity among Christians with the very formation of the Church as the realization of a communion of churches and of the issues that arise out of the delicate nature and balance of relationships that need to exist within this communion.

Father Bliss crafts his text with a clear and precise style but without compromising the necessary nuances and subtleties which are needed for a theological heuristic construct. In the first two chapters, he sets the scene for what will be the birth of the ecumenical movement in the second half of the twentieth century. He has the obvious objective of presenting a clear picture of the evolution of the Catholic Church especially in its Latin Western form. In so doing he does not avoid the thorny issues surrounding the development of the papacy nor the unfortunate schism between East and West. Moreover, by identifying the theological issues and problems underlying the schism, he confronts them straight on. This later theme is taken up again in a more complete theological critique in chapter four entitled "Estranged Sisters." Throughout we can find a blend of historical information coupled with a concise theological analysis. This period of Church history is extremely important not only for the development of a theology of communion in theory but especially in practice. From his examples we may come to appreciate the grandeur of the delicate balance of the theology of *koinonia* as it begins to take shape in the lives of individual churches and eventually its misery as it begins to splinter when churches begin to drift apart, living more and more in isolation from one another and beginning to act unilaterally. Without being simplistic, Bliss honestly looks at the failures on both sides of the divide which begins to widen starting with Christmas 800, and the unilateral decision of the Western church to crown Charlemagne Holy Roman Emperor. We all know only too well how this terminates in the tragic events of 1054 when the estrangement of sister churches became official. This event of history is not an irreversible one, but it is one which requires much patience and charity: Today it is in the process of being turned around. Ever so slowly (and not without pain) the Church is learning to breathe with her "two lungs" once again.

While not analyzing the full contents and all of the events of Vatican II, Bliss seriously considers the relevant texts of the Council which are germane to his project. He shows how the Church, in obedience to Christ's will 'that all may be one that the world may believe', has been moved by the Spirit to an awareness of the need to actively seek the re-establishment of full communion with other churches. In this context, Father Bliss looks at the concrete contribution that both individuals and movements have made to this search (chapter two). It becomes clear that the determination but also obedience of people like Père Congar was the fruit of the Spirit of prophecy in this century. Often these individuals suffered personally for their convictions. Nevertheless, their persistence can be seen with hind sight as also the work of the Spirit. These pioneers blazed trails for many of the Council fathers who would put the Catholic church on the path to Christian unity.

Father Bliss presents a very general overview of the positions of the Reformation both on the Continent and in the British Isles. In the contexts of each phase of the Reformation, Bliss shows the link that existed between the principles of the individual reformers or reformation wings within the Church and the contemporary dialogues that have been established since the conclusion of Vatican II.

The need for the reform of the church's structures is put into its historical and theological context by looking for those pre-reformation movements within the Catholic church. Such individuals and movements contributed to an atmosphere that existed within the church that would eventually lead to the Catholic reformation at Trent. Unfortunately this reform came too late and was far too cautious (remember it took some twenty-five years to get things moving at Trent!). In chapters five and six of his survey, Father Bliss explores the full gamut of Reformed positions: from Martin Luther to the Seventh-Day Adventists. In short, Bliss has attempted to present the full ecclesial situation of all churches actively engaged in ecumenical dialogues today, even those only hesitatingly so.

Bliss brings his work to a close (or rather to the opening of a new frontier) by looking at what the future might hold for the churches in their attempt to conquer the divide! In his last chapter the progress being made by church mergers and union schemes is studied. Moreover, in this section he takes a closer look at the workings and roles to be played by the World Council of Churches and the Pontifical Council for Promoting Christian Unity. To complete the picture, Bliss takes a sweeping look at the interreligious dialogues currently in progress. While not properly belonging to a study on ecumenism, the interreligious dialogue provides important information for the ecumenical dialogues especially in the area of clarification of certain key concepts which have been challenged by our interfaith relationships with other religions.

Documentation

This general overview of the ecumenical movement will not only adequately introduce the reader to the history, theology, and actuality of the search for Christian unity but will allow for a further deepening of the facts, issues, problems and proposed solutions. Bliss has provided an up-to-date documentation of the more important works in his notes. Without being overly technical or too generic, the sources permit continued personal study. In short, what we have here is a well balanced introduction to the issues of ecumenism today in their historical and theological context. The already initiated will likewise profit from the new insights into the ecumenical movement offered by the author. These provide the incentive to deepen an appreciation of the need to go forward on the path to Christian unity.

—James F. Puglisi, S.A.
Centro Pro Unione
Rome, Italy

*"Let us come together.
Let us make an end of our divisions."
(John XXIII)*

🔲 🔲 🔲

*The icon used on the cover and for
the chapter openers of this book is of the
two leading Apostles, Saint Peter and
Saint Paul, who are portrayed standing,
holding the Church in their hands while
above them Christ makes the sign of
benediction with both hands. The work is
by an accomplished painter and judging
from its style it should be assigned to the
seventeenth century. The icon, which
comes from the monastery of the Saviour
on the isle of Prinkipos, is found in the
second floor.*

Introduction

This book is written for ordinary people who want to understand why the Catholic Church decided to become ecumenical and what she is doing about it. It is widely known that great changes came upon this church as a result of the Second Vatican Council, but it is still not fully appreciated that the program first involved a refashioning of her self-understanding and, inevitably, of her relationships.

Those actually involved in the Vatican Council enjoyed an immense advantage over the rest of the Catholic and Christian world in coming to appreciate the processes that were at work. Before the opening of the council on October 11, 1962, for example, nearly four years of intensive work went into the preparation of papers on a broad range of themes. Add to that the years of the council itself, which closed on December 8, 1965. During those seven years, the participants enjoyed a singular experience of being a church in search of its identity.

The broad context of the participants' discussions was the discovery that the Catholic Church could no longer speak of her institutional boundaries as being the outer limit of every possible expression of "church." There were, they came to understand, forms of church in other Christian communities. This meant, of course, that relationships had to be named and cultivated.

The arrival at a conciliar statement about this renewed understanding of the church did not come easily. In fact, a network of documents was required to state as fully and accurately as possible the actual identity of the Church of Christ. The creation alone of the Decree on Ecumenism, *Unitatis Redintegratio,* extended over three years and involved intensive work by bishops and scholars whose suggested modifications added up to three volumes, for what came to be the three chapters of a twenty-five page official statement.

Chapter 1 of this book, titled "A Church to Change," is an overview of how the Catholic Church, in the course of time, narrowed the ecclesial (or church) definition to coincide with her own boundaries, thereby isolating her from other Christians and from the world. Chapter 2, "A Changing

Church," identifies those prophetic people and movements of the nineteenth and early twentieth centuries that challenged the Catholic Church to rethink her definition and to follow through on the consequences of the redefining. Chapter 3, "Uniform No Longer," suggests that true unity and uniformity are not to be confused. This chapter lays the scriptural and patristic foundations for a proper contemporary acknowledgment of a legitimate unity and diversity in the church.

Chapter 4, "Estranged Sisters," speaks about the eleventh-century rupture of the one church into two distinctive units, east and west. It sets a pattern, followed in the next two chapters, of examining the historical circumstances contributing to the east-west division, the advent of the Orthodox Church and its subsequent development, and the historical efforts undertaken to heal the breach. Particular focus is then given to the present-day ecumenical program that has been agreed upon by the Orthodox Church and the Catholic Church.

Chapter 5, "Reform to Reformation," names those people and movements that sought renewal of the church well before the Reformation. It examines the actual Reformation according to its four phases: Lutheran, Reformed, Radical, and Catholic. As in the previous chapter, some attention is given to the history of each phase and to an identification of the main churches and ecclesial communities that emerged in the Protestant Reformation. This chapter concludes with a study of the ecumenical efforts that are operating between each of them in their contemporary relationship with the Catholic Church. Chapter 6, "Reformation in England," follows the pattern of the previous two chapters.

The last chapter, "Leaning Toward the Future," considers a variety of proposals for shaping the work of the united church. It recognizes that problems still stand in the way of completing the unity program and so names several agencies dedicated to continuing the ecumenical task. Although not under the umbrella of "ecumenism," the matter of inter-religious dialogue is discussed, partly to complete this study of the Catholic outreach to church and world, but more importantly to encourage people to understand that ecumenism and inter-religious dialogue now belong to the church's fullest identity.

You will note that chapters 3, 4, 5, and 6 are prefaced by brief studies of documents, doctrines, or strategies. For example, ecumenical documents are named at the beginning of chapters 3 and 5; the variety of dialogues, symbols, and church models are described in chapters 3, 4, and 6; and the marks of the church and the hierarchy of truths are mentioned in chapters 5 and 6.

Given the breadth of material covered in this overview, it has not been possible to offer in-depth studies of the many subject areas that have been included. For those who want to pursue further reading, the entire text has been heavily footnoted, with the intention of offering study leads for serious students. Given the abundance of these references in the actual text, no bibliography has been included.

I wish to express thanks to those who helped me in the preparation of this work. I am most grateful for the encouragement and suggestions given me by friends and colleagues to proceed with the preparation of the book, and I am indebted to several students in Rome who, on many occasions, rescued me when the complexities of the computer world threatened to overwhelm me. I wish to thank in a special way Sister Monica Cooney SMSM, full-time Catholic consultant at the World Council of Churches in Geneva from 1990 to 1996, for her generosity in reviewing the entire text and suggesting changes, many of which I have incorporated into the finished product.

—Frederick M. Bliss, S.M.

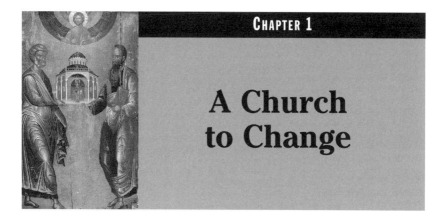

CHAPTER 1

A Church to Change

Catholic involvement in ecumenism is a recent phenomenon. Moreover, Catholic participation, although late, has been generally enthusiastic, including at the level of the bishop of Rome and the Pontifical Council for Promoting Christian Unity (PCPCU).

Entry into what is known as the "ecumenical movement" officially began with the Second Vatican Council. Well before the council, however, initiatives had already been taken, especially in the organizing of prayer programs for Christian unity. Father Paul Wattson,[1] for example, as far back as 1908, while still an Anglican, began the Church Unity Octave in Graymoor, New York. Also, there was the Frenchman, Abbé Paul-Iréné Couturier[2] who, in 1933, introduced in Lyon a triduum (three days) of prayer for church unity. Later in the decade, this became known as the Worldwide Week of Prayer for Christian Unity and continues to be celebrated in the northern hemisphere in January and in the southern hemisphere in July. This "spiritual ecumenism," which is the "soul of the whole ecumenical movement,"[3] was certainly an important prelude to the Catholic Church's eventual official entry into the ecumenical movement. Today, it is the vital accompaniment of all those who are intent on associating themselves with Christ in his prayer "that all may be one" (John 17:20).

1

Since the Catholic Church officially entered the movement, she has demonstrated a developing and deepening commitment to the work of Christian unity. Indicators of such a commitment include: the many dialogues that the Catholic Church has entered into with other Christian churches and ecclesial communities; the ever-deepening theological discussion and debate on the nature of ecumenism and indeed of the church itself; and the multiplicity of writings that have been issued, most especially from the bishop of Rome and the PCPCU. In May 1995, for instance, John Paul II wrote two important documents. The first of these was an Apostolic Letter, *Orientale Lumen*[4] (The Light of the East), in which the pope suggests that the time has arrived for the Orthodox Church and the Catholic Church to deepen their level of communion. This is certainly a significant statement given the lengthy cleavage between east and west spanning nearly a thousand years. The second was an encyclical on ecumenism, *Ut Unum Sint*[5] (On Commitment to Ecumenism), that calls on all Christian peoples and churches to renew their enthusiasm for the restoration of Christian unity. PCPCU has also contributed to these efforts by producing the 1993 *Directory for the Application of Principles and Norms on Ecumenism.*[6]

The recent official Catholic engagement in the movement, as well as the enthusiasm at the level of the leadership, prompts people to ask, "Why is it that, for so long, Catholics were anything but ecumenical? Why so late?" The answers, of course, are many and complex and are found in the tangles of history, which had the Catholic Church developing in isolation from other Christian communities. This isolationism bred a rather strong sense of structured self-sufficiency among Catholics, leading them to define other Christians as "non-Catholics," and members of other religions as "non-Christians." Increasingly, in the late nineteenth and early twentieth centuries, such thinking within Catholicism, alongside the self-imposed isolationism of the church, began to make less and less sense, not just to those beyond Catholic ranks, but most especially to committed Catholics. Action was called for.

A study of these contemporary developments will not make a great deal of sense without some consideration of their background. Hence, the rest of this chapter will focus on five themes: "church" understood as universal and local; the evolution of "families of churches"; the emergence of the papacy; the traditional teaching on "no salvation outside the church"; and a theory on the existence of a Catholic "culture."

Church and Churches

In 1984, eminent Scripture scholar Raymond E. Brown wrote a book titled *The Churches the Apostles Left Behind.*[7] In this work, Brown convincingly demonstrates that local apostolic churches had distinctive identities or personalities, while being noted for the obvious sense of oneness that existed among them. He shows that the very notion of "church" had both a local and a universal meaning. This is something many twentieth-century Catholics have not been used to; they have not associated the word *church* with their local community, such as the diocese. Rather, the Catholic experience has been of only one church, the universal church governed by the pope.

Father Brown explains that once the message of Jesus spread beyond Jerusalem, Christian assemblies, or congregations, came into existence and usually centered on a family home. Thus, 1 Corinthians 16:19 records a greeting from the churches of Asia: "Aquila and Prisca, together with the assembly that meets in their houses, send you cordial greetings in the Lord." Such assemblies were known as "churches," as is indicated in 1 Corinthians 11:16: "If anyone wants to argue about this, remember that neither we nor the churches of God recognize any other usage."

Some of these local churches were predominantly Jewish, others were Hellenistic. They were marked by their cultural inheritance, by the impact of their founders, and by the composition of their communities. In addition to their understandable and legitimate diversity as local churches, each felt a strong sense of belonging to the one church of Christ, and of the need to preserve their unity. In his letter to the Galatians, Saint Paul reminds his readers of the essential nature of this unity: "All of you who have been baptized into Christ have clothed yourselves with him. There does not exist among you Jew or Greek, slave or freeman, male or female. All are one in Christ Jesus." (3:27–28)

An important contemporary church body, the Pontifical Biblical Commission, recently undertook an in-depth study of the New Testament evidence of how "the Holy Spirit brought various local churches to form one communion in one single Church of Christ" (Preface). Their text, *Unity and Diversity in the Church,*[8] relates the New Testament facts to our present experience:

> The Church today is experiencing, more acutely perhaps than in former times, an uneasy tension; but it is a tension that ought to prove fruitful. Local churches, and even certain groups within them, are becoming ever more conscious of their distinctive characteristics within the universal church. There is a growing conviction that the grace of catholicity cannot unfold to its full extent unless a genuine diversity exists between the ecclesial communities within the same communion.

In the four centuries that followed the apostles, known as the patristic period, the fathers of the church—from Clement of Rome (c.94) to Jerome (340–420) and Augustine (354–430)—all testify to a diversity in unity among the local churches. Some of the Greeks, Athanasius of Alexandria (c.293–373) and Basil of Caesarea (c.329–379) for example, both of whom became dedicated bishops of their respective birthplaces, could recite the names of the other bishops throughout the entire Roman Empire, demonstrating their strong awareness of being part of a union or communion. Other bishops were known to have had a kind of register of the churches in the Christian world. Their express task, in addition to caring for their own churches, was the maintenance of "communion" with all these other churches. A common expression of this was the exchange of "letters of communion" among the bishops.[9] If a letter was received from a bishop not on the list—as happened frequently at the time of the Donatist heresy (fourth through the seventh centuries)— the letter would not be received because the bishop was outside the communion. That means he was outside the church.

It is important to take from the scriptural and patristic evidence that diversity is not an end in itself, nor are all forms of diversification good and valid. The Book of Acts, for example, allows for a wide variety in ecclesial organization and ministry, but there are limits, the ultimate test being the reception of one local church by another. If reception is denied, the offending church has obviously taken itself outside the bounds of the Church of Christ.[10] Legitimate diversity is an enrichment of unity, but there is such a thing as illegitimate diversity. Just as Clement of Rome chided the Corinthians for dismissing the presbyters,[11] that is, the lawful ministers in their church, so too, today: we find it difficult to accept precisely as "churches" those communities that are without the episcopal ministry.

Now that we are in an "ecumenical age" seeking to create a model of a united church for tomorrow's world, we must bear in mind the balance that the apostolic and patristic church sought in terms of unity and diversity. There is a major point of difference, however, between the situation of old and ours today. In apostolic and patristic times, it was a matter of living out the unity that already existed among the churches; today, the beginning point is disunity. Any attempt to reconstruct today's united church precisely on the model of the primitive church is entirely out of the question. There are, nevertheless, qualities that are certainly recoverable.

Families of Churches

With the conversion of Emperor Constantine (c.274–337) came a close association of the church and empire, which brought to the church two significant structural or administrative developments. The first related to the way the church became localized, and the second was connected with the gradual partitioning of the universal church into two blocs, east and west.

Provincial and Patriarchal Families of Churches

Geography, language, and a variety of other social forces influenced the creation of the empire's political divisions into provinces, or eparchies. The church's new identity, beyond having the regular local church boundaries—which today we call dioceses—involved the creation of larger units that coincided with the boundaries of the political provinces, a development that continued until about the year 400. The major city in each province became the see city, or ecclesiastical capital, of all the local churches and their bishops. In this way, new church entities, that is, ecclesiastical provinces, were created. The bishops of these see cities were known as "metropolitans," a title and function that remains to this day.

The same kind of political ranking that occurred among the cities happened ecclesiastically as well. Thus, Rome in the west and Antioch and Alexandria in the east were first accorded special status, as is acknowledged by the Council of Nicaea: "The ancient customs of Egypt, Libya, and Pentapolis shall be maintained, according to which the bishop of Alexandria has authority over all these places, since a similar custom exists with reference to the bishop of Rome. Similarly in Antioch and the other provices the prerogatives of the churches are to be preserved."[12] Jerusalem, despite its early decline as a place of Christian focus, was always viewed with respect, more so with the attention that Constantine gave to it and the place that pilgrimages played in its life. The consecration of Constantinople as the "New Rome," in 330, brought that city to a level of importance second only to Rome itself.

The bishops of these five cities were eventually named "patriarchs" because their powers extended well beyond their provinces. For example, beginning with the third century, Alexandria assumed responsibility for all the churches and bishops of Egypt, Libya, and Pentapolis; Jerusalem, although insignificant, was patriarchical over three Palestinian provinces; Constantinople, being the new Rome, became the pre-eminent patriarchical see for the whole of the east; and old Rome continued to exercise control over the entire west.

The grouping of churches into provinces with a metropolitan at the headship, or into the larger patriarchical federations under patriarchs, often developed into "rites," that is, "as a complete pattern of ecclesial life in a community."[13] Such rites had their own expressions of theology and liturgy, of spirituality and canonical system, with differences becoming quite evident among them.[14] In theology, for example, Alexandria and Antioch grew as two distinctive schools. Alexandria's theology followed the academic institutions of the city, which saw theology as an intellectual and philosophically based system. Antioch's theological preference, however, was strongly biblical.

Robert F. Taft says that the time after the peace of Constantine in 313 "is the period of unification of rites, when worship, like church government, not only evolved new forms, but also let the weaker variants of the species die out."[15] He goes on to explain that as the federations of churches (or families) developed, *unity within* particular federations increased, as did *diversity among* them. This was true not just in liturgical matters but across the board. The impact on the universal church was not one of uncontrolled diversification, but of unification, as the arrival of the five patriarchates testifies.

These five sees—Rome, Alexandria, Antioch, Jerusalem, and Constantinople—under their patriarchs, were seen by the Council of Chalcedon (451) "as sharing between them the oversight and a measure of jurisdiction over the whole of the known world,"[16] according to the system of government known as the "pentarchy" or "the rule of the five."

Arrival of East and West

Rome clearly emerged as the undisputed leader in the west, but Constantinople, the "New Rome," began to enjoy preeminence throughout the whole of the east. The old Rome's undisputed prominence was expressed in and through the Latin rite, while Constantinople's became evident through the Byzantine rite,[17] although never to the point of displacing the other eastern rites. All of the patriarchates freely chose their own patriarchs who, in turn, consecrated the metropolitans and laid down regulations for clerical and lay conduct within their territories.

It was the ascendancy of Rome and Constantinople that became a new focus. On the one hand, there was the Roman claim, going beyond simple patriarchal authority in the west, to an understanding that it had a ministry of unity to the universal church. On the other hand, there was the eastern reaction to this, expressed particularly by Constantinople which, according to Eric G. Jay, "had no desire to challenge the primacy of the see of Rome, but steadily resisted western attempts to translate primacy into a supremacy over the whole Church."[18]

Political and cultural factors also served to emphasize the growing ecclesiastical cleavage between east and west. The political initiatives of Diocletian (245–316), in dividing the empire into two parts, and Constantine's duplication of the capital cities underpinned the emergence of two cultures, particularly regarding "two ways of being the church."[19]

These two ways of being "church" inevitably led to different approaches in understanding the church's unity. In the east, the presence of several patriarchates, which included churches of apostolic origin, meant that no one bishop was able to claim absolute preeminence over the rest. Church unity "had to consist in the unity of several patriarchates."[20] In the west, however, the point of focus of the whole church was the one western patriarch, the bishop of Rome, who was also the successor of Peter the apostle. In this context it is worth quoting Joseph Ratzinger's assessment:

> The distinct claims of apostolic presidency and of patriarchal competence become, as in the case of Rome versus Constantinople, a competition between two patriarchates, whereby the real question is mistaken on *both* sides. The tragedy of the whole affair is that Rome was unable to separate its apostolic commission from the essentially administrative ideas of the patriarchate. Its claim, therefore, took a form in which it was unacceptable to the East.[21]

Of interest to us in this particular section is not the east-west debate so much as the two patterns of churches that developed and the self-understandings of each of them. Whereas the churches of the east placed great store by the "local church," be it expressed at the diocesan, provincial, or patriarchal levels, the church of the west had an eye to being the "universal church" under the leadership of the bishop of Rome. To this day, eastern orthodox churches still take the names of territories or of peoples—of Serbia, Greece, Cyprus, for example—and it is in these home churches that the strengths of orthodoxy continue to exist. The church of the west, conscious of the need to take the gospel to the ends of the earth, very early on became noticeably more outward-looking or missionary. As a result, the Church of Christ has been taken into territories as yet not developed, and into the new world, as discoveries were made there—according to the western understanding of the church.

In a word, we are faced with two models of church: one observably emphasizing localness in a variety of expressions, the other stressing universality. Is there an ecumenical value to be found here?

Ecumenical Viewing of East-West Ecclesial Understandings

Without a doubt, east and west are very important to each other, not just because their eventual reunion would remove another scandal from Christian witness in the world, but also because of the enrichment they already bring to each other. The west benefits by the eastern stress on local church; the east is reminded of the importance of the universal church.

But further steps can be taken to reduce tension points. Bearing in mind John Paul's invitation to "Church leaders and their theologians"[22] to engage with him in a dialogue about his ministry in the church, an important preliminary step might focus on a serious reappraisal of the patriarchal function of the bishop of Rome. The fact is that this precise ministry has not been taken seriously in the west. The roles of the bishop of Rome—as Rome's bishop, as the patriarch of the west, and as the primate of the universal church—have more often than not all been subsumed under the latter. Distinctions among these roles need to be made, and visibility given to the patriarchal task within the Latin Church. If the east finds this happening, they will see implied in the action, at least, a growing respect for the patriarchal concept that is so important to them. Joseph Ratzinger's assessment is worth bearing in mind:

> The extreme centralization of the Catholic Church is due not simply to the Petrine office but to its being confused with the patriarchal function which the bishop of Rome gradually assumed over the whole of Latin Christianity. Uniformity of church law and liturgy and the appointment of bishops by Rome arose from the close union of these two offices. In the future they should be more clearly distinguished.[23]

A final observation pertains to the type of union that will occur when the Reformation churches of the sixteenth century and the Catholic Church establish full communion with one another. In the one church, as history demonstrates, there is room for a variety of expressions of "church." There is little reason, then, why the Anglican Communion and the Reformation churches should not be considered for patriarchal status in a united church. The advice of Pope Saint Gregory the Great (c.590–604) to Augustine of Canterbury (d.604) demonstrates a breadth of vision that should well be part of the contemporary ecclesial scene. Their communication continued this way:

> Augustine's second question. Even though the faith is one, are there varying customs in the churches? and is there one form of mass in the Holy Roman Church and another in the Gaulish churches?
>
> Pope Gregory answered: My brother, you know the customs of the Roman Church in which, of course, you were brought up. But it is my wish that if you have found any customs in the Roman or the Gaulish church or any other church which may be more pleasing to Almighty God, you should make a careful selection of them and sedulously teach the Church of the English, which is still new in the faith, what you have been able to gather from other churches. For things are not to be loved for the sake of a place, but places are to be loved for the sake of their good things. Therefore, choose from every individual Church whatever things are devout, religious, and right. And when you have collected these as it were into one bundle, see that the minds of the English grow accustomed to it.[24]

In an address given at Cambridge, England, on January 18, 1970, Jan Cardinal Willebrands, then president of PCPCU, quoted the above passage from Bede, commenting that "it seems to me that Pope Gregory, in his famous letter to Augustine, Archbishop of the English nation, opened the way for a new *typos* of the Church in western countries."[25] The cardinal went on to say that the church actually needs a variety of *typoi* because, in this way, the breadth of the church will become more apparent, and she will be rendered more effective. Theologian Yves Congar is in agreement, "given that the axis of Christian faith is assured, one can accept various expressions of it." He wisely adds: "The formula seems ideal; the problems arise when it is put into practice."[26]

It is worth noting at this juncture that two prominent churchmen so far cited in this book, Cardinal Ratzinger and Cardinal Willebrands, have reminded the Catholic world of the importance of thinking more broadly about the church's visible identity. Cardinal Ratzinger spoke of the Catholic Church's "extreme centralization" due to a confusion of the bishop of Rome's petrine and patriarchal functions, which implies, to say the least, that more than one patriarchate can function in the west. Cardinal Willebrands, for his part, is quite explicit about the potential for the western church to be enriched by a multiplicity of *typoi* of churches. An Indonesian Catholic diocese thinks along the same lines, requesting that the 1998 Synod for Asia held in Rome "should explore the possibility of an East Asian Patriarchate endowed with similar autonomy to the patriarchates of the Eastern Churches in communion with Rome." The statement continues: "This would relativise the primacy of the 'Western Church,' and would help the Asian Churches to earth themselves in the local cultures."[27]

It is incumbent upon all of us, therefore, to think beyond the present reality of the church's identity, to the legitimate possibilities for the one church of the future. This is what it means to have an ecumenical spirit, to be of a mind that our task is to continuously ask the Spirit, on behalf of the church, "for the grace to strengthen her own unity and to make it grow towards full communion with other Christians."[28] How that fullness will find expression is a matter for the future.

As we move deeper into the ecumenical age, with all its imperatives, it will be important to draw on history as we contribute to the fashioning of the church of our times, and for each of us to strenuously work for unity, but not for uniformity.

Emergence of the Papacy

The development of a special ministry of headship and leadership by the bishop of Rome was gradual. The first signs of such a ministry date from the second century, when the Roman bishop occasionally arbitrated in disputes among Christians. Instances of interventions include: Clement I (+ c.101), who wrote on behalf of the church of Rome to the Corinthians disapproving of the dismissal of their presbyters; and Victor I (+ 198), more vigorous than Clement, who threatened to break communion with the churches of Asia Minor when they indicated their reluctance to accept the Roman preference for the dating of Easter.

Primacy Claim

The first known claim to a Roman primacy was made by Stephen (254–257), who also contemplated breaking communion with the churches of Asia Minor for rebaptizing heretics. Using Matthew 16:18f, he spoke of himself as Peter's successor and as leader of all the churches. Then there was Damasus I (366–384), Siricius I (384–399), and Innocent I (401–417), each of whom contributed to a developing theological justification for the position. In many of his letters and sermons, Leo I (440–461) argued that Peter enjoyed precedence over the other apostles, that he was the first bishop of Rome, and that his successors were Peter's vicars. Gregory I (590–604), although he referred to himself as the "servant of the servants of God" and saw authority as something to be exercised in humility and service, was also a promoter of the link between the pope and Peter.

Without an imperial presence in the west—despite an increasingly strong papal leadership such as that exercised by Leo and Gregory—the popes began to assume total western power, spiritual and temporal. This peaked with the crowning of Charlemagne by Leo III in 800, the pope being seen as the one who could both give and take away authority.

The medieval popes were clear and emphatic about their roles. Gregory VII's (1073–1085) famous *Dictatus papae* (Rescripts of the pope) listed twenty–seven propositions in which he claimed sovereign rights over the church and over kings and their kingdoms. Boniface VIII (1294–1303), in *Unam sanctam* (There is only one, holy, catholic, and apostolic Church), declared that all must submit to the Roman pontiff in order to attain salvation.

It was clearly the Roman mind that papal authority extended beyond spiritual matters, into temporal affairs—the emperor, for example, being almost the delegate of the pope. But in the thirteenth and fourteenth centuries, a growing nationalism began to signal to Rome the beginnings of what would be the end of papal authority in temporal matters, something that would certainly be achieved by the end of the fifteenth century. There was a new pride ready to defy the church when "whole nations, even those willing to admit guidance in the spiritual realm, were not willing to admit any papal prerogatives in the political arena."[29] This was the eve, it must be remembered, of the Protestant Reformation, when the reformers in their respective nation states would more often than not successfully ally themselves with the political leaders for the furtherance of their own ends.

Trent, in response to the reformers, continued a policy of emphasizing the place of a centralized church ruled from the top. Temporal controls would not be part of the papal mandate, although, when Robert Bellarmine (1542–1621) wrote in his *Disputations against the Heretics of the present time on the Controversies regarding the Christian Faith* (often referred to simply as *The Controversies*) that the pontiff "does not directly and immediately possess any temporal power." According to Jay, his text was nearly placed on the Index of prohibited books by Sixtus V, precisely because of this statement.[30]

The exercise of temporal power by the papacy would eventually die, although papal ecclesial leadership knew only an ascendancy, for as Richard McBrien says:

> The pope was now regarded as a "universal bishop." Each Catholic was directly under the pope and subservient to him, even more than to the individual Catholic's own bishop. The shift of all significant power to Rome occurred at an accelerated pace. Ecclesiastical authority became increasingly centralized. And people were asked to obey because of the status and office of the legislator, not because he and his decrees were obviously prompted by the Spirit. The definition of papal primacy at Vatican I was the culmination of this development.
>
> This understanding of authority prevailed until the Second Vatican Council. Indeed, it could be argued that the so-called Pian popes (Pius IX, Pius X, Pius XI, and Pius

XII) were among the most administratively powerful in all of church history.[31]

It may seem a simplification but the fact is that as papal temporal preoccupations lessened, papal focus on ecclesial life became more intensive. This focus was essentially western, strongly centralized, and pertained to a church that was understood as universal and wholly papal. As a side effect, the proper functioning of two important groups within the church was adversely affected: the bishops and the laity. There are continuing important ecumenical implications in all of this.

Changing Role for Bishops

The early church structure, it must be recalled, provided for bishops to be elected not merely as heads of particular communities, but into a college that was concerned about the whole church. To bring out this collegial dimension of the church, the custom grew—and later became law at the Council of Nicaea— of having at least three bishops co-consecrate a new bishop.

But the heavy focus on papal primacy from about the time of Gregory VII (1073–1085) until the first Vatican Council (1869–1870), with its definitions of primacy and infallibility, suggested that the pope's jurisdiction entitled him to act as if there was no such body as a college and that bishops were, in fact, simply his delegates in the dioceses around the world. Even at Vatican II, certain council members were suspicious of the notion—even vehemently opposed to the possibility—that collegiality could provide a better environment in which the papacy should function.[32]

Over many centuries, then, the story of the western church unfolds as one in which bishops were seen not as the vicars of Christ within their local churches in communion with Rome, but as vicars or delegates of the bishop of Rome, serving the one universal church or society. There was, for example, Hincmar, Archbishop of Rheims (845–882), who resisted ongoing papal interference in matters that regularly would have been decided at the level of the episcopate. He was of the opinion that the college of bishops should be active in the life of the church and not reduced to a passive papal instrument. Hincmar believed the papacy to be of divine institution, although papal decisions must be in conformity with Scripture and with canon law, which arises out of the ecumenical councils. It is in these councils that the bishops carry out their essential collegial task, expressing most effectively the mind of the church.[33]

Not until Vatican II would we get a definition of the identity of local bishops within their particular churches, and a clarification of the notion of the "college of bishops" as having a function within and on behalf of the church universal. Beyond Vatican II, the teasing–out continues regarding the full implications of the fact "that the episcopal college is not external to the papacy; it is a conditioning environment which helps define the nature of the papal role."[34]

Changing Role for the Laity

The early church, dispersed locally, was deeply conscious of being a "community" within which people enjoyed roles that allowed them to fully participate in the building up of the body of the church. Although distinctions were not paramount, participation, or *koinonia*, was highly significant. But before and especially in the Middle Ages, distinctions came to be made between those who were "of the world," that is, concerned about profane affairs, and those who were "of the church," detached from the world and dedicated to spiritual matters. The monks and the clergy, who were the "church," ministered to those of the world, who had about them "a religious element in an otherwise neutral life."[35] Liturgically, for example, it became abundantly clear that the clergy were the active church members, and the laity were "hearers."

Whereas the Reformation brought a level of "emancipation" for Protestant laity, the Catholic pattern was one of a continuing heavy clericalization of the church, so much so that the word "church," according to Congar:

> ...is sometimes understood by the theorists of ecclesiastical power or papal authority as indicating clerics, priests, and the pope. This use of the word was completely unknown to the Fathers and the liturgy. It is a fact that in a large number of modern documents, the word *Church* indicates the priestly government or even quite simply this government's Roman courts.[36]

The long silence of the laity in the life of the church began to break in the early twentieth century when Catholic laypeople in Europe sought a more active role in church and society. Dispirited with the obvious ineffectiveness of their clerically dominated church, in terms of its total mission of relating to and having an effective presence in a strife-torn world, Christian Europe had just emerged from one world war and was on the brink of another. In that climate, the Italian Catholic Action movement, which was implicit in Pius XI's (1922–1939) 1922 encyclical titled *Ubi Arcano Dei* (On the Peace of Christ in the Reign of Christ), earned definition by him in the 1931 encyclical *Non abbiamo bisogno* (On the Apostolate of the Laity) "as the participation and collaboration of the laity with the Apostolic Hierarchy."[37] Through this writing, the Italian-inspired response to the world was extended to the whole of the church, and many laypeople were energized by it.

In hindsight, however, it is clear that the promotion of Catholic Action was a gesture to the laity, and a specially guarded one. According to the understanding of Pius XI, the priest, not the laity, was the soul of Catholic Action. The wait was until Vatican II, in particular its *Apostolicam Actuositatem* (The Decree on the Apostolate of the Laity) to find an express and positive recognition of their role in the church, arising out of their baptism and confirmation.

Implications for Ecumenism

It is the belief of the Catholic Church "that she has preserved the ministry of the Successor of the Apostle Peter, the Bishop of Rome, whom God established as her 'perpetual and visible foundation of unity,'"[38] and that it is the task of Peter's successors "to ensure the communion of all the Churches."[39] This means, of course, that in the work for the unity of all the churches, an essential ingredient in the ultimate "unity formula" has to be the role of the bishop of Rome in the united church. Furthermore, the position he will occupy cannot be reduced simply to a position of honor.

Beyond this Catholic belief is the Catholic experience that the church has been well served by the bishops of Rome. This is succinctly and wisely stated by Yves Congar: "We should

note at this point that if Rome succeeded in obtaining, over
and above her power, the *authority* of her primacy, it was in
large part due to the value and the wisdom of her answers to
all the questions which were put to her from every region of
Christendom. Genuine authority is moral authority."[40]

Although it is important to remember that Rome has never
succeeded in imposing Roman primacy over the entire church,
there have indeed been experiences of excessive use of authority. In the contemporary scene, we are also aware that dialogue
with other churches, despite all agreements reached in a variety of areas, has left acceptance of the Roman primacy an enor-
mous problem. By the same token, it has to be acknowledged
that "authority" is not just a Catholic problem; all Christian
churches continue to grapple with authority. It is a problem of
universal dimensions.

What Catholics and their dialogue partners need to realize
is that in the united church there is not one singular way in
which all the sectors of the Christian church should relate to
the bishop of Rome. Our previous considerations testify to this
and suggest avenues that we must continue to explore.

Ecclesiastical Writing and Liturgical Texts

The emerging imbalances and stresses that came to characterize the church were reflected in both the writings about
the church and in the religious texts that were in use following
the Council of Trent (1545–1563) and Vatican I (1869–1870).
One writer, Giles of Rome, (c.1243–1316), described the relationship of the church and the bishop of Rome in these terms:
*Summus pontifex qui tenet apicem ecclesiae et qui potest dici
ecclesiam* ("The supreme pontiff who is at the summit of the
church and who, in fact, can be called the church").[41] Another
theologian, James of Viterbo (1255–1308), who produced the
first known writing on the church as such (*De regimine
Christiano*), not only dedicated the work to the bishop of Rome,
but particularly stressed the church's power and its government. More than two centuries later, after the Reformation,
Robert Bellarmine (1542–1621) penned a theology of the
church, the chief ideas of which have stayed with us into the
twentieth century. This work, *De controversiis christianae*

fidei,[42] referred to earlier, stressed both the visibility of the church and its leadership, most especially its Roman headship. Peter's power was directly transmitted to the Roman bishop, whereas the bishops of the world received authority in their dioceses by delegation from Rome, not as successors of the apostles.

The same strong Roman focus became particularly evident in the teaching and liturgical texts of the western church. Following the Council of Trent, Pius V (1566–1572) published the *Roman Catechism for Pastors*, the *Roman Breviary*, and the *Reformed Roman Missal*, while Paul V (1605–1621) issued the *Roman Ritual*.

The use of the word *universal* as descriptive of the church at this time has to be understood. It did not mean that Christ's church had necessarily spread into every sector of the globe. Rather, the European, Roman cultural experience of being church was present in many parts of the western world. In his "lifeline" of the church, Karl Rahner[43] identifies three epochs:

> From the theological standpoint, we can say that there are three great epochs in church history, the third of which has only just begun and was authoritatively brought to notice at Vatican II: 1. The short period of Judaeo-Christianity; 2. The period of the Church in a particular cultural group, that of Hellenism and European culture and civilization; 3. The period in which the Church's living space is from the very outset the whole world.

The first of these, from about 32 to 100 A.D., saw the proclamation of Jesus, his death, and his resurrection as being done "in Israel and to Israel." Paul's mission began the radically new and second epoch of Christian history, "a Christianity that grew out of the soil of paganism." Rahner explains that such a major transition in the history of Christianity is happening now, and only for the third time, as the Christian church of Europe becomes "an actual world religion." The extensive period of a mainly gentile church meant that wherever the church existed, she was recognizably western, European, and Roman. Her ways of celebrating and speaking, of ministering and ruling, of meeting and reaching authoritative decisions, of dressing and honoring ministers, were clearly European and Roman.

At Vatican I (1869–1870), for example, not one indigenous bishop from either Africa or Asia was present. Rather, each of these continents was represented at the council by western missionaries. The first Chinese bishop was appointed in 1926, the first Japanese bishop was appointed in 1939, and the first Indian bishop was appointed after the Second World War. John XXIII created the first local African cardinal in 1960, and Paul VI created the first Pacific Island cardinal in 1973.

All these various emphases, which came to characterize the church, also pointed to certain neglects and needs for change. Where jurisdictional and visible concerns become a preoccupation, the spiritual can be overlooked or underestimated. For example, when the church is increasingly recognized simply by its head, then the body's place and purpose will be neglected, and rarely understood or appreciated. Where the church is defined as clerical, the laity is certain to be relegated to an unimportant and uninvolved level. When the church universal, and Rome, commands center stage, then local churches and their bishops assume secondary roles.

Vatican II announced the transition of the church from being so identifiably western to being a world church. In the light of this explanation, the title of this chapter—A Church to Change—should begin to make a little more sense. Yet, before we can delve into Vatican II and the ecumenical outreach it initiated within the Catholic Church, there are other important historical items that need to be investigated.

"No Salvation Outside the Church"

To grasp Catholic teaching and practice concerning the salvation of people traditionally called "non-Catholics," we need a brief historical overview. As will become evident, the doctrine that evolved profoundly affected Catholics in their relations with all people in the world, and it was not until the Second Vatican Council that the need for a radical restatement became obvious, and was actually addressed.

Some Explanations from the Fathers

The famous phrase "outside the church there is no salvation" can be traced back to Ignatius of Antioch (+ c.110), for whom "willful and guilty separation from the Church is clearly the reason for exclusion from salvation,"[44] and to Origen[45] (c.185–254), whose thought on the matter was not always clear. Further development of this teaching as part of Catholic belief belongs to other Fathers of the church, notably Cyprian, John Chrysostom, and Augustine. A concern of the times was the relationship of the church and salvation, and in particular the question of the extension of salvation to Gentiles and Jews. Often enough, an elaboration of the theology was prompted by the challenges coming from schismatic and heretical groups.

Cyprian (c.200–255), for example, had to contend with the Novationists who so exaggerated the church's "mark" of holiness that they ended up defining the church in terms of the holiness of her members. According to them, only holy people made up the church. Inevitably, the Novationists developed into a distinct sect, which led Cyprian to teach that unity with the bishops was foundational to both the church's identity and the right of her members to salvation. Beyond this recognition of church, according to Cyprian, there was only "nonchurch."

John Chrysostom (c.347–407) was also forthright as to who enjoyed both church membership and the possibility of salvation. Because of those people in his own community who considered him to be too severe, Chrysostom formulated precisely their question and answered it. Why are pagans and Jews not recipients of the salvation Christ has won for all? Because they freely choose not to believe. Chrysostom, like most church leaders of his time, understood that all people, even Jews and pagans, had been given the opportunity of hearing the gospel, but had rejected it and thus were guilty. Their fate was in their own hands.

Augustine (354–430) had to face many challenges, such as those from the Donatists who were noted for their puritanical outlook, including a view which said that sacraments celebrated by priests who collaborated in persecutions were invalid. Augustine also had to deal with the Pelagians, those who rejected the doctrine of original sin and insisted that divine grace is given in proportion to human merits, man having an innate capacity to do good. While Augustine agreed with Cyprian's teaching on "no salvation outside the church," he adopted a more pastoral and conciliarity approach to the Donatists, recognizing their sacraments as valid. Despite their errors, he said, the validity of their sacraments placed them in a kind of dormant relationship with the church. Their sacraments would once again become life-giving only upon their reconciliation with the church. It was during his dealings with the Pelagians, however, that Augustine started to take a much firmer line. Unbelievers, he said, even those who had never heard of the gospel, were beyond the bounds of the church and the possibilities of salvation.[46]

Teachings from Church Councils and the Papacy

The central core of the patristic teaching persisted for many centuries, eventually to find further elaboration in conciliar and papal settings. The Fourth Lateran Council (1215), for example, was quite emphatic: outside the church, "no one at all is saved." Innocent III (1198–1216) gave an added twist, so to speak, to what church membership meant. For him, a significant component of "church membership" involved submission to the bishop of Rome. Boniface VIII (1294–1303), in his renowned *Unam sanctam* (There is only one, holy, catholic and apostolic Church), emphatically taught that submission to the Roman pontiff by every person is altogether necessary for salvation. Then, the Council of Florence (1438–1445) said that the church:

> …firmly believes, professes, and preaches that all those who are outside the catholic church, not only pagans but also Jews or heretics and schismatics, cannot share in eternal life and will go *into everlasting fire which was prepared for the devil and his angels,* unless they are joined to the catholic church before the end of their lives; that the unity of the ecclesiastical body is of such importance that only for those who …abide in it do the church's sacraments contribute to salvation and do fasts, almsgiving, and other works of piety and practices of the Christian militia produce eternal rewards; and that nobody can be saved, no matter how much he has given away in alms and even if he has shed his blood in the name of Christ, unless he has persevered in the bosom and the unity of the catholic church.[47]

The underlying presumption, from third-century Cyprian to the fifteenth-century Council of Florence, was that every person had heard the gospel, that some freely entered the church, and that others knowingly refused to do so. But sixteenth-century global discoveries revealed that vast numbers of people had not, in fact, heard of Christ or the church.

In response to this challenging pastoral scene, Robert Bellarmine spoke of two ways of belonging to the church: by fact and by desire. The latter category was comprised of those unbaptized people of goodwill who desired to do what was right to obtain salvation, but who, for reasons beyond their control, had not actually entered the church. The presumption was that the great majority of people beyond the actual bounds of the church had such a positive disposition.

Geographical discoveries, and the pastoral and theological developments coinciding with them, prompted yet another fundamental question: What is the true nature of the church? The questioning persisted through the nineteenth century, into the twentieth, where it got stated in another way: What is the relationship between the Catholic Church and the Church of Jesus Christ? Understandably, many theological debates occurred, centering on both the precise question and the surrounding issues. Fortunately, the responses not only shed light on the nature of the church, but reached into related questions, such as the quality of Catholic living and the relationship of Catholics and their church with others, especially other Christians. But before Vatican II, Pius XII (1939–1958) gave, as some thought at the time, a definitive answer.

The Teaching of Pius XII in *Mystici Corporis Christi*

In his 1943 encyclical *Mystici Corporis Christi*[48] (The Mystical Body of Jesus Christ), Pius XII sought to bring an end to the debate about the nature of the church, most especially about the precise relationship of the Church of Jesus Christ and the Catholic Church. "We desire to make clear why the Body of Christ, which is the Church, should be called mystical"(60). He identified them as one, the sole source of salvation. The only way for "non-Catholic" people to secure salvation was for them to have an "unconscious desire" for membership in the church.

Instead of quelling the inquiries of Catholic people about their proper "church" identity and their relationships with other Christians, however, the teaching of Pius XII served to stimulate Catholic thinkers to doubt. They began to raise questions about our twentieth-century understanding of life and relationships, and the completeness of Pius XII's answer. People began to ask questions like, "What is the appropriate way for Catholics to relate to people not in the Catholic Church? Does Catholic teaching seriously distinguish among Orthodox, Protestant, and Anglican Christians, or does it just identify them all as 'non-Catholics'? Is it wrong for these other Christian peoples, in their respective churches, to lay claim to a 'church identity'? Why is the twentieth-century ecumenical movement, acceptable in Orthodox, Protestant, and Anglican circles, so unsuitable for Catholic membership? Is it correct to place all the people of other religions that are not Christian in one simple category, for example, Jews, Muslims, and Buddhists? If, in fact, it is better for Catholics to have only minimal contact with other Christians and with people of other religions, then what kind of relationship should Catholics be cultivating with the entire world? Is it realistic for Catholics to disengage from the world, as so many writers and preachers suggest they do?"

These questions—very real questions—surfaced in the decades prior to Vatican II. The hard facts are that the pre-Vatican II answers from the Catholic Church did not offer a great deal of comfort to other Christians and to people of other religions regarding their salvation journeys and the relationships they wanted to establish with Catholics. Nor did Catholics find a great deal of help in the teaching of their church as they desperately tried to relate more fruitfully to all peoples and, indeed, to the world. People of goodwill—members of other religions, Christians who are not Catholics, and most especially Catholics—in their collective consciousness, were decidedly uncomfortable with the Catholic teaching. They were questioning!

The Catholic Culture

The gradual growth of a Catholic culture took place over several centuries. The process climaxed in the nineteenth and twentieth centuries and extended even into the pontificate of Pius XII. Catholicism was more than a church; it was a culture, indeed a counterculture. Alarmed at the invasion of liberalism upon the world scene, and later of socialism and communism, the church saw definite threats to some of her main concerns, namely the sacred and religion, tradition and authority. The choice she made, unwittingly perhaps, was to become a counterculture, and the model she selected was an idealization of the "Christian civilization" of the Middle Ages. (Joseph A. Komonchak examines this in a paper he prepared for the American Academy of Religion.[49])

The Catholic Subculture

To further this intent, papal writings abounded with condemnations of the "world" on the one hand and support of the notion that the church is the source of true civilization on the other. In 1878, Leo XIII's (1878–1903) first encyclical, *Inscrutabili Dei Consilio* (On the Evils Affecting Modern Society), regretted that modern society had rejected "the holy and venerable authority of the Church, which in God's name rules mankind"(51). He viewed the church as the mother of civil society, in which the rights and freedom of the Holy See should "be restored to that condition of things in which the designs of God's wisdom had long ago placed the Roman Pontiffs"(58). He invited a comparison of the present age "so hostile to religion and to the Church of Christ, with those happy times when the Church of Christ was revered as a mother by the nations"(53). Similar sentiments were expressed in *Immortale Dei* (The Christian Constitution of States, 1885), in *Sapientiae Christianae* (On the Chief Duties of Christians as Citizens, 1890), and in *Graves de Communi* (On Christian Democracy, 1901).[50] His successors, including Pius X and Pius XI, endorsed this kind of thinking and writing.

Not finding a place and role in modern society along the lines these writings wanted, the church, under Roman leadership, then energetically pursued the establishment of her own subculture. Catholicism became characterized by a series of developments, the totality of which created a peculiarly Catholic environment. Among them was the strong growth in Marian piety, not entirely religious in intent because it was also promoted as a means of delivery from the turbulence of the times. Leo XIII wrote sixteen documents on the Rosary, pointing out that this prayer was a remedy for social and political ills. Similar motivation accompanied the promotion of the growing devotion to the Sacred Heart. In the love of Jesus, Catholics would find a remedy to the divisions caused by the greed of the rich and the envy of the poor.

Catholic associations came to exist, some devotional in intent, others for charitable purposes or for Catholic social action. Some had social and political goals, including opposition to socialism and communism, and, without any doubt, the encouragement of social contacts among Catholics. The Catholic school system, among other things, fulfilled this protective role by keeping Catholic children together.

It was argued from Rome that, because the challenge from liberalism was more than national, the only agency capable of responding appropriately was the papacy. This interpretation brought with it an increasing centralization of Catholic life, with special emphases on Rome and on the person of the pope. Rome enjoyed not only an oversight of the church, but a very definite hands-on control of teaching and discipline as well. Catholic identity was certainly "Roman."[51]

Catholic Isolationism and Negativity

In their various allocutions, consistories, encyclicals, and apostolic letters, the popes attacked rationalism, socialism, and other current philosophical trends. The famous *Syllabus of Errors*, written in 1864, was constructed out of the many writings of Pius IX (1846–1878). Among the eighty errors condemned in this work was the directive "that the Roman pontiff can and should reconcile himself with progress, with liberalism, and with modern civilization!"

Similar negativity was evident in Pius XI's (1922–1939) 1928 encyclical *Mortalium Animos* (On Fostering the Religious

Union), in which he outlined why Catholics do not participate in conferences such as the first World Conference of Faith and Order, held at Lausanne in 1927 and involving 108 churches. Pius XI also explained why Catholics choose not to be part of the recently formed ecumenical movement, which he labeled "panchristian." There is in it, he said, evidence of relativism in doctrine, modernism in theology, and indifferentism in ecclesiology. He said:

> It is clear why this Apostolic See has never allowed its subjects to take part in the assemblies of non-Catholics. There is but one way in which the unity of Christians may be fostered, and that is by furthering the return to the one true Church of Christ of those who are separated from it; for from that one true Church they have in the past fallen away....Furthermore, in this one Church of Christ no man can be or remain who does not accept, recognize, and obey the authority and supremacy of Peter and his legitimate successors.[52]

If this thinking and writing reflected the church's attitudes about her relationships, then her dominant spirituality certainly revealed fundamental and widespread Catholic preferences. In a footnote to an article titled "The Idea of Holiness in Christianity," Herbert Alphonso observes that from the end of the fourth century "even lay Christians who aspired to holiness strove to mould their lives on a kind of 'flight from the world' *(fuga mundi)*," adding that there remains "a permanent challenge to maintain that authentically Christian balance which organically integrates love of God and love of neighbor."[53] In other words, a combining of a reverence for heaven and earth. George Tavard endorses this thinking: "Christian writers have commonly denounced the world as a place from which one should escape in order to ascend to God."[54] This is evident in one well-known Christian text, *The Imitation of Christ*,[55] which says:

> Esteem the whole world as nothing; prefer the attendance on God before all occupations...You must be sequestered from your acquaintance and from your dearest

friends...and keep your mind disengaged from all temporal consolation (Book III, 53).

The more a man desires to be spiritual, the more this
present life becomes distasteful to him; because he better understands and more clearly sees the defects of
human corruption (Book I, 22).

Beyond Thomas à Kempis (c.1380–1471), much of the writing
emphasized a spirituality of detachment which, more rather
than less, called for a withdrawal from the world. In *The Three
Ages of the Interior Life*, Reginald Garrigou-Lagrange
(1877–1964) has as his thesis that the spiritual life is an intimate conversation with God, achieved through a threefold
process of passing successively through the purgative, illumi-
native, and unitive ways. At the first level one detaches from
the lower appetites which tend to drag one down, to achieve
union with God, when the soul is progressively illuminated.

From the moment he ceases to converse with his fellow
men, man converses interiorly with himself...As soon as
a man seriously seeks truth and goodness, this intimate
conversation with himself tends to become conversation
with God.[56]

In contrast to these spiritualities is that of Teilhard de
Chardin (1881–1955), who remarked that the more "intensely
he came to know and experience the world, the closer God was
to him," the whole world being a "divine milieu." In his book
bearing that exact title, he says:

The Church is like a great tree whose roots must be energetically anchored in the earth while its leaves are
serenely exposed to the bright sunlight. In this way she
sums up a whole gamut of beats in a single living and all-
embracing act, each one of which corresponds to a particular degree or a possible form of spiritualization.[57]

In a personal meditation, de Chardin underlines, in rather com-
pelling words, not just the relationship which a priest should
seek with the world, but the kind of deep, almost visceral inti-
macy which will come to characterize him:

> Every priest, because he is a priest, has dedicated his life
> to the work of universal salvation. If he is conscious of the
> dignity of his office, he should no longer live for himself
> but for the world, following the example of him whom he
> is anointed to represent. To the full extent of my power,
> because I am a priest, I wish from now on to be the first to
> become conscious of all that the world loves, pursues and
> suffers; I want to be the first to seek, to sympathize and to
> suffer; the first to open myself out and sacrifice myself—to
> become more widely human and more nobly of the earth
> than any of the world's servants.[58]

Teilhard de Chardin was not alone in promoting a love and reverence for the world. Thomas Merton, contemplative by profession, developed an increasingly positive attitude toward the
world. The very title of one of his books, *Contemplation in a
World of Action*,[59] suggests that the deeper prayer life of
Christians is world-related. In the chapter titled "The
Contemplative and the Atheist," Merton is moved to remark:

> Christian contemplation is not merely lost in God. It also
> includes in its vision an eschatological understanding of
> the world redeemed in Christ. It sees the world trans-
> formed in the divine light, it sees all things recapitulated
> in Christ (Ephesians 1:10).

Another chapter, "Ecumenism and Renewal," portrays
Merton's developing view that not only the church-in-action
but the contemplative arm of the church as well had a major
contribution to make to the building of bridges among
Christian churches. His insight relates not so much to the prac-
ticalities of Christian reunion, but more to the integrity of the
process, to which monasticism had a contribution to make.

> Two important lines of development are, one hopes, going
> to intersect in monasticism: one, the lived theology which
> is the monastic experience, and, two, the expansion and
> opening of perspectives which lead to a lived unity, the
> common sharing of Christian grace in crisis, irrespective
> of Church divisions.[60]

While isolation from the world began to characterize the church of the nineteenth and twentieth centuries, it became evident that this same isolation was breeding an ecclesial negativity, rendering the church less and less fruitful. Significant people were reading the signs, and each of them, as well as the movements they often became part of, were certainly instrumental in writing an agenda for Vatican II. Such is the subject of the next chapter.

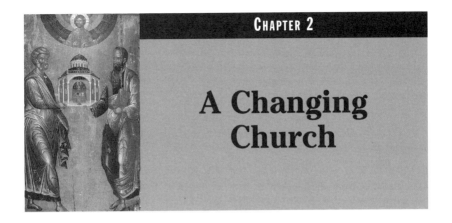

CHAPTER 2

A Changing Church

In hindsight, it is easy to reflect on a scene and identify the symptoms and causes of what is wrong with it. In the same way, we are tempted to look at the past and state categorically what should have been done to remedy certain ills. It is much more difficult, however, to be part of a particular time, immersed in its daily life, and remain free enough to reflect prophetically and critically on the new directions that should be taken.

Over the past century, the Catholic Church has been richly endowed with people who fulfilled such prophetic and critical roles. Although reluctant at times to hear them, let alone heed their advice, the official church was eventually confronted with the inevitability of their message: renewal has to be a constant in church life.

Prophetic People and Movements

Through the centuries, there have been those prophets who were convinced that Christian unity should be a priority. They made it so in their own lives, and they called on the wider church to do the same. Also, there were theologians who fearlessly worked to provide a rationale for the church's renewal, calling her to find her roots and to broaden her vision. Finally, a variety of movements, some scholarly in orientation, others pastoral, revealed to the church the vastness of the ecclesial panorama that is her proper evangelizing field. Our intention here is to consider examples within each of these three categories.

Catholic Prophets of Unity

The first chapter began with reference to two people, Father Paul Wattson and Abbé Paul Couturier, both of whom contributed significantly to the movement of prayer for Christian unity. *UR*, after acknowledging that "there can be no ecumenism worthy of the name without a change of heart" (7), goes on to say that "this change of heart and holiness of life, along with public and private prayer for the unity of Christians, should be regarded as the soul of the whole ecumenical movement, and can rightly be called 'spiritual ecumenism'" (8).

In the encyclical, *UUS*, John Paul II develops the same theme at length (21 to 27). Conversion, he points out, takes us to God *and* to our brothers and sisters, including those as yet not in communion with us. Inevitably, a change of heart comes about, and because we pray together, the goal of unity seems closer and the envisioning of the church much richer. It is a matter of constantly reminding ourselves that conversion and prayer are partners. This will be borne out in the lives of some of these pioneers of unity we will now consider.

Maria Gabriella Sagheddu (1914–1939): Born in Sardinia and entering the Trappists of Grottaferrata near Rome at the age of twenty-one, Maria probably never met an Orthodox, Protestant, or Anglican person, although she knew of the movement of prayer for Christian unity as promoted by Abbé Couturier. Nevertheless, Maria was inspired by her Mother Abbess, who spoke about unity, and by an elderly sister in her community who offered her life for the cause. So inspired was she that, as a newly professed sister, Maria chose to make the same dedication. Shortly after making her offering, Maria developed tuberculosis which was to claim her life just three years after entering the convent.

Maria did nothing extraordinary for unity—no writings, no speeches, no works. Instead, she chose what is called "the little way of ecumenism," her own conversion away from selfishness and pride, which are at the root of divisiveness. The church is enriched by such behavior for, as Martha Driscoll writes: "The most effective way to promote the visible unity of all Christians is by promoting the real unity of your own ecclesial group, by learning to become *church*—one Body, one heart, one mind in Christ—by learning to live together in humility and forgiveness, in mutual service and readiness to sacrifice."[1]

Maria's prayer continues to be answered, as the work for unity intensifies at all levels within the church. Her silent witness continues to inspire, for soon after her death, she became the popular patron saint of the ecumenical movement, with others being drawn to follow her example. So great has been her impact that during the Week of Prayer for Christian Unity in 1983, at St. Paul's Outside-the-Walls in Rome, Maria was beatified by John Paul II. In his encyclical *UUS*, he recommends Maria to the faithful as an exemplary model of one who ceaselessly meditated on the seventeenth chapter of John's Gospel, Jesus' prayer for unity.[2]

Désiré Cardinal Mercier (1851–1926): Appointed archbishop of Malines, Belgium, in 1906, Mercier's ecumenical interests began after the war, first with Russian Orthodox refugees who had entered the west, some of whom had settled in Belgium, including some as students at Louvain. His "ecumenical mind" is revealed in a letter he wrote in 1922 to the Russian National Committee in Paris: "Of course the reunion of the Churches which has ever been dear to godly people is close to our heart as it is to yours, but we do not desire it except in a spirit of absolute respect for the conscience of others."[6]

Mercier's interest in the Anglican Communion was expressed in an address he gave in 1919 to the United States General Convention of the Episcopal Church, when he said: "I have greeted you as brothers in the service of common ideals, brothers in love of liberty and—let me add—as brothers in the Christian faith…this fraternal feeling being nothing other than the corollary of the Fatherhood of God."[7] Although Benedict XV (1914–1922) chided him for meeting with the Episcopalians and for using the phrase "brothers in the Christian faith," Cardinal Mercier remained undaunted and, in 1921, became host to the famous Malines Conversations, the first inter-church dialogue since the Reformation.

Two friends, Father Fernand Portal and Lord Halifax, both deeply interested in the reconciliation of the Anglican and Catholic Churches, met with Cardinal Mercier and requested that he organize conferences between representatives of the two churches. With his approval, the first of a series of meetings began in December 1921 and continued for a number of years. Although the subjects discussed are too many for consideration here, we see the mind of Cardinal Mercier revealed in his 1925 letter to Lord Halifax:

> Instead of putting forward opposing formulas we should consider our subjective states of mind. It is a fact that from the time of St. Augustine until the sixteenth century the Church of England formed part of the same body with the Roman Church. In fact even today is it not implicitly united to Rome? If on both sides of the barrier our consciences were to analyze themselves more deeply, would they not find with the help of the Holy Spirit, that they were wrong to consider themselves to be immutably separated? Historical influences, errors of interpretation, ill-founded fears, may they not have created and maintained superficial divergences which without our being aware of it cover and hide from a profound conscience those truths in which we believe. For my part I believe this to be so.[8]

Dom Lambert Beauduin (1873–1960): A pioneer of the liturgical and ecumenical movements, this Benedictine saw an important link between the two, for at the liturgy's heart is the oneness of Christians which is to be celebrated eucharistically. Therein rests a great goal: the achieving of Christian unity so that the celebration may be complete.

Friendship with Cardinal Mercier took Dom Lambert into the Roman Catholic–Anglican conversations at Malines from 1921 to 1926, the unofficial yet very significant talks involving a Catholic prelate and leaders of the Anglican Communion. Father Fernand Portal and Lord Halifax of these conversations became Dom Lambert's firm friends, and it was in this forum that he came up with the then-daring statement: "The Anglican Church united but not absorbed."[3]

His association with Christians from the Orient, and the request of Pius XI to the Benedictines that they mediate the reunion of east and west, had Dom Lambert founding the "monastery of union" at Amay-sur-Meuse in 1925, which moved in 1939 to Chevetogne. Today, it continues as the home of Benedictine monks from the Orient and the Occident, a center for ecumenical study and research, and a house of welcome. In 1926, Dom Lambert founded *Irénikon*, written by specialists and, for a long time, the only Catholic journal devoted to the ecumenical movement.

In the second issue of *Irénikon*, in May 1926, Dom Lambert asked and answered an important question: "In what spirit do we want to work? Neither that of proselytism, nor that of charity, nor that of an imperialist conception." Some years later he elaborated the method of unity he supported: ". . . bringing about this spiritual encounter of minds and hearts through fervent personal work: coming to know, to understand, to esteem and to love our separated brethren, to pray with them for the concord of the holy churches...It means carrying out work of a psychological nature, in all charity and humility, a work which will help dispel prejudices and open up illuminating inroads of confidence and love."[4]

Made aware that Pius XI's condemnation of the ecumenical movement in *Mortalium Animos* (1928) was aimed at him as well, Dom Lambert resigned as prior of the monastery in 1928 and, after two years of Roman proceedings against him, he was not allowed to return to his monastery until 1951. Not at all embittered, he lived there until his death in 1960. He is buried on the monastery grounds, and the inscription on his tomb reads: *Vir Dei et Ecclesiae* ("Man of God and of the Church").[5]

Augustin Cardinal Bea (1881–1968): As far back as 1935, this German-born Old Testament expert participated with Protestant scholars in a scriptural congress. In so doing, he helped set a precedent for what would become normal in terms of scholarly collaboration. The combination of scriptural scholarship and a great capacity for building friendships gave Bea an "eye" for others, for seeing their places in the divine plan, and for pursuing the restoration of contacts with them when these had been broken.

Baptism was Bea's starting point for understanding Christian relationships. This sacrament makes all Christians fundamentally members of the church, although not necessarily fully. Within the church, then, Christians are recipients of God's graces, which are distributed among them by the Holy Spirit. Ecumenism will build on the foundation, seeking after the fullness of ecclesial membership for all Christians. One can understand why Cardinal Bea would, in 1960, become the first president of the Secretariat for Promoting Christian Unity.

Bea also had great affection for the Jews, which explains the huge amount of energy he put into the creation of *Nostra Aetate*, broadening its scope to be the first conciliar statement on the church's relationship with peoples of all other religions.[9]

Finally, mention must be made of the Dutchman Jan Cardinal Willebrands who first went to Rome in 1960 to be secretary to the newly established Secretariat for Promoting Christian Unity. His post-graduate work was on John Henry Newman, who is often referred to as the father of Vatican II. His study of Newman encouraged Willebrands to envision reconciliation of Christian churches as something truly possible. Founder and the moving spirit of the European Catholic Conference for Ecumenical Questions, Willebrands was soon recognized by Cardinal Bea as suitable for secretarial posting in Rome. On Bea's retirement in 1968, Cardinal Willebrands assumed the presidency of the council. The third president, now in office, is Edward Cardinal Cassidy.

Prophetic Theologians at the Service of the Church

In addition to the above sampling of Catholic prophets of unity, there were loyal and courageous theologians in the church who read the signs of the times and offered a truly prophetic service, which Vatican II would take very seriously.

The "father" of them all, indeed the father of the Second Vatican Council, as has already been mentioned, was John Henry Newman (1801–1890). In two of his works, he raised matters that would not again be treated seriously until the council got under way. In *On Consulting the Faithful in Matters of Doctrine*,[10] Newman argued for the body of the faithful because it is one of the witnesses to revealed truth, being consulted before the church proceeds to a dogmatic definition. In *An Essay on the Development of Christian Doctrine*,[11] he raised an issue that has taken on considerable importance in our times: that all expressions of revelation are culturally conditioned by way of the thought patterns and language current at the time of the formulation. This means that new insights in new ages may require that a particular doctrinal statement be reinterpreted, although never flatly contradicted.[12]

There were many others preceding the council who recognized that the church had a serious and urgent need for renewal. These people developed their ideas in such a way that, without their foreseeing it, Vatican II would come to embrace their thinking. These included Romano Guardini (1885–1968), Marie-Dominique Chenu (1895–1990), Henri de Lubac (1896–1991), and the poet of the "new theology," Pierre Teilhard de Chardin (1881–1955). Beyond these, four other theologians will be considered, with the intention of illustrating that their work was a Spirit-filled gift to what was becoming a necessity for the church: a conciliar forum. (Coincidentally, all four that we now consider were born in 1904.)

Yves Congar (1904–1995): Made a cardinal a matter of months before his death in 1995 at the age of 90, Congar said that the vast majority of Catholics use the word "church" to mean "the hierarchy." His understanding of the church was far wider than the traditional hierarchical model, however, as is evidenced by the titles he wrote and their dates of publication. For example, *Chrétiens désunis: Principes d'un 'oecuménisme' catholique*, published in 1937 before the Oxford and Edinburgh missionary conferences, displays Congar's original thinking in which he is bold enough to agree "that others are Christian not in spite of their particular confession but in it and by it."[13] In 1950, he wrote *True and False Reform in the Church*, some nine years before John XXIII (1958–1963) called an ecumenical council for the renewal of the church. *Lay People in the Church* was written in 1952 and anticipated a council that had to grow into having a very special regard for the laity. In the mid-fifties, Congar was suspended from a teaching role in the church, a period he described as one of "active patience." John XXIII, however, personally placed him on the preparatory theological commission for the council. During the council itself, Congar became heavily involved in the drafting of at least six documents.

John Courtney Murray (1904–1967): Although he was not formally an ecclesiologist, Murray was an expert on religious freedom and the relationship between church and state. Yet, he suffered at the hands of the Holy Office. He was not allowed to continue teaching on these subjects and was, in fact, withdrawn from the list of *periti,* who were to serve at the first session of the council. Despite these barriers, Murray became the chief drafter of what Paul VI called "one of the major texts of the council." Father Murray himself remarked: "The Declaration has opened the way toward new confidence in ecumenical relationships, and a new straightforwardness in relationships between the Church and the world."[14]

Karl Rahner (1904–1984): Like so many of his forward-looking contemporaries, Rahner was viewed suspiciously for a time, although he was honored with being appointed a *peritus* to the council by John XXIII. Paul VI also regarded him highly. In his 1954 writing, *A Theological Interpretation of the Position of Christians in the Modern World,* Rahner presented to the conference of Catholic publicists at Cologne his thesis on "Christian culture." He argued that people cannot be Christian in virtue of their politics or their culture, not even in terms of their morals, but by a profound faith in eternal life. In his own words:

> In the sphere of secular, worldly living, there is never any period that can be called the Christian age, any culture which is the Christian culture...It is never possible simply to deduce, from Christian principles of belief and morality, any one single pattern of the world as it ought to be. In principle, there is neither in respect of the State nor of economics nor of culture nor of history any one clear, concrete imperative which can be deduced from Christian teaching as the one and only possible right course.[15]

A few years later, in 1959, Rahner wrote about the necessity of free speech, noting the absence of any provision, especially in contemporary canon law, for the expression of public opinion in the church. He added that such a lack did not mean that there was no such thing as public opinion in the church, but rather that the recognition of such opinion—and its status— was an altogether different issue. It was becoming abundantly evident, however, that the mind of the faithful was beginning to express itself and, as such, was a reflection of the real needs of the times. A further comment of his is worth noting:

> Both those of us who are in authority and those who are under authority are perhaps still accustomed here and there to certain patriarchal forms of leadership and obe- dience which have no essential or lasting connection with the real stuff of Church authority and obedience. When this is so, Church authorities may see even a justi- fiable expression of frank opinion about Church matters as camouflaged rebellion, or resentment against the Church Hierarchy. Even those not in authority may dis- like such free expression, because they are accustomed to the old traditional ways.[16]

Leon-Joseph Cardinal Suenens (1904–1996): As the Archbishop of Brussels, when he heard that John XXIII had convoked a council, Suenens wrote a pastoral letter to his people on the state of the church and on its opportunities. This letter became known to the pope and had an influence on the open- ing address John XXIII made to the council in 1962. Hardly had the council begun, however, when Suenens observed to the assembly that the deliberations were very introspective. With that, he called for an adjournment so that the council fathers could reflect on the church's identity and on her relationships with other Christians and the entire world. It is a well-known fact that this speech became the important turning point in the life of the council and in the advent of its Pastoral Constitution on the Church in the Modern World *(Gaudium et Spes)*.

In a text published in 1968, the cardinal was able to pin- point the spirit of the times leading up to the council, the graces which characterized those decades, and something of the nature of the conciliar response:

The Second Vatican Council marked the end of an epoch. Or if one wishes to look back even further, it marked the end of a series of epochs. It signified the end of an era.

We could say that in a certain way, it closed the age of Constantine, the age of medieval Christianity, the era of Counter-reformation, the period of Vatican I. In the context of its ancient past, it marks a turning point in the history of the Church.

On the other hand, in the context of its more immediate past, that is, the first half of our century, it appears not so much as a terminal point as a synthesis. Vatican II was the heir and beneficiary of those great movements of renewal which were and are stirring in the heart of the modern church; we mean the biblical, liturgical, patristic, theological, and pastoral renewals.[17]

Movements Reaching into the Church

There were seven movements that would, each in its own way, significantly signal to the church that ecclesiastical renewal was now becoming an imperative. Interestingly, three of the seven started outside of Catholicism.

The Biblical Movement: This began in nineteenth-century Protestant circles in response to the modernist criticism that the Christian Church was based on falsehood, including biblical falsehood. The Catholic Church's response was twofold: swift condemnation of modernism and rejection of modern biblical criticism, this latter rejection holding into the 1940s.[18] Fortunately, Pius XII's encyclical of 1943, *Divino Afflante Spiritu* (Biblical Studies and Opportune Means of Promoting Them), proved to be a timely Catholic acknowledgment that much about the Bible had yet to be discovered and that biblical criticism would be the appropriate scholarship vehicle through which to do it. This new discipline required deep and honest study and an openness of heart in the reception of the results. From 1943 on, through the conciliar years and continuing today, is a period that Raymond Brown says, "has involved the painful assimilation of those implications for Catholic doctrine, theology, and practice."[19] This recent journey into the more complete meaning of the Scriptures has come to be widely understood and appreciated as an essential ingredient in the revitalization of the church.

The Liturgical Movement: The beginnings of this movement can be traced to the Benedictines at Solesmes in 1832. Its efforts intensified and spread into the twentieth century, especially between the two world wars, and notably into Belgium, Holland, Germany, France, and the United States. The movement recognized that the church's worship had become obscured over the centuries by a variety of accretions. It also understood the need to re-create a liturgy that did not leave the impression that the Eucharist is the priest's sacrifice alone and that the people are mere liturgical bystanders. Pius XII's 1947 *Mediator Dei* (On the Sacred Liturgy) certainly made advances in achieving these changes. But the council's first promulgated document of 1964, *Sacrosanctum Concilium* (Constitution on the Sacred Liturgy), truly committed the Catholic Church to an ongoing program of liturgical reform, which is to be the underpinning of ecclesial reform.

The Patristic Movement: In the first stage of the biblical and liturgical movements, emphasis was understandably given to a study of the context of their ancient texts. The next stage was to seek out the relevance of the biblical and liturgical writings for today's world. It was at this point that the Patristic Movement assumed considerable importance, for the writings of the fathers were known to be rich in commentary on the Scriptures and on the sacramental mysteries, but they were also understood as valuable in having a message for the contemporary world. Henri de Lubac and Jean Danielou, in publishing 320 volumes in the series titled *Sources Chretiennes*, firmly believed that the patristic writings were much more than simple historical documents. These writings, de Lubac and Danielou argued, enjoy an inherent quality that relates them to the present age in a very real way. Among these qualities is the patristic preference for symbols and images. Such a style easily suits the modern-day preferred method for recognizing truth, unlike the traditional theological system of abstractions and categories. Further, the patristic understanding of the church as a "communion" and as a body of believers with Christ as head would eventually underpin a greater recognition of local churches and of the equality of all baptized people.

The Lay Movement: Early in the church's life the "ordinary faithful," or the "laity," was clearly distinguished from the "officials," although all felt a responsibility for the evangelization of the world. Only in the Middle Ages did the distinction between the clergy and the laity take on mammoth proportions. This was seen in the striking differences that evolved between the world of the spirit, personified in "spiritual people" such as monks who assumed a particular dress and lived according to the counsels, and the world of temporalities, where people attended to earthly and profane affairs and lived according to the commandments. The ecclesiastical "ideal" was monastic or clerical, so much so that to take the Christian calling seriously one must "escape from the profane world" altogether. Given this model, evangelizing became a task reserved to the clergy and religious.

In the nineteenth century, with the distancing of church and world and the impotency of the church's traditional style, the laity began to be recognized as an educated Christian resource and as a counter to society's social and moral ills. As we have already noted, laypeople were made instrumental in the creation of the Catholic culture. It was their displeasure that was noted at the time of the world wars, and it was for them that Catholic Action came to exist. Up to the Second Vatican Council the laity's reemergence was viewed principally as an apostolic resource.

What the council would have to initiate was a more fundamental theological reappraisal of the place of the laity as members of both church and world. It would have to lend support to a renewed viewing of the place Protestant traditions had accorded their laity.

The Worker-Priest Movement: Interestingly, in his *Gift and Mystery*,[20] written on the fiftieth anniversary of his priestly ordination, John Paul II speaks of the Worker-Priest Movement as having had an influence on him. Karol Wojtila emerged as a young priest at a time when the new theologians were urging a renewal of the relationship between the church and the world.

Whereas Catholic Action aimed to bring the world to the church, these priests, aware of the level of anticlericalism, sought a way of taking the church into the world. They did this by identifying with the causes of the workers and of the labor movement in general. Between the years 1944 and 1954, these priests sought to take Christ's message into the world, aware that the gulf between church and world was ever widening.

In 1953–1954, the ecclesiastical authorities in Rome required these priests to abandon the experiment. Nevertheless, on behalf of the new theology, the point was made that the church, one way or another, had to become a force within the world. The wait was for the council to clarify that such a ministry more properly belonged to the laity.

The Ecumenical Movement: This movement began among Protestant missionaries, the seeds of the more formalized twentieth-century movement being sown in the late eighteenth and nineteenth centuries. The first of these seeds was the influence of Pietism among a number of churches, each of which sought to improve its interchurch relationships. The aim was not organic union but a fellowship or togetherness stemming from the realization that each of them owed its existence to a Spirit-filled response to Jesus. The second relied very much on nineteenth-century liberalism and positivism, out of which arose an appreciation of the imperative that Christians must assume a common response to the great social ills of the times. The third was missionary, a belief that what had been received had to be proclaimed as well. The main tool would be the Bible, hence the advent of Bible societies that, by and large, were interconfessional and ecumenical.

The formal ecumenical movement traces its beginning to the World Missionary Conference held at Edinburgh in 1910. Although there had been similar conferences before, this one was missionary and ecumenical in fact and in intent, with pastors from afar showing concern that they were preaching a divided Lord. Two important organs emerged from this conference: Life and Works, and Faith and Order, which combined in 1948 to become the World Council of Churches, a significant force in today's ecumenical movement. While there were, for quite some time, ecumenical stirrings within the Catholic

Church from a number of prophetic figures, ecclesiastical authorities did not move until prompted to do so by the Second Vatican Council.

The Pentecostal Movement: Dating back to Charles Parham's 1901 Topeka Revival in Kansas and the preaching of his student, William Seymour, at the Azusa Street Revival in Los Angeles, this movement is a twentieth-century outgrowth of nineteenth-century holiness and fundamentalist movements. Broadly speaking, it is a twofold movement. The first is the Classical Pentecostalist group, comprised of a great variety of churches that have sprung into life outside the mainline denominations. The second is called the Charismatic Movement or Neo-Pentecostalism, which dates from the Second World War. This is a renewal movement within the mainline churches, and its presence has been significantly felt within the Catholic Church since 1967. This movement continues to remind Catholics that the Spirit's powerful presence is not only within the church but throughout the entire universe. Furthermore, the work of evangelization, as expressed in the 1991 *Redemptoris Missio* (On the Permanent Validity of the Church's Missionary Mandate), requires a personal and profound meeting with the Savior and an interior change or conversion.

Vatican II in Response

It is no secret that Vatican II's Preparatory Commission worked out of a prior understanding of "church." This is understandable for, as Cardinal Suenens says, it was not until the actual event of the council that such an "age" would pass. Once the council was underway, its members, for the most part, either totally rejected or seriously amended the preparatory papers that were presented for conciliar consideration. The whole council, and each of its documents, had to go through a "process" of emerging from a church in isolation *from* the world, to one that was intent on forging relationships *in* and *with* the world. A look at the council's key documents highlights this process of emergence.

Dei Verbum (The Dogmatic Constitution on Divine Revelation): Until the council, the Bible was not a significant part of Catholic private or public devotional life, nor was it even greatly highlighted in public worship. Stirrings from the world-wide Christian biblical movement, however, aroused Catholic interest that began with *Divino Afflante Spiritu* (Biblical Studies and Opportune Means of Promoting Them) of 1943. Despite the new approach that Pius XII's encyclical advocated, the Vatican II Preparatory Commission's views represented an old-world scriptural preference. Its document was severely criticized and rejected, with a new joint committee taking responsibility for creating a fresh set of proposals.

The outcome was the conciliar decision in favor of a renewed Catholic approach to Scripture, which included both ecumenical sensitivity to other Christian communities as well as an acknowledgment of the wider human family with its variety of religious traditions. The close relationship of "Scripture," which is the written word or text of God, "tradition," which is the way of transmitting that word, and the "church," with its teaching magisterium, was given particular emphasis.

The importance of the Hebrew Scriptures, or the Old Testament, was addressed, taking Catholic thinking beyond seeing them as mere preparatory texts awaiting fulfillment in the New Testament. Appropriate recognition of the Jewish people was given, a matter that would be further considered in *Nostra Aetate* (The Declaration on the Relationship of the Church to non-Christian Religions). God's revelation, it was acknowledged, is not confined to the Jewish and Christian Scriptures, but appears in creation and history as well, and is enshrined especially in other religions whose knowledge of God finds expression in their sacred writings and traditions.

While there was no explicit mention of it in *DV*, the Catholic Church owes a debt of gratitude to many of the Reformation churches for the leads they historically have given to biblical research and scholarship and in making the Scriptures readily available to all the faithful.

Lumen Gentium (The Dogmatic Constitution on the Church): The creation of *Lumen Gentium* (Light of All Nations) was a long and laborious task, involving four drafts, with more than four thousand amendments to the second draft alone. The outcome, however, was the arrival of a very important document that reveals, in the words of Avery Dulles, "the tremendous development of the Church's self-understanding which resulted from the dialogue within the Council."[21]

Whereas the key words descriptive of the prior understanding of church were *society, hierarchy,* and *headship,* the ecclesiology of Vatican II was strikingly *biblical, patristic,* and *ecumenical,* with the church being identified as a *communion.*

The council fathers knew the Tridentine teaching on the church as expressed by Robert Bellarmine, much of it in response to the Protestants. They were familiar with the dogmatic definitions on the church's headship at Vatican I (1869–1870), which favored a monarchical viewing of the church. They were also conscious of the recent teachings of Pius XII in his encyclical *Mystici Corporis Christi,* in which he identified, to the point of exclusivity, the Mystical Body of Christ and the Catholic Church. The development that Avery Dulles refers to is one that takes the conciliar participants to an appreciation of the church in terms, first of all, of "mystery" and "people."

Given the increasing impact of biblical and patristic thinking on the contemporary Christian world, it was inevitable that the church's redefining would begin differently. The broad context must be God's plan of salvation for all that is revealed in Christ through the church. This takes us into the realm of mystery, which explains why the first chapter of *LG* is titled "The Mystery of the Church," and why biblical images and the Pauline teaching about the body of Christ take on such importance in helping us renew and deepen our appreciation of the church. The body of Christ is the people, hence the title of the second chapter, "The People of God," a title that, according to a footnote in the Abbott edition of the council documents:

> ... met a profound desire of the Council to put greater emphasis on the human and communal side of the Church, rather than on the institutional and hierarchical aspects which have sometimes been overstressed in the past for polemical reasons. While everything said about

the People of God as a whole is applicable to the laity, it should not be forgotten that the term "People of God" refers to the total community of the Church, including the pastors as well as the other faithful.[22]

Only then does the document consider the church's hierarchical structure, in particular the papal and collegial components (chapter 3) and the laity (chapter 4). Of particular interest to the subject matter of this book is the statement: "...the unique Church of Christ which in the Creed we avow as one, holy, catholic and apostolic. This Church, constituted and organized in the world as a society, subsists in the Catholic Church"(8). This same section goes on to explain that many elements of sanctification and truth are outside the visible structure of the Catholic Church, and that "these elements, however, as gifts properly belonging to the Church of Christ, possess an inner dynamism toward Catholic unity." This acknowledgment, that there is an existence of "church" beyond the Catholic Church, is the justification for her participation in the ecumenical movement.

Gaudium et Spes (The Pastoral Constitution on the Church in the Modern World): The longest of the conciliar documents, this work was not the product of a preparatory commission. Rather, it arose out of an intervention by Cardinal Suenens at the end of the council's first session. The idea of a link between church and world was still very much confined to the reflection of the movements and the prophets discussed earlier, including Cardinal Giovanni Battista Montini, later Paul VI. The council fathers, once alerted, knew that a definition of the church that promoted isolation from the world was totally inappropriate. The experience of the bishops was of a world scarred by two world wars, by a holocaust, and by the development of frightening weapons. The church, they determined, has and must be seen to have an important and active role to play in this world.

GS was not a revolutionary document, although it did call for a change in strategy, from a tendency to stand in *judgment of* the world to one of *dialogue with* the world. We need only look at the pastoral styles of Paul VI and John Paul II to discover the profound impact that this document made on their pontificates. Since dialogue knows no limits, it extends to "those brothers and communities not yet living with us in full communion," and to all those others "who acknowledge God, and who preserve in their traditions' precious elements of religion and humanity...such dialogue, which can lead to truth through love alone, excludes no one"(92).

Dignitatis Humanae (The Declaration on Religious Freedom): This work began as a chapter in *LG*, then moved to *Unitatis Redintegratio* (The Decree on Ecumenism), and eventually became a document in its own right. Understandably, it experienced a bumpy ride through the council, precisely because the matter of religious freedom, for the conciliar participants, had not been an issue in the church they were brought up in. But this was a council of renewal in which, under appropriate leadership, the council fathers would eventually arrive at a richer understanding of the church's role. Hence, John E. Linnan could observe that "in this brief Declaration the Church returns to a healthier, more realistic, and more evangelical vision of its relationship to the civil society—a vision it once had but lost for awhile in the glamour of its triumph in the West."[23] A truly healthy signal is given in the document's admission that "there have at times appeared ways of acting which were less in accord with the spirit of the gospel and even opposed to it"(12).

Freedom is a natural right and, as such, is confirmed by revelation. It resides not only in individual people but in their social groupings as well, which means that both private and public acts of religion are to be protected by civil authorities and respected by others. Against this background, and in conjunction with other conciliar teachings as expressed in *NA* (The Declaration on the Relationship of the Church to Non–Christian religions) and *Ad Gentes* (The Decree on the Church's Missionary Activity), the church continues to develop a positive outlook on the status and significance of other religions.

Unitatis Redintegratio (The Decree on Ecumenism): Only a brief consideration of this work is made here, simply to give it a context, for the decree needs to be interpreted in the light of all the conciliar documents, especially *LG*. A fuller analysis of *UR* is offered as a preface to chapter 5.

Bear in mind that the Catholic Church distanced herself from the beginnings of the ecumenical movement in the late nineteenth century and throughout the first half of the twentieth century. What's more, it was not associated with the Orthodox Church and the Protestant churches and communities in the founding of the World Council of Churches in 1948. Nevertheless, the many prophets and movements within the Catholic Church continuously reminded her leadership of the need to change. The message began to be heard and respected, as is reflected in the instruction *Ecclesia Catholica* (The Catholic Church and ecumenical contacts) of the Holy Office of December 20, 1949, which allowed for some limited dialogue among Catholics and other Christians while prohibiting official Catholic participation in ecumenical conferences. The instruction's positive but careful approach to the ecumenical movement is in sharp contrast to Pius XI's *Mortalium Animos*, which was quoted earlier in this chapter. The Holy Office document says:

> The Catholic Church takes no part in "Ecumenical" conferences or meetings. But, as may be seen from many papal documents, she has never ceased, nor ever will, from following with deepest interest and furthering with fervent prayer every attempt to attain that end which Christ our Lord had so much at heart, namely, that all who believe in him "may become perfectly one.[24]

The time was approaching to move on from making tentative gestures, and it was soon to happen with John XXIII's founding of the Secretariat for Promoting Christian Unity,[25] which would become an important arm of the Vatican Council. While the preparatory commission suggested a chapter on Protestants in the scheme for a constitution on the church, the secretariat won through with the idea that a specific decree on ecumenism should be created.

In addition to being an educational tool for Catholics into the aims and objectives of the ecumenical movement, the decree pointed to important new directions that the church was now to take. Instead of "returning" to the Catholic Church mentality, all Christians would embark on a pilgrimage toward Christ, beyond viewing the Catholic Church as the only church. They would seek the presence of Jesus and his Spirit in other churches and ecclesial communities and cease to point an accusing finger at those supposedly guilty for causing past division—for that "guilt" was to be shared. So, the important underpinning of whatever action was needed for the achievement of Christian unity would be a change of heart enriched by spiritual ecumenism.

Nostra Aetate (The Declaration on the Relationship of the Church to Non-Christian Religions): This document, initially intended as a brief statement on the Jews, was completely reworked by Cardinal Bea and the secretariat so as to provide a conciliar statement on the relationship of the church with other religions. There was an early fear that a statement solely on the Jews could be a bad political move because of Arab sensitivities and because Christian minorities in Arab countries might be caused some suffering. The strategy, then, was to broaden the scope of the document, diminishing the focus on Judaism and giving attention to Hinduism, Buddhism, Islam, and other traditions in a general way.

Although brief, further attention is given to these other religions in the final chapter of this book. Worth mention here, however, is the fact that a theological advance arose out of a political need. The post-Vatican Council fruit is a developing theology that recognizes the single origin and common destiny of all people who, through their religions, address the mysteries of human existence and encourage the growth in holiness of their memberships. Today, the Pontifical Council for Inter-Religious Dialogue conducts and encourages fruitful discussions and activities in many parts of the world.

※ ※ ※

This chapter has sought to recognize certain aspects of the church that would have to change, interestingly enough in the lifetimes of many of us. Certainly there have been changes over the two millennia but none so intensively and extensively as during and since the Second Vatican Council. Within the council itself, great shifts in understanding happened—the Holy Spirit being a vital part of the total process.

Cardinal Montini, later Paul VI, gave two addresses, one on December 7, 1962, the other a month later. His words capture what has been the focus of this study. The first address was given in Milan, while the cardinal celebrated the feast of Saint Ambrose:

> Yesterday, the theme of the Church seemed to be confined to the power of the Pope. Today, it is extended to the episcopate, the religious, the laity and the whole body of the Church. Yesterday, we spoke of the rights of the Church by transferring the constitutive elements of civil society to the definition of a perfect society. Today, we have discovered other realities in the Church—the charisms of grace and holiness, for example—which cannot be defined by purely juridical ideas. Yesterday, we were above all interested in the external history of the Church. Today, we are equally concerned with its inner life, brought to life by the hidden presence of Christ in it.[26]

In January 1963, Cardinal Montini gave this address to a group of young priests:

> At the Council, the Church is looking for itself. It is trying, with great trust and with a great effort, to define itself more precisely and to understand what it is. After twenty centuries of history, the Church seems to be submerged by profane civilization and to be absent from the contemporary world. It is therefore experiencing the need to be recollected and to purify and recover itself so as to be able to set off on its own path again with great energy… While it is undertaking the task of defining itself in this way, the Church is also looking for the world and trying to come into contact with that society…How should that contact be established? By engaging in dialogue with the world, interpreting the needs of the society in which it is working and observing the defects, the necessities, the sufferings and the hopes and aspirations that exist in men's hearts.[27]

From the beginning, the Second Vatican Council was required to look beyond itself to embrace the world. Within a few days of the start of the council, John XXIII sent a document to the council hall requesting that it be discussed, amended if necessary, and used as the council's first official act. So, on October 20, 1962, nine days into the first session, a council addressed itself—for the first time ever—to all people, not just to members of the Catholic Church. Similarly, the following year John XXIII's *Pacem in Terris* (Peace in the World) spoke to "all men of good will." The council's very first words symbolize so well what the Catholic Church has set out to be: a world church:[28]

> We take great pleasure in sending to all men and nations a message concerning that well-being, love, and peace which were brought into the world by Christ Jesus, the Son of the living God, and entrusted to the Church...Our prayer is that in the midst of this world there may radiate the light of our great hope in Jesus Christ, our only Savior.[29]

If ecumenism is to be properly understood, it has to be against this enlarging vision of the church.

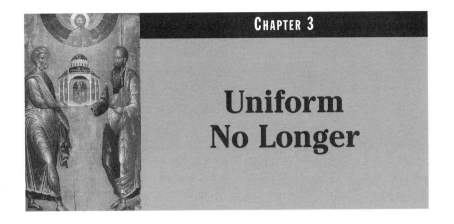

CHAPTER 3

Uniform No Longer

The previous chapter makes it clear that the Catholic Church, as she journeyed into the Second Vatican Council, was called upon to make a great number of revisions. Not the least of these was a revision of her own self-understanding, most especially as expressed in her relationships with other Christians. Aware that the majority of Christian denominations had become part of an ecumenical movement, the Second Vatican Council decided to join that existing movement rather than initiate a parallel one.

Ecumenical Documents

The council placed a great emphasis on setting down Catholic principles for ecumenical involvement. These are stated in the conciliar documents, especially in *Unitatis Redintegratio*, the specific ecumenical document of the council, and in *Lumen Gentium*, one of the two documents on the "church." Both of these were examined in the previous chapter, and *UR* is further analyzed in chapter 5.

"Catholic Principles on Ecumenism" is the title of the first chapter of *UR*, arrived at only in the latter stages of the document's preparation. The chapter had originally been titled "Principles of Catholic Ecumenism," which would have suggested the creation of a Catholic movement parallel to the already existing ecumenical movement that had come into existence outside the Catholic Church. Quite wisely, the council chose not to establish an alternative movement; instead, it enunciated the Catholic principles that would determine the church's way of approaching ecumenism.

A further document, *Orientalium Ecclesiarum* (The Decree on Eastern Catholic Churches), is closely related to *UR* and is concerned with the eastern churches that are in union with Rome: the Armenian, Byzantine, Coptic, Ethiopian, East Syrian (Chaldean), West Syrian, and Maronite. Each is a church in communion with the bishop of Rome, although none of them is "Roman" Catholic. One of the special values of this decree is the clarification it brings to the position of these eastern Catholic churches in the Catholic Church, which is important for the overall good of the church, including the sign it gives to the other eastern churches not in communion with Rome. We return to a study of the east in the next chapter.

Nostra Aetate, which addresses the relations of the Catholic Church with other religions in the world, was originally intended as a chapter in *UR*. However, a broadening of its subject matter beyond just Catholic-Jewish contacts, to take in all religions, created the need for an independent document. In the final chapter of this book, we give further consideration to the rationale for the changing Catholic attitude toward other religions and briefly explore the nature of the contacts that have been put in place.

Since the council, these principles have been further elaborated by the Secretariat for Promoting Christian Unity in a number of its official documents: the *Directory Concerning Ecumenical Matters, Part I* (1967), the *Directory Concerning Ecumenical Matters, Part II* (1970), the *Directory for the Application of the Principles and Norms on Ecumenism* (1993), and *The Ecumenical Dimension in the Formation of Those Engaged in Pastoral Work* (1997)[1], as well as in the two texts of John Paul II mentioned at the beginning of chapter 1, *Ut Unum Sint* and *Orientale Lumen*. In addition to these documents, which give the principles and norms for universal application, there are many well-prepared diocesan directories that take account of the particular circumstances for ecumenism in the local churches. Beyond all of these are the writings of ecumenically minded theologians, the practical pursuits of communities and people, the movements of prayer for unity, and the witness of communities and individuals, many of whom can be described as the contemporary prophets of unity.

Gradually, Catholics are coming to realize that the goal of the journey to full communion will not be a uniform mass of Christians all doing the same thing in the same way. In fact, the picture of the united church of tomorrow is totally beyond our present imagining. There is certainty in all of this, however: the church will not be like it was and it cannot be like it is! Too much has happened over time for uniformity and unity to be equated. The principle has to be "unity in diversity."

This Thing Called "Dialogue"

In his book *Letters to Contemplatives*,[2] William Johnston says that "dialogue" is one of our great modern discoveries. At last we are learning, he suggests, that problems are not solved by argumentation or violence, "but by talking and listening and working things out in an atmosphere of goodwill." Johnston goes on to explain that "authentic dialogue is demanding. It asks us to be completely honest and frank, to respect human dignity, to forgive injuries, to listen and listen and listen, to be detached from our most cherished viewpoints, to compromise if necessary. Dialogue at its highest point asks for what is most painful to human nature: disinterested love. And what could be more in keeping with the Gospel?" Johnston then makes a very telling point: how long it has taken us to discover this obvious aspect of the gospel.[3]

A hallmark of the ecumenical movement is this thing called "dialogue." We could say that dialogue is expressive of the movement, revealing a dimension of unity, the fullness of which is the goal of ecumenism. Churches and ecclesial communities are required to think beyond their own identities and to reflect on and build relationships among themselves. For many of these communities, this involves joint efforts of revisiting past controversies, acknowledging past wrongs, allowing for truer interpretations, and then rebuilding a section of

Christ's church in the light of the discoveries. Let's look at multilateral dialogues and bilateral dialogues.

Multilateral dialogues bring many of the major Christian traditions into a conversational forum where topics are more likely to be general in nature, given the diversity of communities represented. Although the discussions begin in a general way, experience shows that the journey takes the participants into fundamental or foundational issues, such as the very nature of the church. An example is the deepening reflection on the theology of the church that happened during and since the document titled "Baptism, Eucharist, and Ministry" (BEM), or Lima Consultations, including among those communities that hitherto had simply taken "church" for granted, seldom reflecting on its nature.[4]

Multilateral dialogues have triggered a more widespread and wholesome appreciation of the ecclesiastical sciences. The historical-critical method used in the interpretation of Scripture, for example, has enabled the emergence of an agreed biblical basis among many of the churches for the Christian faith. Patristic and historical studies have proved invaluable in taking the churches to important moments and themes in Christian development. This is demonstrated in a multilateral study titled *Apostolic Faith Today.*[5]

It should be noted that most multilateral dialogues have been initiated and supported by the World Council of Churches (WCC), particularly by Faith and Order (F&O), notably the BEM consultation mentioned above. What's more, these efforts have greatly influenced bilateral dialogues because what a church arrives at in the more general forum acts as a discipline in its discussions in a bilateral setting.

A *bilateral dialogue* is best described as a religious conversation at the international level by two world communions (the Anglican–Roman Catholic International Commission, for example), at the national level (the United States Lutheran–Roman Catholic Dialogue, for example), or at the regional level (the Porvoo Conversations between the British and Irish Anglican Churches and the Nordic and Baltic Lutheran Churches, for example). It has only been since Vatican II that bilateral dialogues have come into their own.

Since these conversations involve only two parties, the focus can be more specific than is the case with multilateral dialogues. These exchanges, for example, can—and often do—focus on precise doctrinal issues. What divides can be named, the common ground can be identified, and ecclesiastical disciplines can be employed to advance the dialogue. Specialists can be called upon to present on particular subject areas—be they biblical, historical, or theological—allowing the partners to sometimes arrive at acceptable common restatements of Christian faith and life.

Because individual dialogues can become isolated, one from another, and because of the risk of different directions being pursued, a number of forums have been held by F&O to counter these disadvantages. Thus, the fifth forum on *International Bilateral Dialogues 1965–1991*[6] took the theme "The Understanding of the Church Emerging in the Bilateral Dialogues—Coherence or Divergence?" Four major traditions—Lutheran, Catholic, Orthodox, and Methodist—presented, thus enabling all to become acquainted with ecclesial rethinking across the Christian world. In 1997, the *Seventh Forum on Bilateral Dialogues 1994–1997* issued a document titled *Emerging Visions of Visible Unity in the Canberra Statement and the Bilateral Dialogues.*[7] As well as the group reports, the document contains a series of papers on the vision of unity as understood by the WCC and the Catholic, Orthodox, Reformed, and Baptists traditions.

Unity in Diversity: Scriptural Evidence

As noted in the first chapter, the primitive ecclesial reality was the existence of diverse local churches within the one church of Christ. Later, various groups of churches that had developed into rites continued to enjoy a common membership in the one church. Our present task is to explore something of the nature of the cohesiveness that made these many into one.

Koinonia

Koinonia, or *communio*, is a term used to describe the participation of many churhes in the one church. Though certainly known in apostolic times, this notion waited until the patristic age to be actually articulated.[8] The meaning of *koinonia* needs some exploration because it is now widely used in ecumenism, understood by many as the key to a common theology of the church.

Koinonia goes beyond being a model of the church; rather, it speaks of the nature of the church. Two source documents confirm this thinking. The first document is an F&O discussion document that states: "In many bilateral and multilateral dialogues, as well as within the understanding of certain World Communions, there is a striking, emerging agreement on the use of the notion of *koinonia* to describe the understanding of the Church."[9] The second document reflects a statement from the Congregation for the Doctrine of the Faith: "The concept of *communio (koinonia)*, which appears with a certain prominence in the texts of the Second Vatican Council, is very suitable for expressing the core of the mystery of the church and can certainly be a key for the renewal of Catholic ecclesiology."[10] A brief, readable, and contemporary explanation of the Catholic understanding of the church as a communion can be found in the *Directory for the Application of Principles and Norms on Ecumenism.*[11]

Koinonia has its deepest expression in the Trinity. Thus, because we are made in the image of God, we, as the People of God, are expected to mirror the beautiful unity in essentials of the three distinct Divine Persons. A primary theme of the Hebrew Scriptures is that of God's desire for communion with the whole human race. The covenant with Adam was first (Genesis 1:26–31), then with Noah (Genesis 9), both of them representative of humanity. It continues in God's promise to Abraham (Genesis 12:3), that in him all nations will be blessed. God required the people of Israel to put their trust in him by living in such a way as to express their gratitude to him through their communion with him and with one another (Micah 6:8).

The trouble is, sin intervenes. As a result, divisiveness came to characterize much of human living. Fortunately, however, God has never been daunted by such intrusions. Historically, God has used a variety of strategies to protect unity from the sin of divisiveness. Among the Israelite people, these strategies included a covenant intended to draw all into a relationship with God; a monarchy empowered to rule and make a people one; and priests and prophets to serve that unity and to remind the people of the unity imperatives.

Jesus, for his part, chose twelve apostles as a sign of his desire to reunite the twelve tribes under God's universal kingship. In the first instance, he offered the divine *koinonia* to the children of Israel, and then to diverse people, even to those shunned, like Levi the tax collector (Luke 5:27–32). The universality of the Christ-plan was indeed to the ends of the earth and to all peoples, as becomes evident in the concluding words of 2 Corinthians: "The grace of the Lord Jesus Christ, and the love of God, and the fellowship of the Holy Spirit be with you all!" (13:13)

Paul, the founder of so many churches, was very much aware of the dangers of divisiveness wrecking these communities. Galatians 2 and Acts 15 tell the story of the Council of Jerusalem's agreement on appropriately diverse ways of evangelizing Jews and Gentiles, instead of requiring uniform practices. While the gospel had a national and cultural conditioning that was Jewish, Paul was adamant that these "national" and "cultural" elements were not to be imposed on gentile Christians. The gospel, essentially, has universal applicability, although it has to be encountered locally by various peoples in their particular cultural situations.

Against the background of this brief sketch of Paul's practice, we note the contemporary inquiry of the Pontifical Biblical Commission: "One may therefore ask whether, according to Paul's perspective, different local Churches do not have a responsibility to cultivate their own particular and distinctive charisms, and so contribute to a legitimate and enriching diversity within the one and universal Church"[12] (p 17).

Christ's Plan and Paul's Interpretation of It

Beyond the Pauline experience, for example, there is the epistle of James, which was written to Jewish Christians who worshiped in a Jewish synagogue. Belief in Jesus, it seems to be saying, does not mean disengagement from Judaism, for Jesus himself is the endorsement that Judaism reaches its climactic moment in the person of Jesus, who is the Messiah. An immediate point of contrast demonstrating the richness of unity in diversity is the fourth gospel's emphasis on Jesus as the Son of God and on faith in him, the implication being that Christianity should enjoy a clear distinctiveness beyond its Jewish roots. It is possible to detect in all of this a rather important principle. It says to us that the unity essential to Christianity is not necessarily identifiable at a surface viewing of the church. So, the diverse ways we see of "being church" are likely to be perfectly legitimate expressions of the church in her oneness. The evidence seems clear enough that in the world of the New Testament, diversity was accepted as part of the Christian way.

Unity in Diversity: Patristic Evidence

There is little doubt, therefore, that the use of the word *church* in apostolic times had a twofold application, local and universal, and that its unity allowed for diversity. Christians were aware that they shared a common faith expressed in a variety of ways, and the word describing this was *koinonia* or *communio*. In apostolic times, as we have seen, it was an unspoken word, the people being intent on living as church. In patristic times, however, *koinonia* was actually articulated, so as to be descriptive of the church.

In his essay titled *Communio: Church and Papacy in Early Christianity*, Ludwig Hertling says that the concept of *communio* is key in understanding the early church. The word is richly packed with meaning, he explains, which does not suggest that it was something vague. People knew exactly what they were saying when they used the term. Saint Augustine, for example, picks up on the reality of church and churches: "I am in the Church, whose members are all those churches which, as we know from Holy Scripture, were founded and grew by the labor of the apostles. With God's help I will not desert their *communio* either in Africa or elsewhere."[13]

Churches in Communion in Patristic Times

Without the help of first-hand witnesses such as the apostles, who had by now died, some fundamental questions confronted the churches of the patristic period, to which truly authentic answers had to be given. These issues included the nature of the one God and the fact that the three persons in God enjoy particular and identifiable roles. Churches in patristic times looked for the right words to speak of Christ as God and man, to articulate the identity of Mary and her place in the whole scheme of salvation, and to clearly express the meaning of salvation and redemption. Above all, these churches looked for ways to maintain their fundamental "churchly" character.

These local churches did not possess the network of structures that are so obviously in place today. Thus, to demonstrate their Christian authenticity or orthodoxy, they developed a synodal forum, an arena in which they could articulate their beliefs, reach out to others, and have their beliefs tested and received by others in the one universal church. This reaching out, and beliefs being tested and received, is what gave visibility to the church's universality and was spoken of as *koinonia* or *communio*. "Each synod," according to Werner Küppers, "although possessing its own intrinsic authority, as it were, nevertheless, in order to maintain the *koinonia* (communion), attached great importance not merely to communicating its decisions to other churches but also to having its decision respected by them. This concern and this necessity could not be restricted to the narrow circle around a local synod; they already in principle affected the whole Church."[14]

There is an abundance of evidence that the fathers were deeply conscious of local churches having their particular identities within the universal church. Especially in times of crisis, for example, they sought to demonstrate their worldwide communion with as many other local churches as possible. For example, in writing to the people of Neocaesarea, Saint Basil (c.329–379) listed almost all the countries of the world. Dionysius of Alexandria (+ c.265) drew up a list of all the bishops in communion in the east so as to point out to Pope Stephen (254–257) that he should not break communion with so many churches in one single act.[15] To look at the mix of relationships that came about, the problems that entered upon the Christian scene, and the ways in which local churches responded to the challenges that sometimes threatened to destroy their fundamental unity would make an interesting study.

Without a doubt, the vast patristic experience holds a lesson for us today as we seek to restore to the Christian church its diminished unity. We should bear this in mind as we now look at some of the specific challenges that arose in that period of the church's life.

The threat of schism in Corinth—Rome and Clement I respond: As early as the end of the first century, the local church of Rome felt a responsibility toward the local church of Corinth, where the community had unjustifiably decided to alienate its clergy. Through Clement I (+ c.101), its spokesman, "the Church of God which dwells as a pilgrim in Rome" wrote to "the Church of God in pilgrimage at Corinth," appealing to the entire Corinthian community to end the schism. The call to unity from one local church to another is saying, in effect, that no one church can be a law unto itself. The Corinthians responded respectfully, the letter receiving regular readings even a quarter of a century after its delivery.[16]

Heresy in Antioch—Paul of Samosata: In Book VII of *The History of the Church from Christ to Constantine*, Eusebius records the case of the bishop of Antioch, Paul of Samosata (bishop: 260–268), who taught that Christ was just a common man. Such a teaching disturbed the heads of the other churches and caused them to hasten to Antioch to gather in council. There they spoke of Paul as an "arch-heretic" whom they "excommunicated from the whole catholic church under heaven." Chapter 30 of Eusebius' work explains how they drew up a letter addressed "to Dionysius, bishop of Rome, and to Maximus of Alexandria," which was sent "to all our fellow ministers throughout the world, the bishops and presbyters and deacons, and to the whole catholic church throughout the world under heaven."[17]

In this example it is worth noting that the bishops met with urgency when an assault on the unity of the church was alleged; that the excommunication was from the entire church; and that the letter was first addressed to the bishop of Rome, then to Alexandria, thereby acknowledging the presence of legitimate traditions within the one church. Finally, it is important to realize that all were recognized as church: clergy and laity.

Troubles from Gnosticism and Montanism—Irenaeus and Tertullian: One of the early challenges to the integrity of the church was the heresy of Gnosticism, which made claim to having a secret apostolic revelation. Irenaeus (c.130–c.200) responded that no such secret existed, that the church alone possessed the true apostolic tradition that is publicly and clearly expressed in the Scriptures and in the Rule of Faith. His actual words, in Book I of *Adversus Haereses* (Against Heresies), confirm our theme:

> The church, having received this preaching and this faith, although scattered throughout the whole world, yet, as if occupying one house, carefully preserves it. She also believes these points [of doctrine] just as if she had but one soul, and one and the same heart, and she proclaims them and teaches them and hands them down, with perfect harmony, as if she possessed only one mouth...the churches which have been planted in Germany do not believe or hand down anything different, nor do those in Spain, nor those in Gaul, nor those in the East, nor those in Egypt, nor those in Libya, nor those which have been established in the central regions of the world (presumably Palestine).[18]

Tertullian (c.160–c.220) was just as emphatic with the Gnostics in his work titled *De praescriptione haereticorum* (Against the Heretics), in which he emphasized the great importance of the church's role of unmistakably handing down the truth. Especially noteworthy in the teachings of Irenaeus and Tertullian is that the faith is the same wherever the church is located, although languages and cultures may be different. Later, when he became a member of the Montanists, Tertullian not only expressed concern at a newly arrived laxity in church circles but also sought to undermine one of the church's important identity tags: its hierarchical structure.

In his book *Perspectives on New Religious Movements*, John A. Saliba offers an interesting modern twist to the subject of Gnosticism. He quotes a number of scholars who suggest that "many of the new religious movements, including such groups as the Unification Church and the New Age Movement, are revivals of the Gnostic worldview which is 'again a major competitor for the spiritual allegiance of Christians.'"[19] Scholars are not all of one mind on the subject and, no doubt, continuing studies will be made that should prove beneficial.

Church of Smyrna—Polycarp: The account of *The Martyrdom of St. Polycarp* (+ c.156) offers a different, although relevant, perspective on the question of unity. It begins: "The Church of God which resides as a stranger at Smyrna, to the church of God residing at Philomelium, and to all the communities of the holy and Catholic Church, residing in any place." This passage clearly acknowledges that the one and universal church enjoys local placements all over the world. Chapters 7 and 8 describe the circumstances of eighty-six-year-old Polycarp's final prayer before the hour of his martyrdom "in which he remembered all that he had met at any time—both small and great, both known and unknown to fame, and the whole worldwide Catholic Church."[20]

Novationist problem—Cyprian: A further challenge to the church's unity came in the form of Novationism, which argued that a church lacked the mark of holiness if it was willing to receive back into the community lapsed people or "lapsi Christians," that is, those who renounced the faith in time of persecution. The church has to be a congregation of the holy. In cutting themselves off from the church, the Novationists continued to hold faithfully to the canon of faith, which made a man like Cyprian of Carthage (+ 258) ask a fundamental question: How does one identify the true church? He settled on a simple, straightforward, and perhaps limited answer: The church is comprised of those who are in union or communion with the bishops, and especially with the bishop of Rome. Such became the basis of the western church's self-understanding into the twentieth century, which some would say contributed historically to its heavily sacerdotal and hierarchical identity.[21]

Empire-wide Threats to the Communion

As we have seen, diversity can be an enrichment of the church's unity, but when something intrudes to threaten the very integrity of the church's life, there is a major problem that in no way can be spoken of as legitimate diversity. The intrusions so far identified were serious enough in that they questioned the church's meaning, but since they were localized, they were easily contained. More serious threats, however, had something of an "international" character about them in that they touched the wider church. Clearly, this was a serious matter and called for a more comprehensive response. Such was the case with a number of heresies, three of which we will consider here: Arianism, Nestorianism, and Monophysitism. An altogether new forum—the "general" or "ecumencial" council—responded to each of them.

Arianism and the Council of Nicaea: Lucian of Antioch (c.240–312), head of Antioch's theological school and regarded as the father of Arianism, handed on to his pupil, Arius (c.250–336), the view that the Son did not exist at one time, having been created by the Father. Arius—a priest of Alexandria, eloquent as a preacher, and a ready conversationalist—popularized the view that the Father alone is true God and the principle of all being, the Son not being coeternal with the Father. Rather, the Son was created in order to be an intermediary in the work of creation. As such, therefore, the Son is a creature, even one who is capable of sin. Arius managed quite successfully to propagate his views among clergy and laity alike. He even anticipated twentieth-century techniques by using songs familiar to sailors and travelers to spread his teaching.

The outcome was wide divisiveness across the church, which eventually moved Saint Jerome to observe: *"Ingemuit totus orbis et arianum se esse miratus est"* ("The whole world groaned and marveled to find itself Arian").[22] Local synods did act, one condemning what came to be known as Arianism, others rallying in support of Arius. Emperor Constantine, however, concerned about any threat to the empire's unity, called the first "general" or "ecumenical" council of the whole church: the Council of Nicaea (325). Three hundred bishops joined in this assembly, including the deacon Athanasius (c.293–373), the main defender of orthodox Christianity against Arianism at the council and later, when he became bishop of Alexandria in 328.

The conciliar teaching, long since accepted in the entire Christian world, was first expressed in the Caesaraen Creed (325),[23] and eventually in the Nicaean-Constantinopolitan Creed, dating in its final form from the Council of Constantinople (381). While Arius and the bishops who sided with him were exiled for three years, their return in 328 brought the return of an active promotion of their views. By the middle of the fourth century, there existed three major groupings of Arians: the extremist Anomoeans, who argued that the Father and Son are totally different, the Son being fallible and capable of sin; the Homoiousians or semi-Arians, who taught that the Father and the Son are of "like" substance; and the Homoeans, who retreated from dogmatic precision in stating simply that the Son is "similar" to the Father in all things. Civil connection with Arianism ended when Theodosius I (c.346–395), an ardent Nicene Christian, became emperor and issued the imperial edicts of 383–384. Although Arianism did infect other parts of the world, especially the Germanic tribes, it died by the eighth century.

Nestorianism and the Council of Ephesus: There was a time when "Nestorianism" and the "Council of Ephesus" were subsumed under the word "Nestorian," the Council of Ephesus (431) being a kind of exception in that it alone stood for orthodoxy. This was a simplistic and erroneous viewing of history and an equally wrong classification of people.

Nestorianism has traditionally been explained as a school of thought that denies the hypostatic union of the divine and human natures in Christ, allowing for only "a moral union" of a human person and a divine person. This view suggests that, after the human person and the divine person, there exists a third "person of union." The entire viewpoint carries with it a host of unacceptable implications. Among these is a denial of Mary as *theotokos*, "mother of God," and a denial of the divine in the Eucharist.

Although Nestorius (+ 451) himself was condemned by the Council of Ephesus, there is a great deal of questioning today as to whether or not he was "Nestorian" according to the above understanding. The problem rested, it now seems, not in any denial of the faith by Nestorius but rather in a misunderstanding between Nestorius and his opponent, Cyril of Alexandria, regarding the terms "person" and "nature." This newer understanding is what John Paul II alluded to in his *Angelus* address of November 13, 1994:

> The calm, in-depth dialogue with our brothers of the Assyrian Church of the East made it possible to overcome the misunderstandings that occurred at the time of the Council [Ephesus], and today we share the joy of recognizing that, over and above different theological emphases, our faith in Christ, true God and true man, is one, and equally great is our love for Mary, his most holy Mother.[24]

It is important to realize that the Holy Apostolic Catholic Assyrian Church of the East, to use its precise name, predates Nestorius and the Council of Ephesus by at least two centuries. Scholars are not able to tell us exactly when Christianity first reached the Persian Empire (present-day Iraq and Iran), but it is certain that a Christian community directly linked with earliest Palestinian Christianity was in place there by the middle of the second century. Some suggest that the church's origins reach back even further, to Saint Thomas and his disciples, Addai and Mari.

The association of the Assyrian Church of the East with Nestorian christology dates from a 484 synod that accepted it as the official teaching of the church in Persia. The condemnation of this christology at Ephesus brought with it a persecution of Nestorians who lived mainly in the eastern parts of the Roman Empire. Naturally, many of them took refuge across the border in Persia. The empire and Persia were not on the friendliest of terms, and given the close association of state and religion that characterized the times, the Nestorian teaching inevitably took a firmer hold in Persia, in contrast to the empire's ready acceptance of the conciliar decisions. Without doubt, the isolation of the Assyrian Church of the East from the rest of the Christian world goes back to those times.

Regrettably, the name "Nestorian" has often been applied to the Assyrian Church of the East. Patriarch Mar Dinkha IV, leader of the 400,000 strong church, has expressly asked, however, that it no longer be used. Today, members are spread around the world: in Iraq, parts of the former Soviet Union, India, Lebanon, Syria, Iran, Australia, New Zealand, and across Europe, in the United States and Canada.

Since 1984, important discussions between representatives of the two churches have been progressing, so much so that on November 11, 1994, a *Common Christological Declaration Between the Catholic Church and the Assyrian Church of the East* was signed in Rome by John Paul II and Mar Dinkha IV. Part of the declaration reads:

> The controversies of the past led to anathemas, bearing on persons and formulas. The Lord's Spirit permits us to understand better today that the divisions brought about in this way were due in large part to misunderstandings.
>
> Whatever our christological divergences have been, we experience ourselves united today in the confession of the same faith in the Son of God who became man so that we might become children of God by his grace.[25]

The remarks of John Paul II in his discourse to Mar Dinkha IV, so pertinent to our theme, need to be quoted in full:

> We all recognize that it is of supreme importance to understand, venerate, preserve and foster the rich heritage of each of our Churches, and that a diversity of customs and observances is in no way an obstacle to unity. This diversity includes the power of our Churches to govern themselves according to their own disciplines and to keep certain differences in theological expressions which, as we have verified, are often complementary rather than conflicting.
>
> Together let us ask the Most Holy Trinity, Model of true Unity within diversity, to strengthen our hearts so that we will respond to the call for one visible Church of God, a Church truly universal.[26]

The Mixed Commission, responsible for the ongoing dialogue between the two churches, meets annually. Recent discussions have been about sacramental life, including the Holy Leaven

(Malka) and the Sign of the Cross in the Assyrian Church, and marriage and the anointing of the sick in the Catholic Church. Although these latter two are not numbered among the sacraments of the Assyrian Church's tradition, the members of the commission did reach "a profound agreement on the theological content and significance of these ecclesial acts."

The commission has also deliberated on the Nicaean-Constantinople Creed, including the question of the *filioque* (a term that is further explained in the next chapter), the outcome being that the Assyrian Church has no objection to the Catholic Church's continuing use of this formula in the creed. Discussions about Mary, particularly regarding the Immaculate Conception and the Assumption, reveal that the Assyrian Church acknowledges these two theological "facts." Speaking about them as dogmas, however, raises a wider question, that of papal primacy, which is another and larger issue.

All of this serves to illustrate that present-day Christians who are truly serious about the work of unity and who willingly revisit previous problem areas—even ancient disputes—can find points of "convergence" that hitherto seemed totally out of the question. The goal of the dialogue between the Catholic Church and the Assyrian Church of the East is the fullness of unity, remembering that it has to be a unity lived in legitimate diversity.

Monophysitism and the Council of Chalcedon: In the same way that the title "Nestorian" assumed wider usage than should have been the case, the word "Monophysitism" came to designate a variety of persons and churches that did not deserve such categorizing.

In Greek, *Monophysitism* means "one nature" and has been applied to those who have stressed Christ's divinity to the point of overlooking, even denying, his humanity. The Council of Chalcedon (451) condemned the error, teaching that in "one and the same Lord Jesus Christ, the only-begotten Son, must be acknowledged in two natures, without confusion or change, without division or separation."[27]

Eutyches (c.375–c.454), a monk of Constantinople, has often been referred to as the father of Monophysitism because, in disagreement with the Chalcedonian formula, he taught that the previously existing divine and human natures so blended in the person of Christ that only one resulted: the divine nature. This overemphasis on Christ's divinity could have serious consequences for Christianity, not the least of which would be a denial of Christ's essential identity with us. To be the "second Adam," Christ has to have our human nature.

Beyond the disagreement of Eutyches with the Council of Chalcedon, there was a group of eastern churches that also rejected the christological formula of Chalcedon, that is, "one hypostasis in two natures." This group preferred the wording of Saint Cyril of Alexandria: "the one nature of the Incarnate God." Unfortunately, because they historically did not accept Chalcedon's definition, they have long been called Monophysites, wrongly linking them with Eutyches.

Today, these churches—known collectively as the Oriental Orthodox churches—are the Armenian Apostolic Church, the Coptic Orthodox Church, the Ethiopian Orthodox Church, the Syrian Orthodox Church, the Malankara Orthodox Syrian Church in India, and the Orthodox Church of Eritrea. Together, they have been variously classified as the "Non-Chalcedonian Churches," the "Pre-Chalcedonian Churches," the "Ancient Oriental Churches," and even the "Lesser Eastern Churches," to distinguish them from the Eastern Orthodox Churches.

Modern investigations of this complicated past reveal that the "Non-Chalcedonians" were not, in fact, one with the exaggerated teaching of Eutyches. More precisely, according to the *Common Declaration* (1971) of Paul VI and Patriarch Mar Yacob III of the Syrian Orthodox Church:

> There is no difference in the faith they profess concerning the mystery of the Word of God made flesh and become really man, even if over the centuries difficulties have risen out of the different theological expressions by which this faith was expressed. They therefore encourage the clergy and faithful of their Churches to even greater endeavors at removing the obstacles which still prevent complete communion among them. This should be done with love, with openness to the promptings of the Holy Spirit, and with mutual respect for each other and each other's Church.[28]

The same sentiments were expressed in the *Common Declaration* of Paul IV and Pope Shenouda III, May 1973, regarding the Coptic Orthodox Church:

> We confess that our Lord and God and Savior and King of us all, Jesus Christ, is perfect God with respect to His divinity, perfect man with respect to His humanity. In Him His divinity is united with His humanity in a real, perfect union without mingling, without commixtion, without confusion, without alteration, without division, without separation. His divinity did not separate from His humanity for an instant, not for the twinkling of an eye. He who is God eternal and invisible became visible in the flesh, and took upon Himself the form of a servant. In Him are preserved all the properties of the divinity and all the properties of the humanity, together in a real, perfect, indivisible and inseparable union.[29]

There are, of course, several churches—six in all—which belong to this sector of the Christian world. All of them are in communion with one another while preserving their independence. Since the first agreement in 1967, several others have followed, which means that, according to Ronald G. Roberson:

> The ancient christological dispute between the Oriental Orthodox Churches and the Catholic Church has been substantially resolved. Even though different interpretations of the meaning of the Chalcedonian definition remain, the churches have been able to set aside the old disputes and affirm that their faith in the mystery of Christ which transcends all formulations is, in fact, the same.[30]

Some of these churches, as we have seen, are in dialogue with the Catholic Church and the Orthodox Church, and many of the leaders have visited Rome and other church leaders. They are obviously serious about working for full communion. When this is achieved, the united church will be enriched by having within it diverse liturgical traditions, different spiritual patrimonies, and a range of traditions and customs. In his book titled *The Eastern Christian Churches*, Roberson offers a profile on each church.[31]

❖ ❖ ❖

The scriptures present a rich array of evidence that God does not require people to respond to him in a uniform fashion. God is the creator and respector of legitimate differences, and all of these he gathers into a unity, except when impeded by sinfulness. This has been his way of acting always. The patristic churches, on the one hand, jealously preserved their local ecclesial expressions, yet on the other, they were acutely aware of the urgency of always being in the one church of Christ. In a word, they proclaim for succeeding generations to observe and imitate the important dictum of unity in diversity.

Our study of several ancient Christian traditions—the Assyrian Chruch of the East and the Oriental Orthodox Churches—demonstrates how a blurring of their integrity occurred in ages past which only now, partly in virtue of the principle of unity in diversity, is allowing a rich relationship to develop among them, and with the Catholic Church and other Christian Churches.

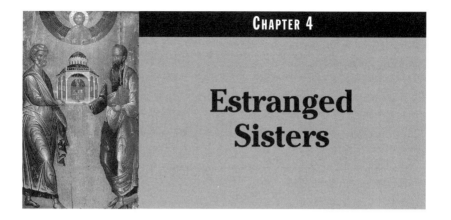

CHAPTER 4

Estranged Sisters

A modern church in the modern world is happening, but not without some pain. The prior institutional model of the Catholic Church, which emphasized her visible and distinctive bounds and structures, clearly expressed the roles among her members and defined her relationships with the world, with other religions, and with other Christians in particular. All these relationships had been worked out over a long period of time and were very much in place at the beginning of the twentieth century. But the model itself, and all its operations, became subject to questioning. The subsequent revision, which became focused in the comparatively short period of time associated with the Second Vatican Council, brought forth renewed definitions of the church, including a fresh approach to the roles of her own faithful, both lay and clerical; an expanded understanding of God's universal plan of salvation; a commitment to the church having a positive attitude toward the world; and an altogether new viewing of her ecclesial boundaries.

The Importance of Symbols

A rather refreshing rediscovery in these times is the place of "symbol" in helping the Catholic Church arrive at a richer appreciation of life and, in our context, of the meaning of "church." Catholics were long used to the dominance of prede-termined categories and measurements, all associated with the mind. Recall the earlier observation of how all people beyond the Catholic Church were so readily classified as "non-Catholics," and even more as heretics, schismatics, dissidents, or infidels. Such was one of the sad side effects of a "one-track" approach to life in all its complexities.

What came to be overlooked was the power of the imagi-nation and the symbols it produces that help people reach life's deeper religious meaning. Christ frequently used symbols to teach the kingdom, and his church continues to proclaim that the sacraments are natural symbols that signify and cause supernatural grace. Stephen Happel explains that people nowadays are coming to appreciate the power of symbols, including their effectiveness in bringing about change. "Knowing that societies are changed more by symbols than by concepts, liberation theology or theologies of emancipation have focused upon the transformative dimension of symbols." He goes on to say that "symbols not only reflect social sys-tems; they change them."[1]

A case in point is the changing mutual assessment of each other by the Catholic Church and the Orthodox Church, which is finding expression in the revival of "the traditional and very beautiful expression 'sister churches,' which local Churches were fond of applying to one another."[2] *Anno Ineunte* (At the beginning of the Year of Faith), a papal brief read in the pres-ence of Paul VI and Ecumenical Patriarch Athenagoras I during a service in Istanbul on July 25, 1967, goes on to say, in the con-text of east-west relations, "And now, after a long period of divi-sion and mutual misunderstanding, the Lord is enabling us to discover ourselves as 'sister churches' once more, in spite of the obstacles which were once raised between us."[3]

A further symbol, probably coined by Yves Congar and cer-tainly used by John Paul II, is at the base of a gradual move-ment away from viewing one another as "other" and "foreign," in favor of a fundamental ecclesial unity that the two already possess, although which needs to be perfected and made visible. That is why Congar was able to say, "Many of us would hold that on the level of the ancient conception of the church as a unity of faith, a sacramental reality and spiritual organism, which the Orthodox retain, it is the same church. I have often suggested this and more than once have wished that the church would begin to breathe through its two lungs, an image which His Holiness John Paul II has also used several times."[4]

Symbols such as "sister churches" and "the church breathing through its two lungs" say a lot. They do not point to divisiveness, suggest guilt, or promote a living out of past antipathies. Instead, they acknowledge and act out of foundational relationships, and they offer rich possibilities for a restoration of that unity that respects legitimate differences and does not call for the absorption of one church by the other. In this way, an envisioning of the future is filled with hope. Not only has the use of symbols helped church relationships, but it has deepened Christian appreciation of what it means to be in the church.[5]

Catholic Arrival at a New Self-understanding

If there was lingering doubt about what should be the Catholic Church's proper self-understanding, two encyclicals of Pius XII certainly offer clarity. *Mystici Corporis Christi* (of the mystical Body of Christ, 1943) and *Humani Generis* (Concerning some False Opinions which Threaten to Undermine the Foundations of Catholic Doctrine, 1950) presented a teaching that seemed to remove forever the ambiguity that had bedeviled discussions on the subject during the nineteenth and early twentieth centuries.

Document of the Preparatory Theological Commission

The Preparatory Theological Commission was entirely faithful to the mind of Pius XII in the text titled *De Ecclesia* (About the Church), prepared for and presented at the opening session of the council in 1962. It stated that "the Roman

Catholic Church is the Mystical Body of Christ...and only the one that is Roman Catholic has the right to be called Church."[6]

It is clear from such a statement that others who called themselves Christian had no "church" identity, according to the mind of the Catholic Church. This explains why she had never developed a theology of ecumenism or evolved an ecumenical program. There simply was no recognition of a church existing beyond Catholicism. In a word, there was no one with whom the Catholic Church could be ecumenical. Unity was still conceived of in terms of all others *returning* to Rome.

This statement of the Preparatory Theological Commission was given a harsh reception, so much so that the council leadership took the opportunity to withdraw it without putting it to the vote. Thereafter, the council became the forum where *Lumen Gentium*, the document on the church, and *Unitatis Redintegratio*, the document on ecumenism, could evolve. A study of the minutes of the council sessions makes fascinating reading, offering insights into the seriousness with which the council members so earnestly searched for a true understanding of the church's identity and for the best possible ways in which to express it.

Development in the Commission's Thinking

A further stage in the process was the presentation in 1963 of a replacement document for *De Ecclesia*. It retained much from the former document, including the statement that the one and only Church of Christ is the Catholic Church. But additional words appeared, such as "many elements of sanctification can be found outside its total structure" and these are things "properly belonging to the Church of Christ." The clear implication here is that a variety of ways of sanctification, which are churchly or ecclesial in character, can and do exist beyond the visible bounds of the Catholic Church. This represents a major development in thinking.

Yet, great difficulties persisted. Not the least of these was the new document's failure to acknowledge that the actual communities to which other Christians belong are the possessors, in some way, of this ecclesial character. Not even orthodoxy was accorded such recognition. Further work had to be done.

In 1964, another draft arrived on the council floor that eventually would be refined to become *Lumen Gentium*. A great development showed up in some of the specific wording in the document that went beyond the thinking of Pius XII as reflected in the statement of the Preparatory Theological Commission "that the Roman Catholic Church *is* the Mystical Body of Christ." The revision read: "The unique Church of Christ ... constituted and organized in the world as a society, subsists in the Catholic Church."[7]

The word "subsists," which was never explained or defined by the council, replaced the word "is." In other words, the prior simple identification of the Catholic Church and the Mystical Body of Christ in an exclusive way could no longer stand. Since then, it has become the church's task to interpret what the council intended by choosing the word "subsists."

A starting point is the constant and unalterable teaching that the Church of Christ exists in its fullness in the Catholic Church. This is foundational to Catholic ecclesiology. But the important point of development is clear: it is no longer right to make a simple equation that the Church of Christ *is* or *equals* the Catholic Church. What is implied, and what is understood very clearly, is that there is an ecclesial or church reality beyond the Catholic Church. In this recognition—of other Christian communities having some elements of the nature of "church"—rests the foundation for Catholic participation in ecumenism.[8] Catholic contact, beyond its own visible bounds, is not confined to other Christians as individuals, but extends to their churches within which they receive their faith and their baptism and where ministry gives to the people their Christian nourishment and support.

Not only has the Catholic Church entered into the ecumenical movement, but she has become a leading voice in many aspects of the drive toward the unity for which Christ prayed. The great range of dialogues, and the very significant progress in so many of them, evidences the level of commitment of the Catholic Church and of her dialogue partners.

And as one reviews the great range of "separated Churches and Communities" (a term no longer acceptable, by the way), to use the precise words of *Unitatis Redintegratio,*[9] it soon becomes obvious that there are levels of closeness between them and the Catholic Church, depending on their retention of those characteristics that enter into the essential definition of "church." Chief among these churches is the Orthodox Church,[10] because of the very close communion that already exists in matters of faith and sacramental life. It is now our task to examine how the Orthodox Church and the Catholic Church came to have an existence apart from each other.

Development of Contrasting Ecclesiologies

The year 1054, which saw the mutual excommunications of the bishops of Constantinople and Rome, has long been cited as the moment of cleavage between the Catholic and Orthodox Churches. It is better to see this date, however, as one of convenience, chosen by the Council of Basle-Ferrara-Florence (1438–1445), where the need was felt to pinpoint an event which its document of reunion, *Laetentur coeli* (Let the heavens be glad and let the earth rejoice), would address. The truth is, two ecclesiastical mindsets developed over a long period of time that, eventually, clashed. Two contrasting east and west "universalist" stances were gradually set in place.

The "Universalism" of the East

Emperor Constantine's (306–337) move of the capital from Rome to Byzantium, renamed Constantinople, and the change within the empire from a federalized structure of provinces and cities to one of centralized control, was the beginning of an imperial control system that was universalist in nature. The Christian emperor increasingly intervened in church affairs, including the convoking of councils and ensuring the reception of the conciliar decrees across the empire. He designated patriarchs and drew up diocesan boundaries. In the minds of many, the move of the capital from Rome to Constantinople generated the idea that ecclesiastical prominence was tied to the location of the imperial capital.

It was not unknown, of course, for emperors to intervene in church and western affairs. Constans II (642–668) imprisoned Pope Martin I because he refused to sign the emperor's *Typos* concerning the nature of Christ. Martin was taken to Constantinople, tried, and then exiled to the Crimea where he died in 655. Again, in the eighth century, a series of emperors forbade the use of icons, and so Emperor Leo III punished the pope for his opposition by annexing the papal lands in southern Italy and Sicily.

The strong identification of empire and church became a hallmark of the east. "Christian society" was understood to embrace all aspects of life, so that any mention of "unity" was always understood to include not just religion, but politics and culture as well. But when the empire began to disintegrate, and there was an inevitable diminution of geographical universalism, the church in the east continued to be culturally and politically tied, now to national entities. For example, Byzantium became the church of the Greeks. Such strong identifications of church and nation—or more accurately, of church and culture—persists today under the umbrella of "autocephalous"[11] churches, which means that local churches have also long enjoyed respected identities in the Orthodox world.

The "Universalism" of the West

Meanwhile, the universalism that emerged in the west was more ecclesiological in character. Imperial moves of one kind or another pushed the church in the west into thinking about its own identity and organization. Before Diocletian (284–313), the one church comprised a communion of local churches, somewhat along the lines of the empire being made up of a federation of provinces and cities. Within these churches, however, there was an awareness of Rome as the place of the martyrdoms of Peter and Paul. This brought to the city a prestige based more on the widely acknowledged religious significance that had come to the city, rather than on the positioning of the capital. There was an ever-deepening awareness of the need to be free of political interference, the church's identity being apostolic and not reliant on the empire. Inevitably, the ecclesiological emphasis shifted from an understanding of the church as *communio,* that is, as a communion of local churches, to a viewing of the church in its universality, that is, of the church in its oneness under the leadership of the bishop of Rome. This is a characteristic of the western and Roman church that has never been lost.

But the understanding did not continue indefinitely as something purely and simply ecclesiological. A continuing fear of secular interference motivated Rome into developing as the empire's rival power, which became abundantly clear on Christmas Day, 800, when Pope Leo III (795–816) crowned Charlemagne the emperor of the west, thereby securing a guardian for the papacy and things western. Added to this was the western church's strong missionary bent, in response to the mandate given by Christ to take the gospel to the ends of the earth. More and more people and territories came under papal influence.

The "imperial Rome" mentality gradually infiltrated the church and, inevitably, the church was identified with the Latin culture. Both of these—the vestiges of imperial Rome and the Latin culture—were to enjoy a long, deeply felt, and universal presence in western Christendom. "Local church" identity was supplanted by the ever-strengthening presence of the idea of the "universal church." The imposition of certain practices and customs of the Latin church overtook local cultures, and papal ecclesiastical rule displaced episcopal and synodal government.

Impact of Contrasting Doctrinal and Nontheological Items

East and west were definitely straining in different directions, inevitably creating for themselves distinctive identities. Then, a series of factors and events leading into the eleventh century lent emphasis to the contrasts. These included doctrinal as well as nontheological items.

Muslim expansion: As Timothy Ware observes, the most striking feature of Muslim expansion was the speed with which it happened. Within fifteen years of the death of Muhammad (c.570–632), Syria, Palestine, and Egypt had fallen to his invading forces, and within a hundred years, his followers had swept through North Africa and Spain, only to be stopped at the battle of Poitiers in 732 by Charles Martel. By the year 700, Islam had managed to suppress the patriarchates of Antioch, Alexandria, and Jerusalem. Although they actually survived, they enjoyed only minimal visibility, thereby leaving Constantinople, the youngest of them, to share with Rome the control of the Christian world.[12] Unable to compete with an ever-strengthening and missionary-oriented Rome, Constantinople failed to look forward. Instead, it chose to reflect nostalgically on a golden past, while at the same time being left to grapple alone with an expanding Islamic presence. In terms of "power," the east was definitely weakening, and the west, under Rome, was strengthening.

Use of the term filioque: *Filioque* ("and from the Son") hails from sixth-century Spanish theologians. It spread into France when Charlemagne (742–814) attempted to make it a compulsory addition to the Nicene-Constantinopolitan creed. Although a series of popes were opposed, sufficient pressure was exercised for the addition eventually to gain papal approval from Benedict VIII in 1014.

While it was right for the Greeks to protest this unilateral western addition to an ecumenical creed, it is an exaggeration for some Orthodox people to claim that the *filioque* is a theological distortion that actually brought about the east-west rupture. The fact is, the word was increasingly in use for five hundred years prior to the 1054 break, during which time west and east remained in communion.[13] As Metropolitan J. D. Zizioulas points out, the *filioque* later became a victim of polemic so as to justify the division.[14]

The core of the matter is not one of theological division but of linguistic differences, as becomes evident in the highly regarded research article prepared in 1995 by the PCPCU. Both east and west recognize "that the Father is the sole Trinitarian Cause or Principle of the Son and of the Holy Spirit," although each tradition has used different words to express the relationships within the Trinity.[15]

In a homily in the presence of Patriarch Bartholomew I on June 29, 1995, John Paul II said: "On the Catholic side, there is a firm desire to clarify the traditional doctrine of the *Filioque*, present in the liturgical version of the Latin *Credo*, in order to highlight its full harmony with what the Ecumenical Council confesses in its creed: the Father as the source of the whole Trinity, the one origin of both the Son and the Holy Spirit."[16]

Metropolitan Zizioulas, in his 1998 address at the University of Saint Thomas in Rome, expressed the opinion that a resolution should soon be possible.

Language and theological style: The *filioque* controversy points to two items of "infrastructure" that highlight the historical parting of the ways between east and west. One is the matter of language, which Yves Congar rightly identifies as a fashioner of ideas.[17] The loss of the Greek language in the west, and of Latin in the east, had a detrimental effect on theological thinking, expression, and communication.

The second item, especially evident from the eleventh century on, is the variation in theological styles.[18] Whereas the west tended to approach theology according to specialities and in a compartmentalized way, the east continued to work with philosophy, theology, and spirituality as one entity.

Fortunately, we live at a time when an improving atmosphere allows for these former problems to be viewed more dispassionately and to be talked about in nonconfrontational ways. Hence, John Paul II felt free enough to refer to the issue in his homily on the feast of Saints Peter and Paul in 1995. He mentioned that the Joint Commission's task "is to explain, in the light of our common faith, the legitimate meaning and importance of different traditional expressions concerning the eternal origin of the Holy Spirit in the Trinity."[19] Because of the insights they shed on the great Christian truths, contrasting theological styles are coming to be appreciated as mutually enriching and complementary, not contradictory.

Disputes: There were other difficulties along the way, such as Pope Nicholas I's (858–867) intervention in the dispute between Ignatius and Photius over the occupancy of the patriarchate of Constantinople. When Nicholas insisted that the two should submit to arbitration, the incumbent, Photius, refused and was subsequently deposed by Nicholas in 863. Photius retaliated in a number of ways, including the convening of a council at Constantinople in 867 at which Nicholas was deposed and excommunicated. Eventually, Photius was reinstated as patriarch. Although relations with Rome did improve, wounds had been inflicted and would continue to fester.

In the eleventh century, a level of east-west cooperation might have been expected because of the common enemy, the Normans. Leo IX (1049–1054) had already experienced defeat at the hands of this enemy that was now threatening Greek-controlled southern Italy. An exchange of letters between the pope, the Byzantine emperor, and Patriarch Michael Cerularius (1043–1058), intended as efforts of communication and cooperation, degenerated into ecclesiastical mud-slinging documents. The last of them was delivered by Cardinal Humbert (c.1000–1061), who was charged with the task of securing reconciliation. Instead of entering into conciliation, and now that Pope Leo IX had died, Humbert chose to place on the altar in the church of Saint Sophia a bull of excommunication of "Michael and his followers." Humbert did this in full view of the congregation on July, 16, 1054. The patriarch responded by excommunicating the authors of the "impious document."[20]

Thus, the year 1054 marks the beginning of the schism. Not until 1965 would the excommunications of 1054 be simultaneously lifted by Paul VI, in Rome, and Patriarch Athenagoras, in present-day Constantinople (Istanbul).

The crusades: Even at this point, the church was still considered to be one. It was the crusades, most especially the fourth crusade (1202–1204), which made the cleavage definitive. Begun by Innocent III (c.1198–1216), control was soon lost when the forces acceded to the request of Alexius IV, who offered rewards to the crusaders if they would secure for him the throne of Constantinople. The city was sacked, the churches were plundered, and Alexius made his way onto the throne. Soon murdered, he was replaced by a westerner, Baldwin of Flanders. Inevitably, a Latin patriarchate was set up and a heavy Latinization program got underway. Western canon law, scholastic philosophy, and Roman rituals invaded the east, with a twofold negative effect: deep hurt to easterners and a denial of the experience of legitimate diversity to westerners.[21]

In reflecting on the long history of the one church before either 1054 or 1204, whichever date one prefers to emphasize, the evidence points to a universal and unwavering attachment to the essentials of the Christian faith. The creeds were born of the one church of the first millennium, and the church's

hierarchical structure, her apostolic succession, the episcopacy, and the priesthood were never subject to questioning.
The area of "mutual incomprehension," to use the words of
Paul VI, is really one: authority, with a range of circumstances
stretching over a number of centuries exacerbating this trou-
blesome subject. The east, for the sake of the church, grew in
appreciation of the roles of the patriarchs, synods, and ecumenical councils; emphasized the communion of the local
churches; and recognized infallibility as a quality invested in the
whole church. The west, also for the sake of the church, paid
particular attention to the emergence of the bishop of Rome
having supreme and universal jurisdiction; to papal infallibility;
and to the universal church, which was at times an earthly
power as well.

When history is allowed to be history, and when review
and dialogue heal the painful memories and correct misunderstandings, these two emphases will contribute to a healthier
united church. We will see that the sufferings of the church of
yesteryear have come to better serve the world of tomorrow.

Attempts at Reconciliation: Eastern Catholic Churches

There is little doubt that a long line of popes and eastern
emperors keenly sought the restoration of unity between east
and west. Their common formula was a mix of politics and doctrine, as will become evident from the two conciliar decisions
in favor of reconciliation, both of which failed because they
could not be sustained in the marketplace.

The Two Councils

The first legislative attempt was at the Second Council of
Lyons (1274). Before this, however, Emperor Michael VIII, seeking a political advantage, engaged in several conversations with
Rome regarding reunion, although the Greek Orthodox episcopate was never party to the talks. Gregory X's (1272–1276)
response was to send agents to Byzantium armed with a doctrinal formula in which the baseline for the negotiation was submission to Roman primacy and acceptance of the *filioque*.

The Greek delegation was placed under heavy imperial pressure to accept the Roman demands, and their patriarch, Joseph, was confined to a monastery and threatened with deposition if he did not consent. At the council's fourth session on July 6, the decision in favor of union was proclaimed, and the imperial party signed a creed that accepted the primacy, the *filioque*, belief in purgatory, and the seven sacraments. Gregory X intoned the *Te Deum!*

While Rome did not follow through with appropriate support for a threatened Constantinople, the union failed. This can be attributed in part to the fact that the Latin occupation was still fresh in the minds of the clergy. More so, because:

> The union had been founded on the theological concept of the Western papacy. Its *plenitudo potestatis* was quite capable of maintaining itself in the West, thanks to its decretalist elaboration, which dominated the resolutions of the council of 1274 in an impressive manner, and which left its imprint still more impressively (in view of the political importance of the papacy) on the Council of Vienne (1311). But it made any union with the Greek church illusory, because it required the Greeks to give up their ecclesiological self-understanding.[22]

As at Lyons, the emperor played a key role—for political purposes—in bringing the Greek party to accept the terms of the reunion at Basle-Ferrara-Florence (1438–1445). Emperor John VIII Palaeologus, conscious of the Turkish threat, knew he needed some form of union with the west to help save empire and city. He realized that involving the Greek church would require nothing less than an ecumenical council.

Pope Eugene IV (c.1387–1447) supplied a fleet to transport the emperor, Patriarch Joseph, and the seven hundred Greek delegates from Constantinople to Ferrara, the city that had superseded Basle as the site of the council. But the plague required yet another move, now to Florence. It was here that the discussion on the procession on the Holy Spirit, recognized as the main obstacle to reunion, took place February through June. Eventually, all but two of the Greek delegation agreed to the Latin explanation, and the decree of union was signed on July 6, 1439.

The agreement did not come to fruition, however. This is explained in part by the failure of the European princes to bring the help promised for the defense of Constantinople, an omission that fed into the deeply rooted Greek dislike of the Latin world. More directly, however, was the action of Bishop Mark Eugenicus of Ephesus, one of those who held out against any agreement at the council. He returned to Constantinople ahead of the emperor and energetically promoted rejection of the conciliar decision among the Greek clergy and people.[23]

In 1484, the union of Florence was officially repudiated in a synod at Constantinople, an action that was not repeated in the west. According to the western church, the agreement still holds, and what has to happen is for the union to be realized.

Regional Reconciliations and the Arrival of "Uniatism"

The last emperor perished in 1453 at the hands of Islam, leaving Rome without a Christian "rival." As a result, Roman relations with Constantinople in the east took on a different character, determined by changing circumstances in the east and new developments in the west. Chief among these was the Protestant Reformation that brought the inevitable reaction, expressed in and through Trent, of an even firmer definition of church membership involving obedience to Rome.

A theological footing, therefore, was in place for missionary work to be undertaken among those Christians not obedient to the bishop of Rome, and these of course, would include the churches of the east. Given the failure of the two councils to bring about reunion, the new missionary strategy aimed at regional reconciliations, a number of which came about. They have often been called "uniate churches," a term which these eastern Catholics today find offensive and which should no longer be used. When spoken of generically, it is appropriate to refer to them as the "Eastern Catholic Churches."

In his book, *The Eastern Christian Churches: A Brief Survey*,[24] Ronald G. Roberson recognizes three basic groups of regional reconciliations. The first was found in the Austro-Hungarian Empire where the work of Catholic missionaries, aided by a pressuring Catholic government, brought about the reconciliation with Rome of a number of Orthodox dioceses. The second model saw the creation, in the Middle East especially, of pro-Catholic cells within the local Orthodox churches. The intention was to bring about the reconciliation of the entire church with Rome, by having bishops elected—and if possible a patriarch—who would be sympathetic to the program. The third model, and the least successful, had Catholic missionaries establishing parallel Byzantine Catholic Churches in the hope that these would eventually replace their Orthodox counterparts. The author also points out that some unions with the Catholic Church came about because of Orthodox initiatives. The Union of Brest in 1595 and the Bulgarian Byzantine Catholic Church came to exist this way.

An important characteristic of these unions was the Eastern Catholic Churches' retention of their own liturgical styles and theologies, of their ecclesiastical disciplines, and of other oriental tonings in line with the notion of "rites" (as discussed in chapter 1). Unfortunately, pressure was brought to bear so that aspects of these legitimate features gradually diminished, in favor of imposed western, particularly Roman, styles.

Eastern Catholic Churches Today

With the passage of time, many of these Eastern Catholic Churches lost contact with their spiritual roots. That is why *Orientalium Ecclesiarum* (The Decree on Eastern Catholic Churches), the Vatican II document on these churches, points out both their importance in the universal church and the need for them to recover their proper traditions. The decree also identifies their special ecumenical task of "promoting the unity of all Christians, particularly Easterners, according to the principles of this sacred Synod's Decree on Ecumenism: first of all by prayer, then by the example of their lives, by religious fidelity to ancient Eastern traditions, by greater mutual knowledge, by collaboration, and by a brotherly regard for object and attitudes."[25]

Some people continue to have difficulty seeing how the Eastern Catholic Churches have "a special role" in promoting Christian unity, especially with the Orthodox Church. On the one hand, the memory is still vivid that the origins of some of them depended on methods quite unpalatable to orthodoxy, and to us. As Roberson points out, there is "some evidence that the official denial of the validity of Catholic baptism by some Orthodox churches can be seen as pastoral responses to the threat they saw in uniatism."[26] On the other hand, there is the problem of the action taken against the Eastern Catholic Churches by communist regimes, especially since the Second World War, and the allegation that some Orthodox people cooperated with the communist authorities in the suppression of these churches.[27] Memories are still fresh.

With the collapse of communism in eastern Europe, tensions between Orthodox Churches and Eastern Catholic Churches, including multiple accusations of proselytism, became such that the Joint International Commission for the Theological Dialogue Between the Roman Catholic Church and the Orthodox Church suspended its regular theological dialogue in order to deal with "the question which is called *uniatism*." The document it made public on July 15, 1993, known as the Balamand Statement, is of great importance, its very title being indicative of significant progress: *Uniatism, Method of Union in the Past, and the Present Search for Full Communion*.[28] Two particular sections state that:

> ...the Oriental Catholic Churches...as part of the Catholic communion, have the right to exist and to act in answer to the spiritual needs of their faithful (3).

> ...uniatism, can no longer be accepted either as a method to be followed nor as a model of the unity our churches are seeking (12).

These two sections, and indeed the entire document, are addressed in the first instance, to those Orthodox churches that have questioned the very legitimacy of the existence of the Catholic Eastern Churches. Similarly, the statement speaks to Eastern Catholics who have come to fear for their own existence because of the contemporary Roman Catholic-Orthodox dialogue that aims at full organic unity. Finally, Roman Catholics who might be embarrassed by the presence of Eastern-rite Catholic Churches in the west are required to rethink their uniformist proclivities and learn to take pleasure in, and be proud of, the richness of diversity of the church in its universality.[29]

Despite the values present in the Balamand Report, however, its arrival has not been without controversy. While some see it as having value in helping overcome the division between the Eastern Orthodox Church and the Roman Catholic Church, others are unhappy with it. A useful analysis of the report and its background, with a series of questions and answers about it, has been prepared by the Orthodox members of the USA Orthodox/Roman Catholic Consultation.[30]

A contemporary example of not allowing past events to have a lasting negative impact is evidenced in the developing positive relationship of the Antioch Catholic Church and the Orthodox Church. Antioch is one of the ancient patriarchates, covering all of the eastern part of the Roman Empire, which would eventually suffer greatly during the Islamic invasions. Then in the seventeenth and eighteenth centuries, because of the work of Catholic missionaries, a "uniate" church was formed in 1724—the Melkite Catholic Church. Today, the two patriarchates have established a joint commission charged with facilitating reunion. They both pray that this step will aid the wider reconciliation of the churches of the east and the west.

The Orthodox Church

There is little doubt that the Orthodox Church and the Catholic Church are one in the essentials, although each has developed particular identifying features. These include variations in theological expressions, spiritualities, and monastic foundations; differences in styles of ecclesiastical government and structuring; and a variety of ways of viewing their responsibilities to the world and to people beyond their own ranks.

Our intention now is not to examine the theological foundations for Orthodoxy's particular identity; we take that for granted. Rather, we take a brief look at some of the more observable features that characterize the Orthodox Church.

The Orthodox Church, known also as the Eastern Orthodox Church (to distinguish it from the Oriental Orthodox), comprises those three hundred million Christians worldwide who are in communion with the ecumenical patriarch of Constantinople.[31] The name "orthodox" has a twofold meaning:

right belief and right worship, which amounts to Orthodoxy's claim to guardianship of true belief and worship.

The church is very much decentralized, local churches having recognizable identities, often as national churches. *Communio*, or *koinonia*, is therefore important, so that the variety of self-governing churches are drawn into and made part of the family. They enjoy this communion with one another and with the patriarch of Constantinople, who occupies a position of special honor as "the first among equals." Constantinople, and its patriarch—the ecumenical patriarch—is the symbolic center of the Eastern Orthodox Churches.

There are fifteen autocephalous, or self-governing, churches. These churches enjoy the right, on their own authority, to solve internal problems and to choose their leadership, including the patriarch, the archbishop or the metropolitan. The four ancient patriarchates, for historical reasons, have a special place. They are Constantinople, Alexandria, Antioch, and Jerusalem. The other eleven autocephalous churches emerged later. Among these are two whose autocephalous status depends on recognition given by the Moscow patriarchate, and not by the patriarchate of Constantinople, which considers that it alone can grant autocephaly. They are the Orthodox Church in the Czech and Slovak Republics (1951) and the Orthodox Church in North America (1970).

There are other churches that do not have full independence, although they are self-governing in most matters. This means that the appointment of the head of an autonomous church has to be ratified by the head or synod of an autocephalous church.

A further group comprises seven canonical churches that have a special link with the ecumenical patriarchate of Constantinople. Their relationship with Constantinople, for the most part, arises out of political problems in their own countries, and the need for them to have the canonical protection of the ecumenical patriarch. In practice, this means that they receive the holy chrism and confirmation of their bishops from Constantinople. There is also a number of churches whose canonical status is in doubt, or others outside of communion with the Orthodox Church.

Orthodox-Catholic Dialogue Today

Historically, each church, Roman Catholic and Orthodox, saw itself as the world's sole source of salvation. Out of this kind of self-realization, they frequently rebaptized converts from one to the other, denied religious freedom beyond their own visible bounds, and developed missionary tactics that resulted in "uniatism," practiced by the Roman Catholic Church, and "protectionism," practiced by the Orthodox Church. It is one of the great graces of the twentieth century that both have felt the stirrings of the Spirit calling for a restoration of the fullness of communion and an abolition of their past unpalatable practices.

Two Churches Approaching Unity

On the Catholic side, the beginnings of change, and the establishment of the theological justification for it, belong to the Second Vatican Council, expressed particularly in *Unitatis Redintegratio* (14–18). Of importance is the document's explicit recognition of the Orthodox as "churches," indicating the arrival of an altogether new ecclesiology in the Catholic Church:

> This sacred Synod urges all, but especially those who plan to devote themselves to the work of restoring the full communion that is desired between the Eastern Churches and the Catholic Church, to give due consideration to these special aspects of the origin and growth of the Churches of the East (14).

An early indicator of the Orthodox Church's commitment to the ecumenical movement was expressed in the 1920 encyclical letter of the ecumenical patriarchate of Constantinople. Its introductory words are:

> Our own church holds that rapprochement between the various Christian Churches and fellowship between them is not excluded by the doctrinal differences which exist between them. In our opinion such a rapprochement is highly desirable and necessary. It would be useful in many ways for the real interest of each particular church and of

the whole Christian body, and also for the preparation and advancement of that blessed union which will be completed in the future in accordance with the will of God.[32]

Just as a League of Nations had been formed, the patriarchate was suggesting the formation of a League of Churches, about which it sought "the judgment and the opinion of the other sister churches in the East and of the venerable Christian churches in the West and everywhere in the world."[33]

The Orthodox Church, however, has had an ongoing struggle, even into the final decade of the twentieth century, of trying to arrive at a revision of its ecclesiology, and therefore of arriving at an understanding of "ecumenism" in tune with the vast majority of other Christian churches. Theodore Stylianopoulos, writing in 1985, is worth quoting at length:

> Traditionally the Orthodox Churches have not developed positive means of relating to other Christian bodies but rather looked upon them in the categories of schism and heresy which would be healed only by repentance and return to the Orthodox Church ... The Orthodox need to realize that this avenue to Christian unity is closed. Rather the Orthodox need to accept the necessity of a long period of growth in a spiritual unity of hearts and minds through authentic dialogue and cooperation, and of witnessing to the key signs of the fullness of apostolic faith and order, while fervently praying for a day when by God's grace other churches may become ready to consider and to discuss communion with the family of Orthodox Churches without surrendering their autonomy. Meanwhile the Orthodox leaders and theologians need gradually to express themselves on the ecclesial status of other churches in the spirit of Vatican II or at least on the fundamental signs of ecclesial reality in any separated church, if the Orthodox ecumenical commitment is to have deep value, and if the Orthodox witness to the fullness of the apostolic faith, life and order is to carry ringing conviction.[34]

Contributing to the revision of Orthodox ecclesiology were the Pan-Orthodox Conferences that began in 1961. One idea behind such conferences was that in future relations between the Orthodox and other Christian churches, the Orthodox would be equipped to act out of an agreed policy. The second of these conferences, at Rhodes (1963), accepted the principle of "a dialogue on an equal footing" with the Catholic Church.

Dialogues are proving very helpful to the churches and ecclesial communities of our times because the very nature of these discussions calls on the partners to explain, even justify, their traditional beliefs. Furthermore, partners are asked to accept that the principle of the development of doctrine is also a very necessary part of church identity.[35]

Nevertheless, it is one thing for dialogue members to reach agreements; it is another for their conclusions to be received by both the body of the faithful and the respective church leaderships. A case in point is the 1993 Balamand meeting that provided the forum in which the delegates of both churches were able to say:

> On each side it is recognized that what Christ has entrusted to his Church—profession of apostolic faith, participation in the same sacraments, above all the one priesthood celebrating the one sacrifice of Christ, the apostolic succession of bishops—cannot be considered the exclusive property of one of our Churches (13).
>
> It is in this perspective that the Catholic churches and the Orthodox churches recognize each other as sister churches, responsible together for maintaining the church of God in fidelity to the divine purpose, most especially in what concerns unity. According to the words of Pope John Paul II, the ecumenical endeavor of the sister churches of East and West, grounded in dialogue and prayer, is the search for perfect and total communion, which is neither absorption nor fusion but a meeting in truth and love (14).[36]

The Dialogue of Charity

The arrival at this mutual ecclesial recognition was aided by a resolution at the third Pan-Orthodox Conference in 1964, also held at Rhodes, which suggested that a "dialogue of charity" is necessary if the right atmosphere is to be created before an official dialogue can get underway. In 1967, Patriarch Athenagoras began his address at Saint Peter's in Rome, acknowledging the earlier visit on July 25 by Paul VI who brought "from the West to the East the kiss of love and peace."[37] It was in Rome that the patriarch said, "We render you the kiss of the charity and peace of the Lord Jesus and bring you the tribute of our high regard." He went on to say that "we are called upon to continue and intensify the dialogue of charity, so as to make this a reality antecedent to theological discussion."[38] Ever since, the two churches have made a point of expressing to each other appropriate greetings, sympathies, and esteem as can be seen in a book like *Towards the Healing of Schism: The Sees of Rome and Constantinople (Public statements and correspondence between the Holy See and the Ecumenical Patriarchate 1958–1984).*[39]

It soon became evident that this "dialogue of charity" was basic to all other possible advances, most especially to the "dialogue of doctrine" to which Patriarch Athenagoras referred. Both of these dialogues rely on an explication of the theology of "sister churches" that describes in symbolic language the rediscovered relationship that should characterize the two churches.

Sister Churches

Beyond the scriptural and patristic foundations, an explicit use of the words *sister churches* is found in a Byzantine protest in 1136 against papal imperialism, which spoke of the "Roman church, to which we do not refuse the primacy among its sisters."[40] Then in 1206, Patriarch John X Camateros wrote to Innocent III, saying "There are five great churches adorned with patriarchal dignity, that of Rome is the first among equal sisters."[41] An opponent of papal infallibility at Vatican I, Monsignor Papp-Szilegyi, expressed concern at a possible impact of a definition on relations with the Church of the East that "has been our sister."[42]

Within four days of his election as bishop of Rome on June 21, 1963, Paul VI had Cardinal Bea, first president of PCPCU, write to Patriarch Athenagoras to advise him of the election.[43]

In September of the same year, Paul VI wrote to Patriarch Athenagoras, in his own hand, expressing his intention to do all he could to restore unity.[44] The patriarch published the letter in the bulletin *Apostolos Andreas* under the title "The Two Sister Churches." The patriarch had already used the term in a letter to Cardinal Bea the previous year. Such were the first uses of the term in modern times.[45]

Paul VI's papal brief titled *Anno Ineunte* (1967), quoted at the beginning of this chapter, explains that it is in virtue of the gifts we share in common—faith, baptism, priesthood, and Eucharist—that we enter into the Trinitarian communion, which is then lived out in each of the local churches. These churches, then, are "sisters." In 1979, Cardinal Willebrands acknowledged the historical factors that have taken us away from each other and spoke of the fundamental communion that remains: "If over the centuries and for reasons which were not always strictly religious, canonical and doctrinal differences have developed between our Churches, we always remain nonetheless 'sister churches.'"[46]

One example lies in what we have now come to see as complementary theologies of the church. Whereas the west tends to emphasize the church as a pilgrim people journeying toward the end-time, when the kingdom will be established, the east views the church as a people who are living the eschatological event in the present. *Ut Unum Sint* (57) recognizes these two emphasizes as complementary insights, or ecclesial emphases, that should be seen as gifts we can share with each other.

The Dialogue of Doctrine

Practical signs of the intentions of both churches to work together—even to re-establishing full communion—were first given in 1975 and 1976, ten years after the lifting of the anathemas imposed on one another in the eleventh century. In these two years, the Orthodox Church, followed by the Catholic Church, formed commissions to prepare for an official theological dialogue of doctrine. A coordinating group set down the objectives and methodology to be followed by the Joint International Commission for Theological Dialogue, announced by John Paul II and Dimitrios I in Istanbul on

November 30, 1978. From these efforts have come four mutually supported statements.

The first agreed statement, issued in Munich in 1982, is called "The Mystery of the Church and of the Holy Eucharist in the Light of the Mystery of the Holy Trinity."[47] Especially pleasing about this document is its mutual recognition of the centrality of the Eucharist providing a foundation for agreement in many areas of church life. No longer is it appropriate to see the church predominantly according to sociological categories. Rather, the emphasis falls in favor of a sacramental reality that enjoys local placement. These local churches, under the leadership of their bishops, are in communion within the universal church. Herein lies a difficulty yet to be resolved: the place of the bishop of Rome in this communion of churches.

Beyond this Munich statement, but also in 1982, was the appearance of the Lima document of the Faith and Order Commission of the World Council of Churches, titled "Baptism, Eucharist, and Ministry" (BEM). Two years later, Orthodox and Catholic scholars in the United States issued a response to both documents. Because these scholars were able to identify a high level of agreement on baptism, Eucharist, and ministry, as indicated in the Lima document, they were moved to recommend "that our two churches explore the possibility of a formal recognition of each other's baptism as a sacrament of our unity in the body of Christ, although we acknowledge that any such recognition is conditioned by other factors."[48]

The second agreed statement, of Bari in 1987, is titled "Faith, Sacraments, and the Unity of the Church."[49] Faith is both a gift from God and a human response and, at its deepest understanding, is an ecclesial event. The content of the faith, as articulated, can quite legitimately bear out a richness of diversity without bringing damage to the *koinonia* of the one church. Likewise, legitimate diversity of practice in the administration of the sacraments of initiation is not harmful to mutual recognition or to the *koinonia*.

The third statement was formulated at Valamo in 1988 and was titled "The Sacrament of Order in the Sacramental Structure of the Church, with Particular Reference to the Importance of Apostolic Succession for the Sanctification and Unity of the People of God." Some of the significant theological advances made in this document include an emphasis on the relationship of Christ and the Spirit, the Spirit being responsible for Christ's presence and ministry in the church, a ministry that peaks in the Eucharist. The ministries of bishops, priests, and deacons, and the work of Christian initiation, all culminate in the Eucharist. The particular task of the bishop is to gather all into a oneness, a unity that reaches beyond the local to the universal communion of churches.

As suggested earlier in this chapter, the regular sessions of the Joint International Commission were suspended in Munich/Freising in 1990 because of the insistence that the question of "uniatism" be addressed. The outcome, as we have already discussed, was the fourth document of significance: the Balamand Report of 1993. On the matter of the reception or rejection of this document, *The Quest for Unity* offers a useful reminder that "while the crisis over 'uniatism' did deflect the Joint International Commission from its original agenda for dialogue, in the long run it may help bring a note of realism to its work. Certainly it has shown how fragile ecumenical dialogue can be if it is not rooted in the actual life and experience of the churches."[50]

Should we remain optimistic? Indeed we should. So many advances have been made since the 1920 letter of the ecumenical patriarchate and the 1965 Vatican II document, *UR*, that it falls to all of us today to continue the work until unity between the Orthodox Church and the Catholic Church is achieved. What should sadden us—and what we should energetically resist—is any suggestion of a suspension of dialogue because of real or imagined offending behavior.[51] The agreed statements so far achieved are signs of progress, to such an extent that Cardinal Cassidy[52] was confident enough to remark in 1997 that "I would venture to state that the restoration of unity between Orthodox and Catholics is primarily a matter of healing past memories. To help overcome such difficulties Pope John Paul II has stressed the need for repentance and conversion, for *metanoia*."[53] It is in this spirit that Pope John Paul II and Ecumenical Patriarch Bartholomew I made their 1995 Common Declaration:

We urge our faithful, Catholics and Orthodox, to reinforce the spirit of brotherhood which stems from the one Baptism and from participation in the sacramental life... Such a spirit should encourage both Catholics and Orthodox, especially when they live side by side, to a more intense collaboration in the cultural, spiritual, pastoral, educational, and social fields, avoiding any temptation to undue zeal for their own community to the disadvantage of the other. May the good of Christ's Church always prevail![54]

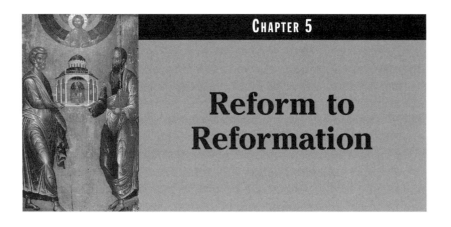

CHAPTER 5

Reform to Reformation

The study of Orthodox-Catholic relations, while recognizing the reality and importance of the church's oneness, also acknowledged how the visible unity became blurred toward the end of the first millennium. Christians in the west are also aware of the even more serious and radical damage to the church's unity that happened in their part of the world from the sixteenth century onward.

The Marks of the Church

It is important to remember that the church Christ founded was gifted with three identifying properties or marks other than unity. These divine gifts of holiness, catholicity, and apostolicity, with unity, are part of her very nature. As such, they remain with her always and can never be destroyed, although their visibility can certainly diminish.[1]

The visibility of the church's "holiness," for example, was badly tarnished before the Reformation. Numerous cries were made for its restoration, but the process of making holiness visible again became such a preoccupation that the other marks of the church began to suffer. New ecclesial structures came into existence at the time of the Reformation, which certainly blurred the church's catholicity and unity. In many instances, her apostolicity suffered as well.

Unitatis Redintegratio: The Church's Text on Unity

Before embarking on a brief study of the far-reaching effects of these inbalances in the Reformation, it will be useful to take a close look at the contemporary Catholic Church text on unity titled *Unitatis Redintegratio* (The Restoration of Unity). The Decree on Ecumenism, as it is classified and known, points out that there is a variety of ways in which unity can be damaged, requiring therefore, different starting points in working toward reestablishing unity. Structurally, the document consists of an introduction that acknowledges the existence of the "ecumenical movement" and, in three chapters, explains the Catholic approach to this Spirit-inspired work.

The first chapter of the decree, "Catholic Principles of Ecumenism," is doctrinally important because, as the title suggests, it sets out the Catholic understanding or principles of ecumenism. Church unity is spoken of as a "communion" in faith and sacrament that is to be experienced visibly and invisibly. "This unity," the decree says, "dwells in the Catholic Church as something she can never lose" (4). Given that this quality has always been identified as part of the Catholic Church's self-understanding, it is reasonable to ask, "What is different today?"

The great advance of the council, as we observed in chapter 3, was to take the Catholic Church beyond seeing this essential "churchly quality" as something exclusive to the Catholic Church. The quality of "unity" can also be found in other churches and ecclesial communities, although "imperfectly." The actual words of the decree are that other Christians "who believe in Christ and have been properly baptized are brought into a certain, though imperfect, communion with the Catholic Church" (3). The aim of ecumenism is to make visible again the unity of the entire church of Christ by eliminating the imperfection.

The second chapter of *UR*, "The Practice of Ecumenism," offers a range of suggestions and gives high priority to the need for a change of heart among all the faithful. Christians of all churches need to realize that the "imperfection" also resides in their relationships. Hence, no one, neither an individual Christian nor a community, is exempted from the task of strenuously working to eliminate the barriers that are so often deeply rooted in human hearts, carried as baggage from the past. The change will be increasingly reflected in the language Christians use regarding one another and in the spirit of cooperation that will become evident among them.

The third chapter, "Churches and Ecclesial Communities Separated from the Roman Apostolic See," acknowledges that many Christians share a great deal in common, including faith, baptism, the Scriptures, and the creeds. It then goes on to identify how the various churches and communities actually relate to the Catholic Church, acknowledging that there are various degrees in the relationships. The Orthodox Church and the Catholic Church, as the last chapter points out, have a very close communion that portrays them as "sister churches" and as "the church breathing through its two lungs." What is so significant about the high level of their closeness, beyond baptism, the foundational sacrament, and the Eucharist, which is validly celebrated by an ordained ministry, is the presence in both churches of all the sacraments by virtue of "apostolic succession."

The decree takes a more guarded approach when expressing the nature of the relationship with "the Churches and ecclesial communities which were separated from the Apostolic See of Rome during the very serious crisis that began in the West at the end of the Middle Ages, or during later times" (19). The words *church* and *ecclesial communities* are deliberately chosen in acknowledgment of the fact that some have a greater identity, in terms of structures, with the Catholic Church (22).[2]

In summary, it is true to say that the separation between the Catholic Church and the Orthodox Church was of a juridical kind. However, the separations in the west, from the sixteenth century on, are not only juridical but also theological, depending on the presence or absence of the sacraments of holy orders and Eucharist in these churches and communities.[3]

Against this background, the remainder of this chapter will look at the calls for reform before the Reformation, the three phases of the Protestant Reformation (with attention to the churches and ecclesial communities that came to exist and which have a relationship with the Catholic Church today), and a final look at what has been named the "Catholic Reformation."

Calls for Reform Before the Reformation

In the two to three centuries before the Reformation, calls for reform in the western church were becoming louder and more emphatic. This behavior points to the fact that virtue and vice coexisted.

Good people were upset at the extent of abuses, such as nepotism and simony. They voiced their concerns regarding a poorly educated, ill-disciplined, and graft-infected clergy; a monastic way of life that bespoke luxury and indulgence; a papacy and a curia that were evidently preoccupied with the affairs of the world; and the practice of selling sacred practices.[4]

Inevitably, the thinkers among them went beyond decrying the abuses and began questioning the very nature of the church within which corruption was commonplace. The tendency was to look back to a kind of golden age in the church's life, to those times when she seemed young and fresh. They wondered if such a church could be re-created.

Individuals spoke their minds about the church as they saw it and as they dreamed about it; *groups* of people experimented with what they believed to be more authentic ecclesial lifestyles; and *theories* came to be formulated as to what shape the true church should take. All of this was happening well before the Lutheran reform was even thought about, so it is to a consideration of examples of each of the three that we now turn.

Individuals Calling for Reform

Bernard of Clairvaux: Although he was a committed churchman, Bernard of Clairvaux (1090–1153) was an outspoken critic of ecclesiastical abuses. He was not at all approving of the papacy's imperial style, and he warned his former pupil and fellow Cistercian, Pope Eugene III (1145–1153), not to immerse himself in secular affairs. Bernard's abiding wish was to see, before he died, the church return to its primal condition of ancient days.[5]

John of Paris: In anticipation of the conciliarists, John of Paris (+ 1306), a Dominican and author of *On the Power of Kings and Popes,* taught that God gifts the whole church with authority. That which is exercised by the pope and bishops is a power that is theirs only indirectly, the church being the direct recipient. He was reacting to the current papal understanding of the church, including the claim that even temporal powers are derived from the spiritual, which in effect means through the papacy.[6]

Dante Alighieri: A layperson, Dante Alighieri (1265–1321), used his *Divine Comedy* to graphically portray his disdain of Boniface VIII (1294–1303) by placing him in the inferno because of the sin of simony. He disapproved of the use of papal power for family ends, and argued that temporal power is not derived from the papacy, for it comes directly from God.[7] In his treatise, *Monarchia,* Dante was emphatic that the empire, and not just the church, is a sacred institution made so by God and not through the ministrations of the church. Both had different and distinctive purposes: the church's task was about heavenly happiness, the empire's about earthly happiness.

William of Ockham: Franciscan philosopher and theologian William of Ockham (c.1285–1347) offered a definition of the church as a faith-inspired community of people, not as a Mystical Body. Like other writers, he denied papal claims to the fullness of power in temporal affairs and went further, denying such claims in the spiritual arena as well. He was at pains to preserve the liberty of all the people who make up the church, expecting that the entirety of Christendom would have elected representation at a general council. Luther was later to acknowledge his debt to William of Ockham.[8]

John Wyclif: Relying on Augustine's prior teaching on the church as the invisible body of the predestined, John Wyclif (1330–1384) went a step further to make an identification and a distinction. He identified the Mystical Body with the church of the elect, and he made a distinction between this invisible church and another church: the church of "prelates and priests." Although people were members of the church, and some held office in it, there was no guaranteed membership of the invisible church. Even popes could be among the reprobates, which meant there was no need to obey them. Toward the end of his life, Wyclif called for the abolition of the papacy, the authority of the Bible replacing it.[9]

John Hus: From Bohemia, and a great promoter of Scripture and preaching, John Hus (c.1369–1415) was indebted to Wyclif for his ecclesiology, but without Wyclif's radical leanings. He became the latter's leading exponent, the two of them having an influence on Martin Luther. Neither Hus nor Wyclif espoused what would become Luther's doctrine of justification by faith alone. Deeply concerned at episcopal and papal corruption, Hus called for the abolition of neither the institutional church nor the papacy, but for their reform. The response he got was, regretably, condemnation to death by the Council of Constance (1414–1418). He was burned at the stake in 1415.[10]

Groups Calling for Reform

Albigensians: Groups upset at the wealth and laxity of the church included the twelfth-century sect from Albigeois in Aquitaine, which became known as the Cathari or Pure Ones or Albigensians.[11] This sect's converts came from among those who were upset at the excesses that had come to characterize the church. Many of these people, unwittingly perhaps, were drawn into a very unorthodox understanding of "church." At the base of the thinking was a revival of third-century Manichaean dualism, which allowed for two gods—and therefore two churches. One of these churches was the church of the "good" God the Father, as established by Christ. The other was the church of the "evil" god, related to Satan and identified with the church of Rome. The Albigensian church had two types of members: the "perfect," from which the ministers were chosen and among whom marriage was not allowed, and the "believers," as yet incapable of perfection.

Innocent III (1198–1216) sent legates to the Albigensians, and when one of them was assassinated, a crusade and an inquisition followed. The complete demise of the Albigensians was achieved by the middle of the fourteenth century.

Spirituals: A radical Franciscan branch imbued with Saint Francis' ideal of poverty called themselves "Spirituals." They held to a futuristic view of the church in what they termed "the third age of the Spirit." They identified themselves as this future church's forerunners. Their radical approach to poverty, their harsh criticism of contemporary church leadership, and their futuristic thinking fed into yet another piece of idealism that became Reformation material.[12]

Waldensians: The Waldensians of the twelfth century, also known as "the poor men of Lyons," were founded by Peter Waldo (the name "Peter" chosen to demonstrate his connection with Peter the Apostle[13]). A merchant of Lyons, Valdes gave up his riches to become a mendicant preacher. In the early stages, the Waldensians accepted Catholic doctrine and order, and their preaching called for ecclesiastical reform through a return to the simplicity of the early church.

At the same time, other strains were developing within the group, including strong perfectionist and antisacerdotal characteristics, the efficacy of the sacraments being tied to the moral quality of the clergy. In this thinking, they went further than Wyclif and Hus. Eventually, they came to define the church as the invisible church of the elect, although there was never a rejection of the church as a visible institution. Whatever was not explicitly found in Scripture—such as the authority of the pope, prayers for the dead, and the veneration of saints—were all rejected as valid parts of Christian worship.[14] They sought ecclesiastical recognition at the Third Lateran Council (1179), but because they were refused permission to preach by Alexander III (1159–1181), they chose not to obey. The Council of Verona (1184) excommunicated them.

In 1532, the Waldensians accepted the Reformed Church structure. Today, they number about twenty-three thousand and are found in Italy (where they are the largest Protestant denomination), in some countries of western Europe, and in Uruguay, Argentina, and North America.

While there is no official dialogue between the Waldensian community and the Pontifical Council for Promoting Christian Unity (PCPCU), an increasing number of fruitful contacts have taken place, especially over the last decade. As expected, the papacy is a problem, not only for Waldensians but for many other Christian churches as well. Hence, a brief focus on the papacy will afford readers an opportunity to better appreciate the nature of this problem as it is seen from the perspective of other Christians.

In 1993, for example, Cardinal Ratzinger met with Rome's Waldensian community, their spokesperson being Professor Paolo Ricca, who holds the chair of church history in the Waldensian Theological Faculty in Rome. Their positive and fruitful exchange included this remark by Dr. Ricca, which highlights not only variations in appreciation of the church and of the papacy as a problem, but the recency of contact between the two churches. He said:

> You know who we are and we too know who you are. We are meeting for the first time but we have known each other for eight centuries. We both, and you more than we, more than I, have a history behind us; indeed, we are part of that history ... We have challenged each other on the very nature of Christianity on each other's way of under-standing it, of living it, and of bearing witness to it. Our quarrel, which continues, is not over details or frivolous marginal questions but touches the substance of things. We represent two different poles of the Christian con-science, two different expressions of faith, of the one faith, two different projections of Church, of the one Church. So we are perfectly aware of our diversities. And yet we are here together....
>
> It is no secret that the Papacy is the crucial node of the ecumenical question because on one hand it forges Catholic unity and on the other it impedes—to use a bru-tal expression—Christian unity.[15]

Ricca was able to take up this theme again in responding to John Paul II's 1995 encyclical, *Ut Unum Sint*. The occasion was the inaugural address of the 1996–1997 academic year, which he delivered at the Catholic Pontifical University of St. Anselm in Rome. In the encyclical (95–96), the pope invites other Christian communities to work with him to discover how the papal ministry may come to be of service to all Christians.

Ricca's response is to suggest that the papal institution needs to undergo a conversion. He explained that:

> ... "conversion" is much more than "reform." "Conversion" means: while remaining yourself you become what you were not. The papacy would remain itself: a structure at the service of unity. But it would become that which it was not: a structure at the service of Christian unity, and not simply—as it has been till now—at the service of Roman Catholic unity. This hypothesis, although at first glance somewhat bold because it implies a kind of death and resurrection of the papacy, could in the final analysis turn out to be the most realistic, if one takes seriously— as the pontiff certainly does—the unbreakable requirement of the conversion of "Peter."[16]

What it is that Ricca precisely intends would have to be explored further with him. In 1997, however, some useful Catholic initiatives were taken. One was taken by the Italian Catholic Bishops' Conference, the organ responsible for maintaining Catholic contact with the Waldensians. Representatives of the conference apologized for the twelfth-century burning at the stake of eighty members of the Waldensian community who did not obey Alexander III's (1159–1181) order that they not preach. The Waldensian moderator, Gianni Rostan, welcomed the apology as well as John Paul II's apology given in Paris in 1997 for the Saint Bartholomew Day massacre of Huguenots more than four hundred years ago. The moderator welcomed both of these moves as "helping to promote ecumenical dialogue."[17]

At the join synod of the Waldensians and Methodists— which a Catholic bishop and an archimandrite from the Italian Greek-Orthodox Church attended for the first time—reached an agreement to enter into dialogue with the Catholic Church to address common problems. The first of these problems to be addressed would be that of interchurch marriages. Further developments are likely, including consideration of student exchanges.[18] The first meeting was held in 1998.

One would hope that the positive moves on both sides are laying the foundations for a dialogue that will one day lead to full communion.

Theories about the Nature and Mission of the Church

We will consider two theories: curialism and conciliarism.

Curialism: In the words of Timothy George, curialism "was a theory of church government that invested supreme authority, both temporal and spiritual, in the hands of the papacy."[19] It was Pope Gelasius I (492–496) who wrote to Emperor Anastasius I (491–518) in 494, stating:

> Two there are, august emperor, by which this world is chiefly ruled, the sacred authority of the priesthood and the royal power. Of these the responsibility of the priests is more weighty...And if the hearts of the faithful should be submitted to all priests in general ... how much more should assent be given to the bishop of that see which the Most High wishes to be pre-eminent over all priests, and which the devotion of the church has honored ever since.[20]

In the Middle Ages, four popes particularly echo most fully the papacy's claim to worldly preeminence. Gregory VII (1073–1085) issued his famous *Dictatus Papae*,[21] making twenty-seven famous claims. In summary, the document says that all bishops, clerics, and laypersons, including rulers, are subject to him. Innocent III (1198–1216) referred to the pope as the Vicar of God,[22] thereby strategically placing himself between divinity and humanity. Innocent built up an efficient organization of legal and financial officers in Rome, his delegates and emissaries penetrating into every part of western Europe. The most famous of the four was Boniface VIII (1294–1303) who produced the bull *Unam sanctam*, in which he said: "We declare, state, and define that it is absolutely necessary for the salvation of all men that they submit to the Roman Pontiff."[23] Finally, Clement VI (1342–1352) declared his viewpoint when, for example, he demanded of the Armenians an acknowledgment that the pope enjoys the same level of jurisdiction that Christ did during his earthly life.[24]

Conciliarism: This theory of the fifteenth century affirmed the superiority of an ecumenical council over a pope—understandable, one would think, given the outrageous claims made by the four pontiffs mentioned above. Then came the Great Schism (1378–1417), when three individuals made claim to the papal throne at the same time. Now the whole world saw the need for reform, in head and members, and conciliarism was one expression of that rising demand. The theory distinguished between the universal church, which was represented in a general council, and the church of Rome, with the pope and its curia.

Canonists and others in the late fourteenth and early fifteenth centuries who were working for the end of the Great Schism openly demanded a general council.[25] These included thinkers such as Pierre of Ailly (1350–1420), Jean Gerson (1363–1429), and Dietrich of Niem (c.1340–1418). Thus, conciliarism was born, the theory which says that authority is invested in the whole body of the church. Such authority can be given over to one man, the pope, but in the event of abuse, the church, through a general council, can resume the exercise of its God-given authority. Papal heresy or a disputed papacy would justify such action.

The Council of Constance (1414–1418) deposed all three of the claimants to the papacy, and elected Martin V (1417–1431). So ended the Great Western Schism. The council passed *Sacrosancta* (1415), which required all in the church, including the bishop of Rome, to obey a general council. It also passed *Frequens* (1417), which saw the importance of councils in God's work and, therefore, required future councils to be convened on a regular basis.

The Council of Constance solved the immediate problem of three popes, but its teaching about the superior powers of a general council was not received by Martin V, who actually closed the council in 1418, or by Eugenius IV. The death knell came in the bull *Execrabilis*, promulgated in 1460 by Pius II following the Council of Florence. Both this council and the papacy strongly affirmed the primacy of the bishop of Rome.

Reform Calls Continue

As the sixteenth century neared, the church continued to suffer under the burden of widespread and intensive corruption. The calls for reform became more demanding, characterized by a high level of urgency. As we proceed to examine the various phases of the Reformation, it will become clear that the cries of some of the individuals already mentioned begin to be heard. We will also see how the movements and theories took on a variety of forms, sometimes beyond the bounds of the visible church.

People like Desiderius Erasmus (1466–1536), Martin Luther (1483–1546), and Jean Calvin (1509–1564) made their calls for reform of the church as members of the historic Catholic Church. They did not, early on, entertain any idea of departing from the church. Their only aim was reform. But those in high places, including the papacy, were not free enough to respond. They had become ensnared in corrupt practices and had great difficulty extricating themselves so as to serve the church more worthily.

Furthermore, by the early decades of the sixteenth century, papal power across Europe was on the decline, so much so that "universal" reform of the church was beyond Rome's resourcefulness. Nation states were coming to exist with a corresponding emergence of "national churches" in countries such as Spain, Portugal, Denmark, and Germany. The pope was incapable of controlling them.

As the reformers emerged, they frequently looked to local governments or rulers to help achieve their desired reforms. Such was the case with Luther who looked to the German princes; Zwingli, who called on the Zurich city council; and Calvin, who insisted on church and civic authorities working hand in hand. To this day, the Reformation churches are foundationally identified with particular nationalities. Besides, it is difficult to speak of one Protestant understanding of "church," although the nature of the church was the over-riding concern of all of them. What happened was far from a common reform; rather, there was a splintering into movements, something that has bedeviled Protestantism from Luther into our own times. Hence, it will simplify matters if we name the various phases of the Reformation and then identify the main ecclesial bodies that emerged from them.

The First Phase of the Reformation

The immediate cause[26] of the eruption of the Reformation was Leo X's (1513–1521) granting of indulgences to those who would contribute to the building of Saint Peter's in Rome. Needing an expensive dispensation himself, Archbishop Albert of Mainz (and of Magdeburg, where Wittenberg is located) was a willing cooperator in the venture. Part of the money generated would be for Saint Peter's and part for the bankers, to whom Albert was indebted. He arranged for Johann Tetzel, Dominican preacher, to promote the cause throughout Germany, but the Elector Frederick of Saxony forbade such preaching in his territory. Martin Luther (1483–1546), siding with the elector, became angry when some people chose to cross the border to hear the message. These people returned thinking they had no further need of penance because of the indulgence they had been granted. Luther's reaction was to write the famous ninety-five theses which, on October 31, 1517, according to Philip Melanchthon, Luther attached to the door of Castle Church in Wittenburg.

Luther and the Birth of Lutheranism

Martin Luther's attack on indulgences arose from his long-standing personal agenda that had earlier—long before the indulgence issue—driven him to ask the question: "How can I find a favorable God?" This search took him beyond the arena of theological subjects to an abiding question: "How can one be certain of salvation?"[27]

What happens now is a rapid development from a focus on Luther's personal journey to an issue with ecclesial ramifications, and from an effort to reform certain behaviors in the church to a questioning of the very nature of the church. Luther embarked on the development of a new doctrine of the church, which would become embodied as the Lutheran Church. We can best follow this development if we consider it under four headings:

Luther's fundamental doctrine: Pauline in character, Luther's fundamental doctrine came out of Romans 1:17. There, in response to his question about a favorable God, he personally discovered a forgiving, justifying God.[28] This doctrine, often spoken of as "Justification by faith alone," or *sola fide*, continued to be developed by Luther, to the point where he described the church as the assembly of those who enjoyed justification by faith. The church was not identifiable so much through external acts of religion, but as a community that had a mind and heart of faith.

The progression is interesting. Luther shared his personal discovery in his teaching at the University of Wittenberg, where he was concerned about reforming the theology as it was taught there. When he posted the ninety-five theses, he gathered about himself—probably unwittingly—a wider audience. Thus was alerted the Diet of Worms, which condemned his teaching in 1521. In the following year, he became the leader of a new movement: the Lutheran Reformation.

Luther's structure of the church: Given his foundational description of the church as the assembly of the justified, Luther then attempted to localize the church. He began with the notion of "grace," that justification is a free gift or grace from God. So the church is wherever God offers this grace in Christ.[29] Succinctly expressed, the church is found where "the Gospel is rightly taught and the Sacraments are rightly administered," giving rise to the expressions *sola scriptura* and *sola gratia*.

It is useful to remember that Luther's earlier training was nominalist[30] in character, which was anti-Aristotelian, anti-Scholastic. He inherited a discomfort with the traditional links between faith and reason, especially as it was expressed in scholastic philosophy and theology. Scripture was the sole source of truth and doctrine.

Luther's definition of church: Further clarification of the identity of the church was expressed in the distinction Luther made between "the invisible church of the elect" and the empirical or "mixed" church of saints and sinners. He went beyond Saint Augustine in speaking of the invisible church, further describing it as the church of the spirit or soul, which does not need an external and physical identity to be real.[31]

Luther spoke of the "mixed" church as the body of saints

and sinners, a manmade ecclesiastical institution. He maintained that this latter church, in its hierarchical structure, had erroneously claimed to be the embodiment of Christ's kingdom. Members of this church, it is not hard to imagine, were all the members of the hierarchy and all others whose Christianity was connected with this visible body. Surfacing now was Luther's second great dislike beyond scholasticism: the papacy. Roman criticism of his teaching intensified the polarization, leading Luther to identify the bishop of Rome as "anti-Christ."

Given further experience and the influence of Philip Melanchthon, the description of the church in terms of "invisibility" and as subject only to the gospel was seen as super-idealistic. Luther came to accept that the church must have certain visible or institutional signs by which the presence of the "invisible church" could be detected. There are seven of these signs. Preaching of the Word, baptism, and the Lord's Supper are the three primary signs. The secondary signs are the power of the keys, ministry, public prayer, and a Christian life shaped by the cross.

Luther's organization of the church: Luther was not at peace with the traditional Catholic distinction between a privileged and high-ranking clergy or hierarchy on the one hand and the laity on the other. Using 1 Peter 2:9 ("You are a chosen race, a royal priesthood, a holy nation, a people he claims for his own"), he argued that all the baptized are priests and all enjoy priestly power with regard to Word and sacraments.

Ministry, which is divine in origin, emerges with the consent of the community. Very important for Luther was this understanding of the church as a company of believers, various groups within the church having special responsibilities. Among these were Christian princes, who enjoyed a divinely given leadership role. Their task was to implement the reform, given the doctrine of the priesthood of the laity.[32]

The actual organization of the Lutheran Church at the time of Luther, and the gradual emergence of Luther's doctrine, is an immense story in its own right and beyond the scope of this text. The early and ongoing doctrinal development and expression are found in the *Augsburg Confession* (1530), the *Apology*

(1531), Luther's two catechisms (1529), and the *Book of Concord* (1580).

Lutheranism Today

Lutherans today number about sixty-one million, fifty-seven million of these in churches belonging to the Lutheran World Federation (LWF), established in 1947 in Lund, Sweden. The principal tenet, justification by faith alone, continues in place, as does great reverence for the Scriptures. The LWF:

> ...acknowledges the holy scriptures of the Old and New Testament as the only source and infallible norm of all church doctrine and practice, and sees in the three ecumenical creeds and in the confessions of the Lutheran Church, especially in the unaltered Augsburg Confession and Luther's Small Catechism, a pure exposition of the word of God.[33]

There are fifteen million Lutherans in Germany, and more than twenty million in the Scandinavian countries. The Lutheran Church is strong in the United States as well, with a membership of eight and a half million. In both Indonesia and Tanzania, there are more than two million, and more than one million in each of Ethiopia, India, Madagascar, and Brazil. There is more than half a million in each of Papua New Guinea, South Africa, and Namibia. Smaller numbers are found in many other countries.[34] Although the style of worship varies throughout the world, preaching is the principal feature of the liturgy. Church government is synodal, membership comprising clergy and laity.

The importance Lutherans give to ecumenism, and therefore to the unity of the church, is expressed in a variety of ways. For example, Lutherans are striving to heal their own internal divisions. We have seen evidence of this in the United States during this century, when various Lutheran communities merged. In 1998, the two largest bodies in the States—the Evangelical Lutheran Church and the Lutheran Church-Missouri Synod—agreed to formal joint discussions. In 1948, some Lutheran churches joined with other Protestants to become the Evangelical Church in Germany, comprising members of Lutheran, Reformed, and United communities.

The Lutheran Church is certainly a significant part of the world ecumenical movement, engaging in dialogues with the Anglican, Methodist, Orthodox, Reformed, and Catholic Churches. Ecumenical conversations have also taken place with the Baptist World Alliance, the Seventh-Day Adventist Church, and the Mennonites. The ecumenical commitment is unambiguously expressed, however, in the 1990 Constitution: "The Lutheran World Federation confesses the one, holy, catholic and apostolic Church and is resolved to serve Christian unity throughout the world."[35]

International Lutheran–Roman Catholic Dialogue

As we move into this section, you will discover that many of the issues judged to be problems at the time of the Reformation, and in the relationship between the two churches since, have now become items of dialogue. As we talk together and mutually revisit history, we are finding that much of the past is a matter of misunderstanding and misinterpretation. At the same time, however, we have to admit that definite deviations did occur. Given our mutual commitment to the cause of visible Christian unity, the task that lies ahead is to find the ways and means to overcome the misunderstandings, the misinterpretations, and the deviations. This is where "dialogue," not polemic, will help us on the journey. Such is the grace of our age.

In November 1964, during the course of the Second Vatican Council when *Unitatis Redintegratio* was in preparation, representatives of the LWF suggested to the Catholic authorities that a bilateral dialogue be established between the two churches. The one that subsequently began in 1967 was rightly labeled by Harding Meyer as the "father of all the ecumenical dialogues of the Catholic Church at universal level."[36]

Besides the international dialogue conducted on behalf of the Catholic Church by PCPCU with the LWF, national dialogues are also taking place, particularly in Germany and the United States. Both of these are of great help to the international dialogue. For example, the United States dialogue did valuable groundwork on the Eucharist, ministry, and justification, which was readily taken up by the international team. Similarly, German research into the Tridentine condemnations showed that the great majority of them are no longer applicable.

Bearing in mind that the aim of the Lutheran–Roman Catholic dialogue is full visible unity, we proceed with a brief review of four phases in the Lutheran–Roman Catholic dialogue.[37]

First phase: the gospel and the church: The first phase (1967–1972) was very much exploratory, providing a forum in which the traditional problem areas between Catholics and Lutherans could surface: the doctrine of justification, the relationship between Scripture and tradition, reciprocal recognition of ministry, and the question of papal primacy.

The fruits of the dialogue, published under the title *The Malta Report* (1972), reveal a developing convergence on the two subjects of justification and Scripture-tradition. Matters identified as needing more study were justification in relation to Christian freedom, apostolic succession, and eucharistic hospitality and intercommunion.

Second phase: the Eucharist (1978) and ministry (1981): The international forum in this second phase (1973–1984) was served well by the presentation of a number of biblical and patristic papers on the Eucharist. The resulting discussion showed considerable consensus. When it came to a discussion on ministry, however, difficulties began to surface, most especially regarding the Catholic belief in the necessity of the episcopate in apostolic succession. Further analysis indicated that the divergences here actually stemmed from differing understandings of "church." Hence, an important topic was suggesting itself for the next phase.

But during this second phase, joint "occasional papers" were also produced so as to mark certain anniversaries. *All Under One Christ* (1980) honored the 450th anniversary of the Augsburg Confession, and *Martin Luther—Witness to Jesus Christ* (1983) paid tribute on the 500th anniversary of Luther's birth. These two studies point to how well we are learning to interpret the past, not just recount it. We have discovered that the Reformation was indeed a religious event that had an impact on the very nature of the church. As Cardinal Etchegaray reflected in his Marseilles 1983 newsletter, which he wrote on Luther's anniversary:

> Luther is a Christian straight out of the Gospel. He
> wanted the Church to fight for its one true cause: to
> ensure that the Gospel shone through a Church which
> was weighed down with excessive baggage ... But, in so
> doing, he discarded the priceless treasures of the undi-
> vided Church and his heirs have not been able to realize
> the totality of the faith of the Church in its continuity
> down the centuries.[38]

In summary, the twofold study set out to discover and make
presently relevant both the doctrinal content of the Augsburg
Confession and the faith of Luther. Two further documents
issued during this phase were: *Ways to Communion* (1980) and
*Facing Unity—Models, Forms and Phases of Catholic-Lutheran
Church Fellowship* (1985).

Third phase: church and justification: The report of the third
phase (1986–1993) captured, in few words, the mutual problem
on the two decisive questions of justification and ecclesial
structures:

> Catholics ask whether the Lutheran understanding of jus-
> tification does not diminish the reality of the church;
> Lutherans ask whether the Catholic understanding does
> not obscure the gospel as the doctrine of justification
> explicates it.[39]

While not attempting a study of the entire subject of "church,"
a wide range of ecclesiological subjects did arise, affording
each partner an opportunity to explain its position. These subjects included an understanding of the church as the community of believers, the church as the sacrament of salvation, the
church visible and invisible, and the church holy and sinful.
The outcome was a "broad consensus" (165) with some differences remaining.

Of special note was the consensus achieved on how
Christ's salvation reaches people in and through the church. In
the past, Lutherans were so strongly emphatic about Christ
being the unique mediator, that any suggestion of the church's
involvement was interpreted as endangering Christ's singular
role. Today, Lutherans, with Catholics, understand that the

117

church's radical dependency on Christ is precisely for the purpose of mediating his salvation to the world.

Four other controversial topics were raised: the institutional continuity of the church, ordained ministry in the church, the place of binding church doctrine and the teaching role of the ministry, and church jurisdiction. It was agreed that these happen to be realities in the church, although subject to a variety of developments throughout history. In the end, these realities must serve and be seen to serve the gospel. Clearly, convergence is happening in areas that hitherto were considered points of fundamental difference.[40]

A sign of considerable progress on this precise subject of "justification" was given in June 1998, when the "Joint Declaration on the Doctrine of Justification" was made public.[41] The declaration is the result of the work of Scripture scholars and theologians and of the approval given by the authorities of the Catholic and Lutheran Churches. Leaving the polemics of the past centuries aside, the declaration expresses agreement that forgiveness and salvation arise from God's grace, while good works flow from that newly acquired condition in people. Beyond the agreement, it is acknowledged that certain areas still need to be explored and clarified, including the precise nature of the relationship of grace and sinfulness in people and the wider question of authority.

Fourth phase: other topics not yet addressed: Meanwhile, meetings of the fourth phase of the commission, which began in 1995, continue annually. The purpose of this phase is to take up those topics that have not been dealt with sufficiently at the international level. These include (a) the apostolicity of the church, including the episcopacy and a universal ministry for Christian unity; (b) mariology, the saints, sacramentology in general, and the number of the sacraments; (c) a study of certain ethical and moral issues; and (d) a review of matters already considered so as to incorporate new ideas that may have arisen over the more than thirty years of dialogue.[42]

If the results of all these discussions and decisions can filter out and become part of Lutheran-Catholic relations in ordinary communities, an important pastoral accomplishment will be realized. After all, that is where the "church" actually exists, that is where Christ's justifying graces are needed. Such is one of the purposes of a book like this.

The Second Phase of the Reformation

What Luther did soon proved to be just a beginning to the Protestant Reformation, for even within his own lifetime, serious divergences began to occur. The very word *Reform,* for example, often loosely used to refer to all the churches that trace their origins to the sixteenth century, more properly refers to those Protestant communities that came to exist in opposition to Lutheranism (the first phase, which has already been considered) and the Radical Anabaptists (the third phase, which is the subject of the next section). In other words, the development of the Reformed Churches was quite a distinctive aspect of the Reformation. This will become especially evident in the matter of the Eucharist.

Huldreich Zwingli and Martin Bucer

Huldreich Zwingli (1484–1531) is regarded as the third man of the Reformation, after Luther and Calvin, probably because he did not write a great deal. Zwingli claimed that he was not influenced by Luther in developing his reform doctrines. Whatever the truth of that matter, Zurich was a city ready for reform, and Zwingli was the man on the spot.

Whereas Luther retained a reverence for tradition, Zwingli developed an open distaste for ceremony and any externals that traditionally had been used by Christians to aid them in relating to God. He, therefore, developed a new order of liturgy comprising Scripture, sermon, and prayer, with bread and wine no longer on an altar but on a bare table in the nave of the church. Churches were denuded of images, relics, and vestments, the ministers wearing street clothes; hymns were banned because they were not scriptural; and devotions to Mary and the saints were forbidden. Even the organ at Great Minster was removed. God's grace, Zwingli argued, is immediate, so ceremony or intermediaries of any kind become substitutes for true religion.

119

Clearly, Zwingli was more ruthless than Luther, most especially on no less a subject than the Eucharist.[43] For four days in 1529, Luther and Melanchthon met with Zwingli and Martin Bucer (1491–1551) at Marburg to discuss a variety of issues, principally the Eucharist. Their eucharistic agreement was on four points: fuller congregational participation with the cup available to all; the centrality of the Word in the eucharistic service; an understanding of Eucharist exclusive of any idea of sacrifice; and rejection of the term and concept of transubstantiation.

The point of difference was quite serious. Luther, in line with Catholic thinking, insisted that Christ is bodily present in the Eucharist, the word *is* in the words of consecration to be taken literally. Zwingli regarded the Eucharist as no more than a commemorative service in which a community shows allegiance to Christ and remembers gratefully the event of the cross. Strongly into spiritualism, Zwingli argued that the physical reception of a spiritual gift is an impossibility.[44]

Martin Bucer, a leader in both the continental Reformation and the English Reformation, tried to reconcile the Lutherans and the Zwinglians, although favoring Zwingli's eucharistic views. His compromise formula was that Christ is given with, not in or under, the forms of bread and wine. In other words, while the Divine life accompanies the bread and wine, a person without faith receives only bread. This doctrine, which became a feature of Protestants who were not Lutherans, came to be known as "receptionism."

Contact between Luther and Zwingli now ended, the break between the two being definite, and the two centers of Protestantism came to exist: Wittenburg with Luther, Zurich with Zwingli.

Jean Calvin and John Knox

French-born, Jean Calvin (1509–1564) was offered a position as a teacher of Scripture when he was passing through Geneva, the city that would eventually become his home until his death. In Geneva, he continued the reforms begun by Zwingli and came to be known as the father of the "Reformed Churches," which normally are governed by presbyters.

The term "Calvinism," sometimes used as an alternative name for the Reformed Churches, or at least for their religious ideas, is no longer considered appropriate—for two reasons.[45] First, Calvin's ideas were modified by his successors within the Reformed Churches; second, the term was used disparagingly by German Lutherans who were not comfortable with the 1563 Heidelberg Catechism.

Not only was there a growing rift between Lutheranism and the Reformed movement, but Calvin was to arrive at the conviction that separation from the Catholic Church was a necessity. He believed that the Catholic Church failed in preaching the pure word of God and in administering the sacraments just as Christ had instituted them. He also believed that the papacy had assumed the headship of the church, a role that was Christ's alone. Given this negative viewing of Catholicism, Calvin rejected the validity of her orders.

His classical work, *Institutes of the Christian Religion,*[46] went through several editions. The second edition, issued in 1539, presented his first developed ideas on the nature of the church. Aware of the vagueness of Luther, Calvin set out to give the church a definite identity. In this, he probably was influenced by Bucer, who came from a background of considerable ecclesiastical administrative experience. We consider Calvin's doctrine under four heads.

Two ways of speaking about one church: Like Luther, Calvin took up Augustine's notion of the visible-invisible church, although he did not accept Luther's idea of two churches. Instead, he opted for two ways of speaking of the one "church." There is the invisible church, comprising the saints and the elect, chosen from the beginning of the world and being members of the "body of Christ," and there is the visible church of men and women who worship God, including those who relate to Christ only outwardly. He described this visible church as "mother" so that, "away from her bosom one cannot hope for any forgiveness of sins or any salvation."[47] In this one church, of which Christ is the sole head, it is not possible to identify who are the elect.

Union with Christ: This was fundamental in Calvin's thinking. It was a union achieved through the power of the Spirit, and the beneficiary found peace and the beginnings of a transformed life.

121

A program of discipline: Calvin accepted Luther's first three marks of the church: the preaching of the word and the administration of the sacraments of baptism and Eucharist. But "discipline," too, became an important identifying feature of the Reformed Churches, although it was not considered a mark because it is part of the church's organization, not her definition.

For practical purposes, however, discipline became a very distinctive feature of the church, first and foremost in Geneva. An austere and somewhat unforgiving man himself, Calvin extended his personal program of discipline onto the church.[48] Because he set out to protect people from bad influences, sinners were required to undergo penances. These sometimes included excommunication, which had as its ultimate aim the reconciliation of the penitent. To this end, he created the consistory, a supervisory agency for the maintenance of religious orthodoxy.

To achieve his purposes, Calvin insisted that the spiritual and temporal jurisdictions, although distinct, should complement one another and work hand in hand. And so they did, as is evidenced by the close relationship of church and magistrates in Geneva.

A fourfold ministry: Calvin believed that Christ imparted to the church the gift of a fourfold ministry of pastors, teachers (or doctors), elders (or presbyters), and deacons. Interestingly, he regarded ordination as a sacrament, although he explains: "I have not put it as number three among the sacraments because it is not ordinary or common with all believers, but is a special rite for a particular office."[49]

As was the case with Lutheranism, Reformed thinking on the church was subject to developments at the hands of Calvin's followers. That is a subject in its own right, beyond the intent of this work. However, mention must be made of the doctrine of predestination, long attributed to Calvin but, in fact, belonging to his followers.[50] To identify Calvinist thinking as distinct from Lutheran, Theodore of Beza spoke of the "divine decree" to either eternal life or to death. This became the principle from which all else in the Reformed thinking derived. God wills the salvation of the elect, implying that Christ did not die and rise for all, and that those not chosen remain unaware of their plight. This frightening doctrine proved to be a stumbling block to Reform's long-term development.

John Knox (1513–1572) was the leader of the Calvinist-inspired reform as it took root as the Church of Scotland, or Presbyterianism, as it became known. Knox spent time in Geneva, where he had firsthand experience of the Reform movement and of Calvin's thinking in particular. Not an original thinker himself, but renowned as a preacher, he returned to Scotland, of one mind with Calvin, to lay the foundations for the church.

Reformed/Presbyterianism Today[51]

"Reformed" is the name of the Calvinist Churches in Holland, France (where it is the largest Protestant body), Switzerland, Hungary, and other European countries; in Scotland and in the English-speaking world generally, the churches are called "Presbyterian."

In 1970, the World Alliance of Reformed Churches (WARC) was formed from two previously existing groupings of churches holding the presbyterian system. Today, WARC comprises more than one hundred and ninety-three Reformed, Presbyterian, and Congregationalist Churches as well as some United Churches, representing about seventy million people. There is no one exclusive definition of faith among the members, who are drawn into the alliance for purposes of witness and service. The headquarters of the alliance is in the Ecumenical Center in Geneva.

Reformed/Presbyterian Churches are adorned simply. Worship is similarly simple, without liturgical form, and the minister wears a black robe. Very few churches have weekly Eucharist, although monthly celebrations are not uncommon.

Relations between Lutherans and Reformed, in this ecumenical age, are far more positive. Intercommunion is possible, and the Concord of Leuenberg (1973) brought the European churches of both traditions to theological agreement on matters of faith and order. In 1985, the LWF and WARC, at the world level, established a joint dialogue commission. The latest agreement, finally approved in August 1997, is in the

United States between the Evangelical Lutheran (more than five million members), the Reformed and Presbyterian (three million members), and the United Church of Christ (one and a half million). The "Formula of Agreement" allows for the churches to retain their creeds and theological traditions, while recognizing each other's sacraments and clergy, cooperating also in missionary work and social service projects.

Reformed–Roman Catholic Dialogue

There was a reluctance at first for this dialogue to get underway, largely because of what was believed to be fundamental divergences between Catholic and Reformed doctrines on the nature of the church and its relationship with God and with the world. Nevertheless, preliminary talks between WARC and SPCU (now PCPCU) got underway in 1968 when, inevitably, "church" surfaced as the obvious subject to be addressed.

The aim of the Roman Catholic–Reformed Joint Study Commission, unlike the aim of the Lutheran–Roman Catholic dialogue, is not full visible union. It is a matter of finding common ground, clarifying differences, and seeking ways of working together to give common witness. To date, there have been two phases in the work of the commission.

First phase: Presence of Christ in Church and World: The title of the report of this first phase (1970–1977) states the general subject matter of the study. Particular items, however, included the relationship of Scripture and tradition, metaphors and models of the church in the New Testament, the role of the church in God's plan of salvation, and the fact that the church is a pilgrim people who have a eucharistic memorial and a ministry. There was then a pause for seven years.

Second phase: Towards a Common Understanding of the Church: This second report (1984–1990) is regarded as a considerable advance on the first, showing a certain maturing in the discussions. A number of background papers, examples being papers on the reformers and on sixteenth-century Catholic ecclesiology, proved helpful in the work of reconciling or cleansing memories. The report offers a common confession of faith by the dialogue participants, pointing to the already existing areas of agreement: that Christ is the one mediator, that justification is received by grace through faith, and that the church is the community of those called to be redeemed and sanctified. The relationship of the gospel and the church is addressed, although different understandings emerged as to how this church unfolded in history. Finally, the report speaks of common action areas and the challenge that faces the two churches in working toward a concept of unity that can be agreed on.

Third phase: The third phase, which does not yet have a title, began in 1998, the early subject matter being suggestions presented in the report of the second phase. In the eight-year interval when no international dialogue was in place, contacts were confined mainly to invitations to important events in each other's church.

But WARC has held three consultations since 1990, and has included the LWF and PCPCU. The first of these ended with the report titled *Christian Fundamentalism Today*. The second, which PCPCU was unable to attend, was on ethnicity and nationalism. The third, in cooperation with the Mennonite World Conference, was on *The New Dialogue between the First and Second Reformation*. The "first reformation" in this title refers to the reform efforts before the sixteenth century, which we have already studied, including the Waldensians, John Hus, and others. The other party in this dialogue is sometimes referred to as the "radical reformation," including the Anabaptists, the Quakers, and the Church of the Brethren, which we study in the next section.

For its part, PCPCU invited Reformed representatives to attend the December 1991 Special Assembly for Europe of the Synod of Bishops. Two representatives attended, one from the Church of Scotland and one from the Swiss Federation of Reformed Churches. A further invitation was extended for a representation at the Synod of Bishops held in October 1994 on the theme of the consecrated life. This was accepted by Sister Minke de Vries, prioress of the Sisters of Grandchamps of the Reformed tradition. Sister Minke de Vries also wrote the Way of the Cross for the 1995 ceremony, presided over by John Paul II at the Colosseum in Rome on Good Friday.[52]

It should be clear from the above study that the conversation between the Reformed and the Catholic Churches has not only a different aim from that of the Lutheran-Catholic dialogue, but it began less enthusiastically. The choice of Zwingli, Calvin, and others, unlike that of Luther, was to create a tradition even further from Catholicism, resulting in a separation that, at times, was an embittered one. Having begun talking now is a great achievement; the continuation of the same is important in the hope that someday the aim of the dialogue will become a mutual pursuit of the fullness of unity.

The Third Phase of the Reformation

The Lutheran and Reformed movements together are sometimes referred to as the "Magisterial Reformation," in contrast to the "Radical Reformation,"[53] also identified as the "left-wing" of the Reformation. The main complaint of the radical reformers was that the magisterial reformers did not go far enough in refounding the church along strictly scriptural lines. The identity they wanted the church to have would involve a complete break with anything suggestive of a "Roman and papist" connection, a commitment to the pursuit of personal holiness peaking in believer's baptism, a separation from the world and its affairs. It would involve the gathering of small groups for sharing the Word, the breaking of bread, and prayer along the lines of the New Testament "house" communities.

Beginnings of the Radical Reformation

The beginnings of the actual Radical Reformation can be traced to Zurich, 1525. Conrad Grebel (1498–1526), one of Zwingli's more radical disciples, rebaptized Georg Blaurock, thus making "believer's baptism" a sign of the movement. Not only had Zwingli not gone far enough, in their view, but he was suspected of compromising—certainly of changing—his stance on a number of issues. At one time, he promoted the common ownership of property as a Christian ideal, yet within three to five years he became an advocate of private owner-ship. Early in his reforming career, he was a supporter of adult baptism, later changing—vehemently—to an insistence on infant baptism. When the Anabaptists,[54] so named by Zwingli, established themselves in Zurich and chose to rebaptize, the penalty imposed on them was death by drowning at the hands of the secular authorities. Once expelled from Zurich, they spread throughout central Europe.

Subsequently, the name "Anabaptist" (which literally means "rebaptizer") has often been used to identify all these pious groups of people who believed the Reformation should be more radical than what the reformers had achieved, although it must be added that not every group required con-verts to be rebaptized. The Swiss Brethren, for example, in their Schleitheim Confession (written in 1527 by Michael Sattler), held that baptism was to be given to those who repent and who believe in Christ's saving act, whereas the Spiritualist Anabaptists were not convinced of the need even of believer's baptism. These latter were so named because of their pente-costal leanings and their belief in the invisible church. None regarded baptism as a sacrament. Only what is explicitly stated in Scripture is to be believed and practiced: such is *sola scriptura* in the extreme. Given this foundation, Anabaptists professed a radical form of Christian discipleship, including a high level of separation from the world—which was expressed in an unwillingness to assume civic appointments, a refusal to take oaths, and an option for pacifism. All in all, their prefer-ence was for a simple and holy lifestyle, if not one that was somewhat insular.

The spirit of the Anabaptists has continued into our day in a number of presently existing denominations. We now con-sider some of these.

Hutterites and their present-day contacts with Roman Catholics: At about the time the Swiss Brethren were establishing themselves in Zurich, another group was forming in Moravia under the leadership of Jakob Hutter (+ 1536). He organized communities into collective farms where members took on Anabaptist-living in a radical and ascetical fashion, including renunciation of private property. They suffered a great deal of persecution through the years, having to flee in the 1760s into the Ukraine. Then, in the nineteenth century, the Russian members migrated to the United States to avoid conscription, and the German members moved to Canada on the eve of the First World War.

Hutter's followers retain the way of life he set for them in the sixteenth century. After making a confession of faith, they are baptized, at about the age of twenty. Today's forty thousand Hutterites, mainly of German descent, live in colonies of sixty to one hundred and fifty members on farms ranging in size from four thousand to twelve thousand acres. They share a common life without private property, and they engage in only minimal trading, paying taxes but not accepting social security. Communal prayer is a daily event, and on Sundays there is a hymn-and-sermon service in the schools. The Hutterites do use electricity and modern farming equipment, but they do not use radio, television, or film in their personal and family lives.

While there is no official dialogue or conversation between the Hutterite community and the Catholic Church, there are profitable informal contacts between the Bruderhof (the German name for the settlements established by the Hutterites) and various Catholics. In the eighties and nineties, Elder Johann Christoph Arnold had exchanges with Cardinal John O'Connor of New York, in a small local dialogue, and with Cardinal Joseph Ratzinger of the Congregation of the Doctrine of the Faith. After the meeting with Cardinal Ratzinger, Elder Arnold and his group remarked that they were "not merely partners in a discussion but participants in an encounter of deep inner content."

A Catholic group first established in Munich, but with branches elsewhere, calls themselves *Integrierte Gemeinde* ("integrated community").[55] Comprised of laity and priests, married and single people, this group decided to establish a house in New York, motivated by a desire to have closer contact with the Bruderhof. It was their relationship that led to the meeting in Rome with Cardinal Ratzinger. Rather wonderful to read are the words of Elder Arnold:

I long for a new, mutual understanding between the Roman Catholic Church and the Hutterite movement, so that we can again look into one another's eyes and know that the past is forgiven. Then together we will be able to seek more deeply what true and living discipleship of Jesus means as we enter the 21st Century. Most of all, Roman Catholics and Hutterites will be able to encourage and support each other in becoming more dedicated and convinced Christians.[56]

The Mennonites and their present-day conversations with Roman Catholics: Menno Simons (1496-1561), formerly a Catholic, joined the Anabaptists in 1536 to become one of the more outstanding leaders of the Radical Reformation, exercising a twenty-five year long ministry among communities in Holland and in nearby places. Eventually, his followers came to be known as the Mennonites. They are the oldest Protestant free church.

True to the Anabaptist ideal, the Mennonites are opposed to an organized church, favoring autonomous congregations instead. Other characteristics include believer's baptism, the Lord's Supper (although rejecting the Real Presence in the Eucharist) presided over by an elder chosen by the community, and the refusal of military service and the taking of oaths or public offices. Without a common doctrine, what they accept varies from community to community, ranging from unitarian beliefs to trinitarian.

Of their one million members, an estimate of the Mennonite World Conference, the majority reside in the United States and Africa, with smaller communities in Holland, Germany, Russia, Canada, and Mexico. The Mennonite World Conference, which began in 1925 and is held about every five or six years, successfully incorporates most groups, although fragmentation does still occasionally happen.[57]

For some years, there have been occasional contacts between Catholic participants and Mennonite representatives at the Conference of Secretaries of Christian World Communions. More recently, Cardinal Cassidy sent a greeting to Dr. Larry Miller, General Secretary of the Mennonite World

Conference which met in Calcutta in January 1997. The Cardinal wrote: "We are most happy to be represented at the meeting by a member of our staff. It is our sincere hope that there will be other contacts between the Mennonite World Conference and the Catholic Church."[58] It is hoped that a dialogue will get underway.

The Catholic hope was soon to be realized when, for the first time, Mennonite and Catholic theologians met in an international conversation in October 1998 in Strasbourg, France. The sponsors of the consultation were the Mennonite World Conference and the PCPCU. The purpose of this first meeting was to promote a better understanding of each church and to further the task of overcoming prejudices. Two sets of papers were presented: one set describing each church, and the other addressing the sixteenth-century problems between the two churches. The consultations will continue.

Productive encounters go well beyond official or even unofficial "dialogues." A case in point is the 1997–1998 United States–based program titled "Catholics and Anabaptists in Conversation about Spirituality." Several Mennonite scholars feature in the lecture series, and a prominent topic is the work of the Dutch Catholic priest and author, Henri Nouwen (1932–1996), whose writings "have had a major impact upon spirituality movements within Mennonite and Church of the Brethren denominations." [59]

The Amish: It was the Swiss Jacob Ammann who became disillusioned with Mennonite "laxity" and withdrew his membership in 1693 to form a stricter group. This group became known as the Amish Church. Insistence was on a severe discipline, which included separation from those under the ban of excommunication, even family members. They began immigrating to America in 1720 and settled primarily in Pennsylvania, Ohio, Indiana, Nebraska, and, in fewer numbers, Canada.

The Old Order Amish Church is especially noteworthy for the characteristic plain, dark clothing; the beards and dark hats of the men; and the bonnets and aprons of the women. Members are pacifists, decline social security benefits, worship rotationally in private homes, and forbid marriages with people outside of the community. There have been separations, the new groups favoring less rigid forms of discipline and the use of modern inventions.

Today, there are about one hundred and thirty thousand members of the Amish Churches. There are no significant contacts between the Catholic Church and the Amish.

The Religious Society of Friends (Quakers): The Religious Society of Friends began in about 1650 in England, under the leadership of George Fox (1624–1691). Although they do not belong to the Anabaptist tradition as such, many Anabaptist beliefs were incorporated into Quaker thinking. Among their views, for example, are those of Caspar Schwenckfeld (1489–1561), a prolific Anabaptist writer who, among other things, rejected the eucharistic presence of the body and blood of Christ in favor of an "inner feeding" on the celestial food.

Fox, likewise, was a devotee of the "inner light," which superseded external forces. This enabled the brethren to assume the title of "Friends," in line with John 15:14: "You are my friends if you do what I command you." Great importance is given to the Inner Light, for it enables them to be freed from sin, thus uniting themselves to Christ so as to have a good moral character and perform good deeds.

Apparently, the name "Quaker" was descriptive of people who tremored in ecstasy, and Fox is said to have ordered a magistrate, before whom he was on trial for his beliefs in 1650, to tremble on hearing the Lord's name.

The churches had fallen so far away from the truth, according to Fox, that recovery of their true form was far from possible. The Friends, therefore, would relate directly with Christ, a kind of firsthand religious experience. Their disposing of intermediaries included the Bible, creeds, and the sacraments. As a result, there is no water baptism and no external Eucharist, only spiritual baptism and spiritual eucharist. They use the Bible, but not as an authoritative source for their beliefs and conduct. No authority of any kind would intervene between them and God.

Local congregational identity is paramount, and membership simply amounts to attachment to a community without any formal acceptance procedures, such as an initiation rite.

Worship is spontaneous, devoid of any liturgical form. Traditionally, silence has been a significant component, with women and men enjoying equal rights in speaking and praying. They are opposed to compulsory church attendance, military service, and the taking of judicial oaths. The Friends are socially active, their members often occupying leadership roles in prison reform efforts, opposition to slavery, care of minority groups, relief work, and world peace.

Schisms have happened among them, often depending on the emphases different communities have chosen to give to themselves, be they evangelical, social, or intellectual. They are favorably disposed to ecumenical endeavors, but their formlessness, especially their opposition to external state-ments of belief, make headway difficult. The Friends World Committee for Consultation, which began in 1937, meets every three years. It represented the Friends at the Second Vatican Council.

Persecutions led many to immigrate to the United States where William Penn (1644–1718) founded Pennsylvania. Today, there are two hundred and fifty thousand Friends in the world, about half of which are in the United States. Friends-Catholic contacts do not go beyond the Faith and Order Multilateral Dialogue and the annual conference of Secretaries of Christian World Communions.

Baptists and their present-day conversations with Roman Catholics: The Baptists are spiritual descendants of the Anabaptists. In Holland in 1609, John Smyth (c.1554–1612), an Anglican clergyman ministering to a small English refugee group, established the "Church of the Baptists." Believer's bap-tism was the basis of membership, with Smyth and his follow-ers seeking entry into the Mennonites, which happened only after his death.

In 1612, Smyth's associate, Thomas Helwyns, along with others, returned to London where they established the first Baptist Church at Spitalfields. They became known as the "General Baptists," being followers of Arminian theology, which teaches that it is God's will that all be saved, in contrast to the rigid predestination thinking of the times. The Particular Baptists also began in London, so named because of their belief that redemption is "particular," that is, Christ died only for the elect. In the late nineteenth century, the General and Particular Baptists came together in the Baptist Union of Great Britain and Ireland.[60]

Those seeking religious freedom immigrated to America in the early seventeenth century. After a difficult beginning, they spread rapidly and increased greatly in numbers, especially during the eighteenth century. Today, the four American conventions together total twenty-seven million, the second largest denomination in the United States after Catholicism. The Southern Baptists are more akin to Particular Baptist thinking in their theology.

Doctrinally, Baptists teach that adults who make a personal confession of faith and who are baptized are received into the body of Christ, the church. Since Baptists are strongly congregational, they go only as far as having unions of churches and conventions, without any central church identity or structure. The Scriptures are the sole source of authority, creeds not enjoying any such role.[61]

There is an international voluntary forum, the Baptist World Alliance, which was founded in 1905. Its headquarters are in Washington, D.C. Between the congresses, an executive committee continues the work of coordination, especially in areas of education, missions, and the promotion of freedom and human rights. Not all churches of today's forty million Baptists belong to the Alliance.

Ecumenically, the Baptist starting point is different from that of the Catholic Church. Denominationalism, for Baptists, is not sinful and scandalous. What happened at the Reformation, they maintain, was an appropriate purification of Christianity, and the advent of denominations has enabled the church to be enriched by a variety in the witnessing that can be offered. That is why the president of the Baptist Union, Dr. Derek Tidball, remarked in May 1990 that he anticipated the 1990s as a decade of ecumenism in which he "hoped that we will learn to talk with one another without the imposition of a super-church."[62]

For a long time, Baptists were reluctant to enter the ecumenical movement because they could not agree on the generally accepted endpoint of ecumenism: the full visible unity of the church. However, a decade of discussions in the United States ended in 1989 with *An Agreed Statement from the Southern Baptist–Roman Catholic Scholars' Conversations.*[63] The goal of the conversations, therefore, was not full visible unity, but "understanding and mutual awareness," a stage in the ecumenical process prior to dialogue.

Major differences surfaced, but so did "significant convergences in fundamental attitudes." The conversations have continued since the 1989 report. Among the disagreements is the matter of evangelizing, which Baptists view as missionary work directed at those who do not have a personal relationship with Christ, including members of other churches. Agreements include belief in the divinity, humanity, and resurrection of Christ and on certain moral issues, including opposition to abortion, pornography, and racism. The dialogue team actually published five pamphlets offering biblical reflections on social issues such as the environment and racism.

The first phase of an international dialogue (1984–1990) between the Baptist World Alliance (BWA) and PCPCU ended with the report titled *Summons to Witness to Christ in Today's World.*[64] Some South American Baptists who were not in favor of the conversations at the outset renewed their opposition when the report was released. Such opposition made it difficult for the BWA to agree to a second phase, a suggestion being that just now regional dialogues might be more appropriate, such as those underway in the United States and France.

Returning to what others see as the Baptist practice of evangelizing or proselytizing, the fact that it is being done in traditionally Catholic and Orthodox areas is a source of real tension. The BWA has clearly stated its intention to establish Baptist churches in southern and eastern Europe, although a further statement about opening more churches in Nepal carried the hopeful note that its intent was not the winning of converts from existing Christian churches.[65]

Further signs of hope have arisen from two workshops held at the 1995 Baptist World Congress in Buenos Aires. The first carried a self-criticism by Baptists for their being tardy in entering into ecumenical matters, suggesting also that there should be more in-house ecumenical workshops for Baptists. The second was a review of the BWA's international conversations, including the Catholic one. As yet, a second-phase conversation has not begun, but it certainly is a Catholic hope that it will happen.[66]

Seventh-Day Adventists and their present-day contacts with Roman Catholics: When Baptist preacher William Miller (1782–1849) predicted the second coming of Christ would occur in 1843, and it didn't happen, a small group who remained faithful to him formed the Seventh Day Adventist Church. These people were Joseph Bates, James White, and his wife, Ellen, who is considered a prophetess and whose writings are still regarded as an important doctrinal source among the Adventists.

Characteristics of this two-million-strong church include acceptance of the Bible as the sole rule of faith, believer's baptism, congregational government and tithing, Sabbath worship, and the mortality of the human person, immortality being a gift of Christ to the just. There is a General Conference with headquarters in Washington, D.C.

Traditionally, the Seventh Day Adventist Church has not been involved in the ecumenical movement, but an exploratory conversation with the LWF in Toronto in 1996 suggests the beginning of change. At their two world conferences, at Indianapolis in 1990 and at Utrecht in 1995, a representative of the Catholic Church was present.

Christian Church (Disciples of Christ) and their present-day dialogue with Roman Catholics: The beginnings of the Christian Church, or the Disciples of Christ, can be traced to Thomas and Alexander Campbell (1788–1866). This father and son left Presbyterianism in the United States to merge their followers with an earlier group called "Christians," under the leadership of Burton W. Stone, in the early nineteenth century.

Although the theological roots of the Disciples rest in reform, our consideration of the church in this context is due to their practice of believer's baptism, also by immersion. They are strongly committed to the Scriptures as the one authoritative source of Christian beliefs, and they are equally dedicated to bringing church practice into line with the New Testament. Hence, Acts 2:42 offers the appropriate model for worship: "They devoted themselves to the apostles' instruction (teaching) and the communal life (fellowship with congregational government), to the breaking of bread (Eucharist), and the prayers (led by anyone)."

The membership is one and a half million, united in the World Convention of the Churches of Christ (Disciples), which was started in 1930.[67]

The Disciples have long been committed to the unity of the church and are dedicated contributors to the ecumenical movement. The dialogue with the Catholic Church has as its goal, as stated at the first meeting, the developing of "relations between the Disciples Churches and the Roman Catholic Church that the unity willed by Christ may be attained and given visible expression." It began in 1977, and so far there have been three phases.

The report of the first phase, *Apostolicity and Catholicity in the Visible Unity of the Church* (1977–1982), highlights three areas that would be basic to future discussions: the nature of baptism, the importance of spiritual ecumenism, and the relationship between faith and tradition.[68]

The commitment of both sides of the commission to the full visible unity of the church is very evident in the report of the second phase, *The Church as Communion in Christ* (1983–1992). This union, identified as "communion," exists first and foremost in the Trinity and is extended to the world in a salvific way through the church. The church, which is a eucharistic community, is both the sign and instrument of this salvation. In all of this thinking, there is a remarkable level of convergence.[69]

But there are also differences in understanding. The Disciples do not view the episcopacy, for example, as necessary for the maintenance of the church's unity. Nor do they view creeds and doctrines as the Holy Spirit's way of continuing to guide the church into a unity of faith. Finally, there is considerable divergence on the important matter of the Eucharist. In contrast to the Catholic position of allowing only ordained priests to preside at the Eucharist, and of permitting only those within the Catholic Church to receive the sacrament, the Disciples provide for nonordained ministers to preside and for any person attending the service to approach the table. These are examples of some of the matters that will need attention at subsequent meetings.

The third phase began in 1993, and "The Individual and the Church" was chosen as the theme. This focus enabled the commission to take up the unresolved issues that surfaced during the second phase, especially those that seem to point to fundamental theological differences. Faith, so important in any Protestant self-definition, places the believer in a relationship with the church. What is the nature of the relationship? What is the role of the church in nurturing the faith of the individual? What is the relationship of Word and sacrament in the church? Besides addressing questions like these, the commission has to deal with matters such as the interpretation of Scripture, the right of the church to teach, and the role of ecumenical councils, ordained ministry, and the church's magisterium.[70]

The 1998 meeting addressed the topic, "The Teaching Office of the Church." Two important papers were presented at this gathering, one by Jean-Marie Tillard on "How Is Christian Truth Taught in the (Roman) Catholic Church?" and one by William Tabbernee on "Alexander Campbell's Teacher-Bishops and the Role of Scholar-Pastors Among Contemporary Disciples of Christ." The discussions that followed saw both acknowledging that, in teaching the Word of God, some members of the community enjoy empowerment to minister in this way. This specific task in the Catholic Church is given to bishops; for the Disciples, it is the function of the ordained ministers. In both churches, when doctrinal or pastoral problems arise, these pastors have authority to direct the community, while being conscious of the sense of the faith, the *sensus fidei*, of the whole Church of God.

These very fruitful discussions continue, with the 1999 subject being God and the formation of conscience. The commission's goal is to have an Agreed Statement in place by 2001.

Of course there are continuing questions and difficulties. Without the dialogues, however, there would be even more. What is happening in so many of these dialogues is a clarification of issues, an overcoming of misunderstandings, and an acknowledgment that ongoing convergences are possible.

The Radical Reformation, although it did draw great numbers of people from allegiance within the traditional Christian and Catholic beliefs, did not take people into a vacuum. By and large, the members of the various communities were asked to embrace holiness of life by committing themselves to Christ in a self-sacrificing way—and they did.

There are variations in emphases from community to community, as we have seen. For Catholics and those Christians with whom they are in a dialogue or conversation, it is important to continue deepening the bonds. At the same time, they must accept the challenge of creating that kind of atmosphere in which they can begin to engage in dialogue with those they do not yet have a fruitful conversation.

The Fourth Phase: The Catholic Reformation

The question has often been asked, "Was the Catholic Reformation a reaction to the Protestant Reformation, or was it an in-house and independent renewal of Catholicism?"[71] Modern scholarship tends to favor the view that the church had succumbed to such a degree that "renewal" or "reform" had become a universal imperative, bringing forth a twofold effect: the Protestant Reformation and the Catholic Reformation. In the words of Owen Chadwick, "the Reformation came not so much because Europe was irreligious as because it was religious."[72]

The Council of Trent

The Council of Trent (1545–1563)[73] became the reforming arm of the Catholic Church. It was in this conciliar forum that a level of reaction to Protestantism arose. In theological areas, the council clarified Catholic teaching where there had been confusion and examined the reformers' views on the Scriptures, justification, predestination, and the sacraments, mostly rejecting what they taught. There was a certain acknowledgment of the validity of the reformers' protests about clergy conduct, ecclesiastical discipline, seminary education, and missionary work. Monasteries and older religious orders were reformed, for example, and new ones came to exist, including the Jesuits. Strict laws were put into place governing the granting of indulgences, the administration of the sacraments, and church life in general, including diocesan and parochial life.

The implementation of the Tridentine decrees was entrusted to the pope. Hence, the catechism of the Council of Trent, largely the work of Charles Borromeo (1538–1584), and the creation of standard texts for the missal, the breviary, and the ritual ensured a universal program of reform which, for the centuries to follow, was strictly supervised by the Roman pontiffs.

The Catholic Reformation achieved an immediate purification of the church but the wider reform movement had, by now, moved on from being a call for the removal of abuses within the church to something altogether new. Doctrine, religious liberty, and, indeed, the very nature of the church had become central to the entire process. The result was, as we have seen, the reformers' redesigning of the church according to a variety of patterns, including new definitions of "church," the first of which appeared as Article VIII of the Augsburg Confession.

That the problems of ecclesiology and the papacy were not addressed was a strange conciliar omission. As Yves Congar remarked, the council had to give an answer to the Reformation, yet it failed to take up at the point that really concerned the reformers: the matter of ecclesiology.[74] It was instructed to respond to the individual issues that were subject to attack by the reformers, not addressing this wider matter of the true nature of the church. Only when explaining the Apostles' Creed did the catechism of Trent, in the article titled "I believe the holy Catholic Church," give a traditional exposition of Catholic ecclesiology.

Robert Bellarmine

Reference was made in the first chapter to Robert Bellarmine (1542–1621) and to his famous work, *Disputations against the Heretics of the present time on the Controversies regarding the Christian Faith*. Apologetic as the text is, it reinforced the teaching of the catechism, and together they provided the one expression of Catholic ecclesiology that stayed in place until well into the twentieth century. Reacting to the Protestant emphasis on the church's invisibility, Bellarmine gave great stress to her visibility, defining her in these words:

> ...the congregation of men bound by the profession of the same Christian faith and by communion in the same sacraments under the rule of the lawful pastors, and especially of the only vicar of Christ on earth, the Roman pontiff.[75]

So strong was Bellarmine on the church's visibility that he identified church membership as requiring only an exterior profession of faith and participation in the sacraments, without the need of any interior virtue, although he also spoke of the graces that belong to the soul of the church. This form of expression gave the impression that the church has, on the one hand, a visible and canonical body, and on the other hand, an invisible soul where grace resides. The ecclesiastical disciplines in the centuries to follow emphasized the division, even to the point of bringing about a divorce of the church's "body" and "soul." Canon law became the discipline under which "church" was thought about, and "virtues" was the heading under which "grace" was considered. In other words, people learned not to look to the church for grace. Pius XII, and later Vatican II, gave a great deal of attention to this, the important resolution being expressed in the title of the first chapter of *LG:* "The Mystery of the Church." The church is, indeed, the vehicle of Christ's graces.

The other point of particular emphasis in Bellarmine's ecclesiology was on the pope as the inheritor of the universal authority that Christ gave to Peter.[76] This pronounced insistence on the headship of the universal church carried with it a corresponding de-emphasis on the local church and on the place of the bishop as its leader, as we studied in the first chapter.

Trent, and its ecclesiological interpreter Robert Bellarmine, bequeathed to the Catholic Church a particular and limited viewing of "church," one which stayed in place through the First Vatican Council and up to Pius XII and his encyclical *Mystici Corporis Christi.*

◈ ◈ ◈

Three main ecclesiological emphases have come to exist out of the early scriptural and patristic patterning of the church. In the first instance, there is the Orthodox understanding, as studied in chapter two; the variety of Protestant expressions which we have begun to consider in this chapter; and the Catholic ecclesial expression and teaching, which backgrounds this entire text.

The privileged task of modern-day Christians, therefore, is to seek a reconciliation of all these ecclesial expressions so as to make the church clearly one again. Many people, as we have seen, are taking this work seriously. An essential prerequisite to the task is the empowerment to move beyond seeing Christianity solely in terms of one particular community's explanation, as if that one explanation can provide "all we need" in order to fulfil religious duties and so attain salvation. Christians are to enter the depths of the reality that, just as God reconciled all things to himself in Christ, so the church's mission is to make that reconciling action of God visible. Ecumenism is not an optional extra.

But the picture of fractured Christianity is as yet incomplete, for there is another reformation to consider, that of England and its ramifications, which is the subject of the next chapter.

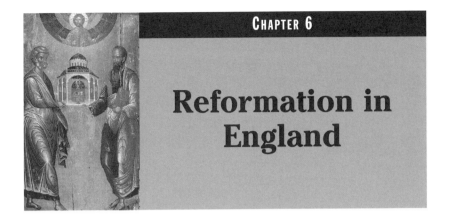

CHAPTER 6

Reformation in England

Parallel to the church's search for a suitable unity model is the world's growing awareness that it, too, must seek a certain oneness. We hear this latter aspiration expressed in terms like "global consciousness," which is a way of saying that we must become better neighbors and truly a human family if we are to survive. A second worldwide characteristic is a deepening appreciation for pluralism's rightful place in society, which can be expressed by the respect we have for our linguistic, cultural, and ethnic differences.

Which "Model of Church" Should Suit the Future?

These two worldwide yearnings no doubt heighten the church's sense of vocation, that is, her mission to the legitimate groupings of people on the earth, to the total human community, and to the whole created order. At the same time, however, the church sees in these yearnings a reflection of her own internal ecclesial task. In a word, she is prompted to look for a formula that will assist the passage of all the churches and ecclesial communities into a unity, while preserving—and not destroying—the legitimate traditions among them that have grown up over the centuries.[1] We turn now to a consideration of some of the models that have been proposed at various times.

The Return Model: Two former ecclesial models are no longer acceptable. One of these, the "Return Model,"[2] has featured in both the Catholic Church and the Orthodox Church, based on their respective and exclusive claims to being "the church." If the idea of "return" is to have any ongoing validity today, instead of each church imposing it as a requirement, it could be better expressed in a mutual journey toward each other. Thus, both churches would more properly live out their rediscovered sisterhood in the family of the one church. In this way they would offer to other churches and ecclesial communities a fitting example of church union.

The Uniate Model: The other model, also unacceptable in the contemporary scene, is the "Uniate Model" because the advances made in Orthodox-Catholic thinking means that "a revival of uniatism would lack a basis in Catholic ecclesiology,"[3] as we discussed in an earlier chapter.

The Model of Reconciled Diversity: Keeping in balance the two notions of "one church" and "legitimate diversity or pluralism" is a difficult task. Some contemporary unity models, however, so emphasize diversity, that denominationalism is, in fact, being kept alive. One such model, first suggested in the mid-seventies, is called the "Model of Reconciled Diversity." It came about, in part, as a reaction to the idea that the "one church" goal of the ecumenical movement might mean uniformity, centralization, and loss of confessional identities. What is primary, according to this model, is the preservation of the post-Reformation thinking that the only legitimate expression of gospel diversity is denominational. Unity is to be expressed through the continued existence of the various churches, although now marked by a spirit of cooperation, including a common teaching about faith and ethical issues, by table fellowship and, in some instances, by the formation of federations among them. The writings of one advocate of this model, Harding Meyer, has Yves Congar remarking that for Catholics "the idea of 'reconciled diversities' thus remains a question mark."[4]

The Conciliar Fellowship Model: The primary aim of the "Conciliar Fellowship Model" is the organic unity of all the churches, while continuing to respect their confessional identities. Still holding to their traditions and to their particular and recognizable gifting to the Christian scene, the special focus within this model is the reconciliation of the churches at the point of the divisions among them. The forum where this will be achieved is a conciliar one, which will also be an expression of their newly acquired communion. There is a great deal that is vague about the model, including its failure to define organic unity and its inability to recognize the need for a headship in the reunited church.[5]

The Typology Model: Koinonia or *communio*, scriptural and patristic in its earliest definition as we saw in chapter 3, became the central idea of the Vatican Council ecclesiology, especially as expressed in *UR*. After the council, writers like the Belgian Benedictine Emmanuel Lanne expressed the theology in terms of a "Typology Model." He wrote: "It is clear that we must try to discover together in what manner and measure God intends the unity of his church to express also diversity and pluralism in a single communion of faith and church life."[6] In the first chapter, we referred to Cardinal Willebrands' 1970 speech at Cambridge, England, on this precise subject. In that address, he offered an explanation of a *typos* of church:

> Where there is a long coherent tradition, commanding men's love and loyalty, creating and sustaining a harmonious and organic whole of complementary elements, each of which supports and strengthens the other, you have the reality of a typos.[7]

Cardinal Willebrands details the elements in a *typoi:* "A characteristic theological method and approach...A characteristic liturgical expression...A spiritual and devotional tradition...A characteristic canonical tradition."[8] In the bilateral dialogues of the Catholic Church and other traditions, the *koinonia* theology has underpinned the discussions, revealing a Catholic

145

respect for the various *typoi*. This is especially evident in the dialogues with the Orthodox and Anglicans, with some mention of *koinonia* appearing in the Methodist and Pentecostal conversations.

At the Seventh Assembly of the WCC in Canberra (1991), *koinonia* was adopted as a key notion to describe the unity sought after. This thinking was developed further by the Fifth World Conference of Faith and Order, Santiago de Compostelo (1993).[9] Here it was acknowledged that the concept of *koinonia* had long been prominent in the ecumenical movement, although the conference set out to clarify and develop Faith and Order thinking on the subject.

It would be true to say that the *koinonia-typoi* theology is now widely accepted as offering the most appropriate model for the unity the church is seeking. Having said this, it must be acknowledged that the concept is not without problems, but it is the task of church leadership and theologians to work toward a refinement of the model and make it a workable option.

What Is the "Hierarchy of Truths"?

The conciliar teaching on the "hierarchy of truths" is located in *UR* (11), which surely implies that the subject is intended to have importance for ecumenism. The fact is that it has great importance and, in summary, we might describe it broadly as a formula that seeks to preserve the church's unity in the inevitable and important context of diversity.[10]

The way into understanding the subject is not by drawing up a list of truths alongside each other and attempting to evaluate their importance. Rather, the starting point is found in identifying the central or foundational doctrines of our salvation, and subsequently relating the various other doctrines to that beginning point. These central truths are, on the one hand, about the mystery of God the Father, Son, and Holy Spirit and the person of Jesus and the salvation he won for us through his death and resurrection; and on the other hand, about how the human person is created by God and is re-created in Jesus and about the church and its role in dispensing Christ's salvation in the world.[11]

To realize the richness of meaning in these truths, we look first to the Scriptures, where they are recorded, and then to the apostolic and early post-apostolic communities, where we find a "lived interpretation" of them. These two, the Scriptures and the testimony of the early Christian communities, are the two significant reference points for us today as we search together to better understand the foundational truths of the Christian faith.

As the church's life has unfolded through the centuries, teachings have also emanated from ecumenical and general councils, from the ecclesiastical magisterium, and from other sources, much of it being expressed in dogmatic statements, confessions of faith, liturgies, spiritualities, and canonical pronouncements. Not all of these truths, religious though they may be, are equal in importance to the central Christian truths. For example, the Catholic dogmas of the Immaculate Conception and the Assumption are not and should not be placed on a critical and equal footing with the central doctrines cited above.

Sometimes, greater emphasis is given to one truth over others, thus relating it more prominently, and improperly, to the center. This is the case with people who think the certitude of their faith, and therefore their salvation, depends on the doctrine of papal infallibility, instead of on the doctrine of the mercy of God. Similarly, differences occur among communities in their ordering of teachings in relation to the center. They do not dispute, for instance, the centrality of the universal Lordship of Jesus, but they disagree over how Christ feeds the flock through appropriate leadership in the contemporary Christian community. Instances such as these have led to Christian divisions in the past.

An ecumenical task, therefore, is to better understand why other Christian communities have ordered in particular ways their believing and living in relation to the center, while also deepening their own self-understandings. The outcome might well be a realization that the unity of faith held in common is deeper than the diversities that divide.[12]

Theologians acknowledge that, despite the value of the theory of the "hierarchy of truths," it remains terribly difficult to apply. How much diversity can there be while ensuring the preservation of the unity of faith? On the one hand, there is the

Orthodox, with whom Catholics do not enjoy full communion. The Orthodox believe in and celebrate the dormition of Mary but do not accept either of the Marian dogmas. Yet, the Catholic Church, in virtue of *UR* (15) and the Directory 124, can permit and, where appropriate, encourage worship in common and eucharistic sharing with the Orthodox. It needs to be remarked here that normally the Orthodox do not encourage, nor permit, Catholics to receive the Eucharist in an Orthodox liturgy, given that we are not in full communion.

On the other hand, the difficulties experienced by the Lutheran and Anglican communities in accepting the Tridentine understanding and expression of the Eucharist prompts the question: Is Trent's teaching the only possible expression of Catholic eucharistic faith?

Against this background, the remainder of this chapter looks at the story of English Reform. We review the arrival of Anglicanism and consider the work of ARCIC I and II (the Anglican–Roman Catholic International Commission), which is the official dialogue between the Anglican Communion and the Catholic Church. We also take a look at Methodism: its birth within Anglicanism, its development into a fully independent denomination, and the state of the dialogue with the Catholic Church. Finally, we consider the Salvation Army, the Evangelicals, the Pentecostals, and the Old Catholics, as well as the nature of the relationship between each of them and the Catholic Church.

The Story of English Reform

It took a French philosopher to observe that the English are not very religious. That is why they invented cricket, he said, to give themselves a sense of eternity. Fictional though the story might be, the fact is that the beginnings of the English Reformation—unlike the continental one—were not religious. This was so, even though many of the forces that impelled Europe toward reformation were also present in England. To simplify this study, we will briefly examine the chief contributing events and characters of the English Reformation in four chronological stages.

First Stage: Designing a Change

The design stage of the Reformation and the laying of the foundations of the Church of England have always been associated with King Henry VIII (1491–1547), who had a political agenda behind his personal and pressing need. Politically, Henry had a major problem in that one-third to one-fifth of the land of his kingdom was in the control of churchmen, disadvantaging both king and people. At times, Henry resorted to the papacy as an ally in order to control the monasteries and orders that were the principal landowners. The outflow of taxes to Rome, however, and the disenchantment of the people with the corrupt Cardinal Wolsey, also chancellor of the realm, were not at all helpful to Henry. What made matters worse, and led to his fall in September 1529, was Wolsey's failure to secure Pope Clement VII's (1523–1534) permission for Henry to divorce Catherine of Aragon, which would free the king to marry Anne Boleyn. Instead, parliament and certain strategic appointments would help Henry achieve his objectives.[13]

Two appointments now gave a certain religious bent to this "planning" stage of the English Reformation. One was Thomas Cromwell's (c.1458–1540) appointment as royal secretary and viceregent. Totally committed to the idea of royal supremacy, and under the act bearing that name, he proceeded against Thomas More and John Fisher, also sending many others to their deaths. He lent support to the reformers who were beginning to appear on the scene, and he required that an English translation of the Bible be placed in every parish church.

The other appointment was that of the scholar Thomas Cranmer (1489–1556) as Archbishop of Canterbury, who came to be described as the principal architect of the Reformation. Also a believer in royal supremacy, Cranmer quickly declared Henry's marriage to Catherine null and void and crowned the king's new wife, Anne Boleyn, queen in 1533.

The 1534 Act of Supremacy meant that the papacy diminished as a point of focus and Henry, now as "supreme head on earth of the Church of England," secured a closer liaison of church and state. The legal rights of the pope were transferred to the crown, including the "first-fruit" taxes, the clergy as well being made subject to the laws of the land.

Cranmer was in a dilemma. On the one hand, he was committed to the king who remained quite Catholic in much of his thinking, especially with regard to the Eucharist and the doctrine of transubstantiation. Cranmer had to go along with the king. On the other hand, he was influenced by and sympathetic to those who had gone off to Germany and Switzerland to study the continental reform. Among these were William Tyndale (c.1491–1536), who printed the first English translation of the New Testament in 1535, and Miles Coverdale (1488–1569), who completed a translation of the entire Bible into English by 1535. Cranmer penned a liberal preface to the English Bible and accepted the doctrine of justification by faith. He disbelieved transubstantiation, which became especially obvious after Henry's death in 1547, and favored the Calvinist view that the Eucharist is a "spiritual gift to the heart, not in the hand."

Second Stage: European Contributions

Planning became more earnest when Edward VI (1537–1553), Henry's nine-year-old son, ascended the throne in 1547. The kingdom was now effectively in the hands of regents who were able to promote Protestant doctrines relatively unimpeded. Cranmer persuaded Martin Bucer to accept the divinity chair at Cambridge, and other continental refugees also enjoyed the freedom to promote their beliefs, publish tracts, effect changes in church decor, and displace the ancient liturgies with continental-type services.

The 1549 prayer book, of which Cranmer was the principal author, was modeled in part along Lutheran lines, incorporating some eastern liturgical ideas and elements from a medieval Roman rite. Yet, the year before it was published, Cranmer had become more Zwinglian in his thinking. Thus, within two years a simplified Swiss-influenced replacement liturgy was being advocated.

Inevitable, then, was the rapid arrival of a revised prayer book in 1552 containing elements of the reformed-style liturgy, brought about partly by Bucer's critique of the 1549 version. It was not yet the simplified sermon, prayers, and psalms of Zurich, yet it did require the removal of the altar and the substitution of a table. It included the Black Rubric, which explained that Cranmer's insistence on communicants having to kneel "is not meant thereby that any adoration is done ... unto any real and essential presence there being of Christ's natural flesh and blood." A difference between the two books is shown in these words:[14]

> 1549 prayer: The body of our Lord Jesus Christ which was given for thee, preserve thy body and soul unto everlasting life.

> 1552 prayer: Take and eat this in remembrance that Christ died for thee, and feed on him in thy heart by faith, with thanksgiving.

Despite these developments, it would still be true to say that by 1553 England was not a Protestant country. Indeed, changes were happening rapidly—but not so rapidly as to impact just yet on ordinary people.

A short-lived Catholic restoration happened when Mary Tudor (1516–1558) arrived on the throne. In her first year, she prevailed on parliament to nullify all the Edwardian religious legislation. Some time later, she also had Henry's laws revoked, except those pertaining to the monastic lands. Those opposed to the restoration, including Cranmer, were burned at the stake, about three hundred in all, thus causing people to associate Rome with the defeat of heresy or schism at any cost.

In summary, then, Edward's reign exposed the populace to the possibility of a Protestant England, and Mary's reign exposed them to the resumption of Catholicism. The lasting effect of both was to create a chasm between Protestants and Catholics. Elizabeth I was to follow in 1558, but she did not heal the breach; instead, she reinstated the Edwardian approach.

Third Stage: Real Beginnings of the English Reformation

The real beginnings of the English Reformation belong to the reign of Anne Boleyn's daughter, Elizabeth I (1542–1603). Here, too, is found the origins of the Church of England.

Elizabeth's early wish, in line with her father's thinking, was to have Catholicism without the pope—a royal supremacy by which she would be supreme governor in all spiritual, ecclesial, and temporal affairs; a celibate clergy; and the doctrine of the Real Presence in the Eucharist. Hence, the 1552 prayer book was amended and reissued, omitting the Black Rubric,[15] although retaining the Zwinglian communion formula, preceding it with the words: "the Body of our Lord Jesus Christ which was given for thee."

The attempt by Mary Stuart of Scotland to take the English throne, and Pius V's excommunication of Elizabeth in 1570, made Elizabeth resolute to establish the Church of England, although she still wanted it to retain a range of Catholic characteristics, not all of which she succeeded in having. So it was in 1559 that a definitive Protestant settlement was put in place with the passing of the Act of Royal Supremacy over the church and a new Act of Uniformity, which restored the English liturgy and authorized a revision of The Book of Common Prayer.

Inevitably, legislation penalizing Catholics and others was put in place, so much so that by the end of her reign, only about two hundred thousand Catholics and a few Puritans remained in England.

The actual shaping of the Church of England in its beginnings was principally the work of three men: Michael Parker, Richard Hooker, and John Jewel. Michael Parker (1505–1575), the new Archbishop of Canterbury, whose ordination has long been an issue in the debate over the validity of Anglican orders, was a true devotee of the *via media* and a contributor to the formulation of the Thirty-Nine Articles.

But it is theologian Richard Hooker (1554–1600), the Thomas Acquinas of the Anglican Church, according to Congar,[16] who is widely regarded as the father of the Church of England. He set himself the task of resisting the efforts of some to install only Calvinist thinking in the church, and of preparing the classical Anglican theology: *The Laws of Ecclesiastical Polity*. In writing this book, Hooker was much influenced by his teacher, John Jewel (1522–1571), bishop of Salisbury, who had written *An Apology of the Church of England*. Jewel related the Church of England more to its Catholic roots, and Hooker related it to the Puritan influences of the times. With these perspectives, Jewel and Hooker devised the Church of England's hallmark, the *via media*: that the church is "catholic," retaining all the essentials of the early church; that the church is "reformed," ridding itself of the excesses of medieval times; and that the church is "*troika*," acknowledging the necessity of Scripture, tradition, and reason in contrast to the Protestant reliance on Scripture alone.

Fourth Stage: Anglican Identity[17]

The Anglican Communion's subsequent history saw her trying, often desperately in the face of the many internal demands that she be all things to all people, to stay close to the *troika* as if it were an anchor. All members of the church accepted the judgment of Scripture as primary, but then the evangelical wing indulged in a disproportionate favoring of the Bible. All in the church respected the link with the primitive church and its creeds, the common episcopate, the Thirty-Nine Articles, The Book of Common Prayer and other founding documents, and the moral authority of the Archbishop of Canterbury, but some sought to revisit the Catholic connection. All acknowledged the importance of reason in discerning truth, but the sometimes liberal and radical conclusions drawn were seen as disturbing.

The absence of an effective magisterium within the church, at least from the Catholic viewpoint, greatly disadvantaged the Anglican Communion's drive for internal unity. Having said this, it must be acknowledged that there are some who will argue that such diversity is the "particular vocation" of the Anglican Church. Yet, a writer like Jean Tillard is of the opinion that even that role is diminished, with the Anglican Communion now "living through one of the deepest crises of its history," because of recent disregard for "three cements, all considered essential." Those are the "Book of Common Prayer, shared by all with only very secondary variations; the common episcopate, consecrated according to this prayer book so that the sacraments could be celebrated everywhere according to the tradition; and the moral authority (in a sort of honorary primacy) of the Archbishop of Canterbury, charged with the task of preserving the other bishops within one communion."[18] Tillard then asks: "Does 'communion' still exist in these three fundamental registers?" In answer to the question, he says that the unity of the prayer book has been broken, the episcopate is divided over the question of the ordination of women, and provincialism has assumed a greater importance than the common good of unity. Further comment on these issues follow in the next section.

The Anglican Communion Today

The name "Anglican" was probably first used in 1851 and refers not to language and culture but to the common origins in the Church of England of the thirty-seven autonomous national churches that today make up the Anglican Communion. All of them, with their total of seventy-three million members, are in communion with the Archbishop of Canterbury.[19] Of this figure, only twenty-six million are in the Church of England, whereas in the continents of expansion, such as Africa, there are thirty-one million, and more than six million in Asia.

These churches are given a variety of names throughout the world, for example: the Episcopal Church of the USA (ECUSA), the Church of Ireland, the Scottish Episcopal Church, the Nippon Sei Ko Kai (the Holy Catholic Church of Japan), Chung-Hua Sheng Kung Hui (the Holy Catholic Church of China), and the Igreja Episcopal do Brasil.

Since the Anglican Communion is not a confessional body as such, and does not have a centralized authority, it relies on a variety of means to achieve a unity in the midst of its characteristic diversity. The Archbishop of Canterbury does not have a universal ministry to the communion as such, but simply a position of honor among equals. What is more, there is no specific Anglican confession of faith, and the prayer book, once common, now differs from province to province.

The Anglican Communion relies on three forums to further unity. Chief among these is the Lambeth Conference, which began in 1867 and meets every ten years. It involves all the bishops and is presided over by the Archbishop of Canterbury. The most recent such conference was held in 1998. The second forum is the pan-Anglican Congress, dating from 1908, which is attended by clergy and laity. The third body is the Anglican Consultative Council, which has a liaison role in the communion, also representing it in ecumenical meetings. None of these three has any executive authority.[20]

It is true to say that Anglicanism continues to try to bring together Protestant and Catholic traditions and teachings. But as already indicated, the two strands have not blended so as to form a distinctive church. Instead, the shades of opinion are reflected in two different expressions of Anglicanism.

One is the Anglo-Catholic wing, a name that dates from the Oxford Movement (1833–1845). Members are strongly committed to the notion of continuity with the early church, to apostolicity, and to the creeds and the sacraments. They favor close relations with Orthodoxy and Catholicism and are, for the most part, disposed to their understandings on the nature of the church. The other wing is Evangelical. Members have a strong belief in the authority of Scripture and place much store by the preaching of the word. In line with Protestant thinking, they seek after a deepening faith in the saving work of Christ, conscious as they are of the doctrine of the fall and of justification by faith alone. There is a wide range of thinking on church, ministry, and sacraments.

Wide divergences in beliefs and practices can, therefore, be found within the Anglican Communion. Authority is one such issue,[21] especially as it relates to the ordination of women to the priesthood and the episcopate. In some countries, the gap has widened between those who favor such ordinations and those who do not, with great damage being done to the communion among Anglicans. The consequences include the creation of "episcopal visitors," for example in England, to minister to congregations that do not accept the ministry of their diocesan bishops because they ordain women. Some protesting bishops and sections of the Anglican community have formed autonomous and independent churches, and others have left Anglicanism altogether, even entire congregations in the company of their priests.

Anglican–Roman Catholic Dialogue

Since the Chicago-Lambeth Quadrilateral of 1888, there has been a high level of ecumenical interest within the Anglican Communion. This is demonstrated in recent times by the growing closeness of Anglicans and Methodists and by the Porvoo Declaration of 1993, which involved an agreement to establish communion between the British and Irish Anglicans with the Nordic and Baltic Lutherans.

In 1960, before the Second Vatican Council, the Archbishop of Canterbury, Geoffrey Fisher, visited Pope John XXIII. This was the first time a leader of a sixteenth-century Reformation church visited a pope. Interestingly, there was no joint communique and no photographs.

But the council singled out the Anglican Communion alone for special mention in *UR*. This document speaks of the many national and denominational communions that separated from Rome in the sixteenth century and adds, "Among those in which some Catholic traditions and situations continue to exist, the Anglican Communion occupies a special place" (13).

The year after the conclusion of the council, Archbishop Michael Ramsey and Pope Paul VI issued a "Common Declaration" (March 1966). In this declaration, they stated that it was the time to begin removing the causes of conflict and to seek after unity and that they would "inaugurate between the Roman Catholic Church and the Anglican Communion, a serious dialogue" that "may lead to that unity in truth, for which Christ prayed."[22] Their statement said that the dialogue should embrace theological issues, including Scripture, tradition, and liturgy, looking also to practical matters that may be hindering closer relations between the two communions.

It is clear, then, that the aim of the dialogue is full visible unity. Our study can be organized under three headings.

Joint Preparatory Commission: A Joint Preparatory Commission was established with the purpose of suggesting a procedure to be followed in future talks. Over three meetings, the commission identified three doctrinal areas that need to be explored: ecclesiology, ordained ministry, and authority. They also suggested two matters of pastoral concern: moral theology and the theology of marriage and mixed marriages. The other recommendation made in *The Malta Report* (1968) was in support of establishing a Permanent Joint Anglican–Roman Catholic International Commission. Having agreed that Anglicans and Catholics have a rich and common inheritance, the members of the Joint Preparatory Commission remarked that "divergences since the sixteenth century have arisen not so much from the substance of this inheritance as from our separate ways of receiving it."[23] Such a significant observation can be a very useful guiding principle to all of us in our efforts to understand our different traditions as we work to rebuild Christian unity.

In personal letters to the Archbishop of Canterbury, both Pope Paul VI and Augustin Cardinal Bea, of the Secretariat for Promoting Christian Unity, affirmed the work of the Joint Preparatory Commission. They made suggestions as to how the work should continue, including acceptance of the idea of replacing the Joint Preparatory Commission by a Joint Commission of Oversight. Similarly, the 1968 Lambeth Conference recommended a Permanent Joint Commission and the appointment of a commission to explore jointly the theology of marriage and mixed marriages. Finally, Lambeth suggested that collegiality be the guiding principle for growth in better relations.

Anglican Roman Catholic International Commission (ARCIC I):
Over a period of twelve years (1970–1981), thirteen dialogue meetings were held in England and Italy. After several of these meetings, reports were issued on "Eucharistic Doctrine, Ministry and Ordination," and "Authority in the Church," including some "Elucidations." The Final Report of all these documents was published in 1981, the preface observing that "from the beginning we were determined ... to discover each other's faith as it is today and to appeal to history only for enlightenment, not as a way of perpetuating past controversy."[24] Wise advice to all of us.

In the introduction to The Final Report, the commission points out that the notion of *koinonia* underlies their considerations of the church. This theme runs through all their statements: "We present the Eucharist as the effectual sign of *koinonia*, episcope as serving the *koinonia*, and primacy as a visible link and focus of *koinonia*."[25]

The 1988 Lambeth Conference, having received responses to The Final Report from the provinces of the communion, stated that Lambeth "recognizes the Agreed Statements of ARCIC I on 'Eucharistic Doctrine, Ministry and Ordination,' and their 'Elucidations,' as consonant in substance with the faith of Anglicans, and believes that this agreement offers a sufficient basis for taking the next step towards the reconciliation of our Churches grounded in agreement in faith."[26]

The Catholic official response was given in 1991 and was more cautious, saying: "It is not yet possible to state that substantial agreement has been reached on all the questions studied by the Commission. There still remains between Anglicans and Catholics important differences regarding essential matters of Catholic doctrine."[27] The report details the areas of concern.

ARCIC II: The ARCIC II Commission (1983–   ) appointed a subcommittee of four to review the queries of the Holy See regarding The Final Report, sending its clarifications to the PCPCU in 1993. Cardinal Cassidy of the secretariat replied to the ARCIC officers, saying that "the agreement reached on eucharist and ministry by ARCIC I is thus greatly strengthened and no further study would seem to be required at this stage."[28] The only matter of continuing concern that the cardinal raised in his letter is the diversity of Anglican practice regarding the reservation of the Eucharist and the attitudes toward the reserved sacrament.

Although many expressed disappointment at Rome's long delay in responding to The Final Report, and others criticized the style and some of the content of the response, the PCPCU has since remarked that questioning by one or other of the dialogue parties is a legitimate part of the reception process. This process continues, sometimes in less formal ways, indicated by concerns in some Anglican quarters that the clarifications given may not be respectful of Anglican diversity. At the same time, Catholic concerns regarding the agreement on the Eucharist are reinforced by the demands made, for example in Sydney, for Anglican lay presidency at the Eucharist.[29]

In its ongoing work, ARCIC II produced two important reports. The first of these, in 1986, is the joint statement of the commission titled *Salvation and the Church*.[30] Although it is not an authoritative document, the commission released it in the hope of receiving constructive observations and criticisms.

The focus of this document is the age-old question of justification, the wider context being the doctrine of salvation, and specifically the role of the church in mediating Christ's salvation to the world. This same topic, as we saw when speaking of the Lutheran–Roman Catholic examination of the question, was fruitfully addressed in the United States dialogue. ARCIC II was able to benefit from these prior discussions. Incidentally, this raises an important point: the conclusions reached in one dialogue cannot contradict those of another. As the preface of *Salvation and the Church* says, "The search for unity is indivisible."

The Congregation for the Doctrine of the Faith (CDF) gave a "substantially positive" response in 1987, pointing out that certain divergences remain, particularly in the areas of ecclesiology and sacramental doctrine.

The second ARCIC II document, *Life in Christ: Morals, Communion and the Church*, was published in 1993. This is the first international dialogue to directly address the subject of morals. The commission began its work against a background of "widespread belief that Anglicans and Roman Catholics are as much, if not more, divided on questions of morals as on questions of doctrine."[31]

However, the principal finding of the commission is that Anglicans and Catholics have a shared vision and heritage, both of which continue to influence their moral choices, an important factor in the partial communion they already share. Again, it is important for them to cherish what unites, as this is so much greater than what divides. Understandably, the sixteenth-century division generated separate developments and the rise of divergences that continue to exist today.

The report says that the differences have not come about because of disagreements over the sources of moral authority or of fundamental values. Rather, they exist as a result of subsequent developments that gave rise to variations in the formation of the moral judgment of the faithful in each communion. After giving some attention to the historical developments, the commission then confined its attention to a consideration of marriage after divorce and of contraception, two areas in which the disagreements had been expressed officially. Yet, it is encouraging to read in the report that, although the differences are serious, "careful study and consideration has shown us that they are not fundamental" (88).

Study continues, with particular attention being given to the inter-relatedness of Scripture, tradition, and the reality of authority in the church. For example, *The Gift of Authority* (1999) builds on the earlier statements on authority that were published in The Final Report (1981) and addresses some topical issues, such as the Anglican Communion's decision to ordain women and John Paul's encyclical *Ut Unum Sint.*

It is important to notice that this dialogue, like so many, is not proceeding at the international level alone. National dialogues are also in place, two especially important ones being those in Canada and the United States. Some dioceses and parishes have been in covenant relationships[32] for years, and bishops of the two communions meet regularly. Study groups are happening in parishes, and a variety of other contacts are ensuring that the pursuit of unity is becoming increasingly the habit of the entire People of God. In the city of Malines, Belgium, for example, ARCIC held its 1996 meeting to coincide with the seventy-fifth anniversary of the famous 1921–1925 Malines Conversations between a group of prominent Anglicans and Catholics. Lord Halifax, with his friend Abbé Fernand Portal, arranged a series of meetings under the patronage of Cardinal Mercier, the aim being the restoration of unity between the two communions.[33]

The Birth of Methodism

There were those in early eighteenth-century Britain who were intent on renewing the Church of England. As they searched for a guiding theology, they looked especially at the teaching of the Dutchman Jacobus Arminius (1560–1609), who followed the optimistic doctrine that, although Christ died for all, people were left free to accept or reject the graces he won for them. This choice of the Arminian belief was in preference to the rigid and somewhat frightening Calvinist doctrine of election and predestination, which stated that Christ died only for the elect.

Work of the Wesley Brothers

It was at Oxford in the 1720s that a small group came together to develop a "religion of the heart," speaking of faith that would express itself in good works. At first, this group involved Charles Wesley and his companions, then more forcefully, the leadership of his brother, John (1703–1791).[34] Others were involved as well, including George Whitefield, who brought with him a strongly Calvinistic touch which was to stay with just a sector of the movement. Their noticeably intense commitment earned the group a variety of names, including the Holy Club, the Godly Club, the Reforming Club, the Enthusiasts, and the Sacramentarians.

The group was happy with the name "Holy Club," and then with the epithet "Methodist," even though the latter was given them, "not in praise, but derision," according to Maldwyn Edwards, who also records that John Wesley later gave it his own interpretation: "A Methodist is one who lives according to the method laid down in the Bible."[35] Their program included the recitation of psalms and prayers, weekly communion (in contrast to the then Church of England practice of communion only three times a year), and the doing of charitable works, including visiting prisoners, providing for the poor, and maintaining a school for children.

They came to appreciate the fact that their charity should not be confined solely to the immediate neighborhood. As a result, the Wesleys and two others accepted the invitation of General James Oglethorpe to visit Georgia, and they set sail in October 1735. In Georgia, they were pastorally busy. John Wesley was so impressed by the inspiring pietistic behavior of a group of twenty-six Moravians he met on board ship, that some of their practices made their way into Methodism, namely religious conversion or revivalism.

Many date the true beginnings of the Methodist movement to May 21, 1738, when John, back in London, had a conversion experience three days after his brother had a similar experience on Pentecost Sunday. That night, John went to a meeting in Aldersgate Street where he described what had happened: "I felt my heart strangely warmed. I felt I did trust in Christ, Christ alone for salvation; and an assurance was given me that

He had taken away *my* sins, even mine, and saved me, from the law of sin and death."[36]

Others identify the start of Methodism to 1744, when John organized his first conference, just outside London, to discuss the theology of sanctification, or perfection, and to give to the movement a certain structure. Although the ties with the Church of England still remained strong, the identifying features of Methodist life and organization were in place by this year.

From this time on, the movement began to spread in the form of "societies" throughout the rest of Britain, and from the 1760s into Maryland, Virginia, Philadelphia, New York, and New Jersey in America. The only admission requirement was the desire to pursue holiness and the living of a disciplined, prayerful life.

Richard Boardman and Joseph Pilmore began their work in America in 1769. Thereafter, two preachers each year were sent from England until the Revolutionary War of 1775–1783 made it impossible for the English to continue with this outreach. Although committed to a continuing place in the Church of England, as Pilmore noted in his diary, the drift of American Methodism from the mother church was beginning to happen.

With the war over, John Wesley asked the bishop of London in 1784 to ordain preachers for service in America. When the request was declined, Wesley, in virtue of his belief that the early church regarded presbyters and bishops of the same order, ordained Thomas Coke as superintendent (later changed to "bishop") of the Societies in America and Richard Whatcoat and Thomas Vasey as elders (priests). American ties with the Church of England were now broken.[37]

In that same year, the meeting known as the Legal Hundred passed the Deed of Declaration, which gave to the conference the right to appoint Wesley's successor in the event of his death, taking the right away from the Church of England. The Methodist Episcopal Church came to exist in America with its ritual, Sunday service, and Articles of Religion all arranged by Wesley, using as his sources The Book of Common Prayer and the Thirty-Nine Articles.

Although Wesley ordained more than twenty individuals for Methodist ministry in England, he and Charles remained members of the Church of England to their deaths. Right through the nineteenth century in many places, chapel services were never scheduled during the hours of Church of England services, Methodists still considering themselves Anglicans, returning to the church for the sacraments. The formal split in England happened only in 1891.

Both in America and in Britain, Methodism has suffered and continues to experience a great deal of splintering. But the twentieth century has also witnessed some mergers, made easier by the fact that the earlier divisions were, for the most part, governmental and not doctrinally motivated. Methodist churches, founded either from Britain or from America, came to exist in continental Europe, whereas those throughout the British Commonwealth took their origin in England.

Methodist Churches Today

Fifty-five million Methodists live in more than ninety countries. The headquarters of the World Methodist Council, which was established in 1951, is located in Lake Junaluska, North Carolina; it also has an office in the Ecumenical Center, Geneva. The council meets every five years—an executive committee meeting between conferences to serve the needs of the wider church.[38]

Methodists consider themselves to be part of the universal church, basing this belief on the doctrine that all believers are priests. The church continues to be inspired by Arminian theology, although there are a few Calvinistically inclined Methodists, particularly in Wales. Wesley was emphatic that salvation is for all, and as Rupert Davies explains, *Arminian* should not be used to describe John Wesley's teaching in the word's vague eighteenth-century sense. Rather, its classical understanding should be applied: "that the grace of God and the Atonement wrought by Jesus Christ are for every man" and "that the doctrine of predestination is a blasphemous fable."[39]

While doctrinal issues do not preoccupy Methodists, explained in part by Wesley's dislike of controversy, it is possible to name four basic doctrines: the universality of Christ's redemption (in contrast to Calvin's doctrine of predestination); justification by faith (in line with Protestant thinking); the reassuring presence of the Spirit in one's life; and the awareness that holiness is personally attainable. Unlike the Catholic preference for expressing belief in doctrinally succinct statements in dogmas, creeds, magisterial statements, and the like, Methodists have a tradition, beginning with Wesley himself, of enshrining their beliefs in hymns. John, and especially Charles, were prolific and talented composers of hymns that are reckoned by many Methodist thinkers to be "liturgical theology."[40]

Modern-day articulation of Methodist belief is a task of the World Methodist Council, although the Apostles' Creed is a standard, alongside modern credal expressions. The *Standard Sermons of John Wesley*, his *Notes on the New Testament*, and the *Twenty-Five Articles of Religion* continue to have some influence.

There are two sacraments, baptism and the Lord's Supper, as well as regular fellowship meetings and a ritual for services, with freedom in prayer forms being encouraged. The singing of hymns is a truly identifiable feature of Methodism, John and Charles Wesley both having composed many hymns that enjoy widespread use in Christian churches today, even beyond the Methodist world. Without a doubt, these hymns are a rich source of Methodist theology and spirituality. Abstinence from alcohol was once universally required, although regulations have been modified in recent decades. Whereas American Methodism has a threefold ministry, and is therefore episcopal in character, British Methodism has one order of ministry and, as such, is nonepiscopal. In 1969, problems over the historic episcopate caused the Church of England to turn down the Methodist-Anglican plan for reunion.

Greater emphasis is given to living out the Christian life and to attending to social needs. Hence, the *Social Creed* of 1908, which has become a model for similar expressions in other denominations.

Methodist–Roman Catholic Dialogue

For a long time, the Methodist Church has been strongly and enthusiastically ecumenical, as is evidenced by the work of men such as G. Bromley Oxnam and John R. Mott, who were instrumental in setting up the World Council of Churches in 1948. This spirit, no doubt, accounts for the healings that have taken place within Methodism itself, both in Great Britain and the United States. It also helps explain the repeated attempts since 1955 at reunion with the Church of England, something that continues today. Several times, the Anglican Communion has rejected the recommended vote on reunion, principally because of the differences in understanding the historic episcopate, as mentioned already. Discussions between the two churches have resumed.

Although the Methodist–Roman Catholic dialogue is one of the oldest, having started in 1967, it has not earned quite the same headlines in the religious press as, for example, ARCIC I or the Lutheran–Roman Catholic dialogue in the United States.[41] Yet, both churches regard it as important, one aspect of the common heritage being identified by John Paul II in his address to a delegation of the World Methodist Council in 1992:

> Concern for holiness has been a significant part of the spiritual tradition of both Catholics and Methodists. Authentic Christian holiness will always remain first and foremost a gift of God ... We may be confident that the effort to live in fidelity to this gift will involve its own ecumenical dynamism, for as the Second Vatican Council observed, the more Christians strive to live holier lives according to the Gospel, "the better will they be able to further the unity of Christians" (*UR* 7).[42]

Changing peoples' lives in and through the pursuit of holiness, so long a feature of Methodism, is an important aspect of the dialogue's earlier stages. The first three reports (every five years the Joint Commission presents a report to the World Methodist Council)—Denver (1971), Dublin (1976), and Honolulu (1981)—all highlight "holiness" or "perfection" as subjects, expressed in themes like Spirituality, Christian Home and Family, and Towards an Agreed Statement on the Holy Spirit. While some dogmatic and moral issues were also addressed, such as Eucharist and Ministry, Authority, Moral Questions, and Euthanasia, there was a shift after 1981 from topics of a pastoral kind to more "traditional" ecumenical themes.

"Church" and "tradition," not strong in Methodist thinking and writing, were given explicit consideration in the discussions leading to the fourth phase and the Nairobi Report of 1986

(*Towards a Statement on the Church*), where it was acknowledged that divisions "are contrary to the unity Christ wills for his Church," but calling for a commitment to seek after full communion. Out of the fifth stage came the 1991 report, titled *The Apostolic Tradition*, which describes how the tradition is handed on in a church that enjoys an ordained ministry. Although difficulties remain, the very existence of the dialogue has enabled advances to be made. Some of the areas of divergence are sacramentality, the ministry of oversight or *episcope*—especially the Petrine ministry—and the ordination of women.

In the sixth stage, a 1996 report was issued by the Joint Commission for Dialogue between the World Methodist Council and the Catholic Church titled *The Word of Life*. Of particular value in this document is the way it relates Scripture and church, the latter being viewed as the servant of the word, dependent on it, and growing as church when it communicates the word to others. Scripture, for its part, is to be interpreted in the context of the church, where it was composed and to which it refers. Scripture is alive in the church today, and it speaks to both bodies, thereby underpinning the reconciliation we are to achieve.

The seventh phase began in 1997 and is expected to report to the appropriate authorities of each church in 2001. Meanwhile, the commission is addressing the question of authority, in particular the matter of who enjoys the right to teach authoritatively.

While full communion of the Catholic Church and the Methodist Church is not an immediate prospect, the discussions are useful in surfacing what it is that Methodists and Catholics already share in common. Furthermore, areas of disagreement that once seemed major are now being spoken about in much more hopeful words. The observation of David Carter is one example. In his article *A Methodist Reaction to Ut Unum Sint*,[43] he says that the more Catholics and Methodists examine their respective ecclesiologies, the greater the likelihood that they will discover that ecclesial reconciliation is not an impossibility.

The Arrival of Other Significant Churches

Ongoing developments in the Christian world continued to express themselves in the formation of further Christian churches and communities, now predominantly those with an evangelical bent. The Salvation Army, for example, combined a strong commitment to the gospel with a concern for the poor and neglected in society. Evangelicalism and Pentecostalism, beyond finding their places in already existing churches, also dubbed off to form new communities. The Old Catholics, of course, do not fit into this scheme of things, but they are considered at this point because of their relative recency and their close association with the Anglican Communion.

The Salvation Army

Described by some as an organization for evangelistic and social work, and by others as a spiritual movement with an acute social conscience, the Salvation Army comprises people dedicated to Christ but who do not have Christian baptism. "Infant baptism is not used because it is believed that salvation must be the result of the free choice of an individual ... Water baptism of adults is also thought unnecessary, and in some cases harmful, since people may come to place their trust in the outward act rather than in the essential inward experience of 'baptism' by the Holy Spirit."[44] Despite this outlook, the Army considers itself part of the Christian Church with its own distinctive government and way of life.

As far back as 1966, Bernard Leeming, in his commentary on the "Catholic Principles of Ecumenism," noted that while *UR* gives special attention to certain Christian denominations, such as the Eastern Orthodox and Anglicans, the general principles of the decree apply to all Christians "if they really accept Christ." That is why, according to Leeming, two groups "occupy a special position, the Friends (Quakers) and the Salvation Army. They do not use any of the normal Christian rites and yet few could doubt that they have much of the authentic Christian spirit."[45]

Founded in London by William Booth in 1865, "The Christian Mission" changed its name in 1878 to the "Salvation

Army." The Army reflects Booth's Methodist background, where he was a preacher, and the Arminian thinking, which underpinned their beliefs.

Booth did not set out with the intention of founding another denomination. Rather, he became acutely conscious of London's East End poor, who were uncomfortably worshipping in class-conscious congregations. Inevitably, a separate entity came to exist. These poor people, Booth felt, needed a special kind of evangelizing, preferably recent converts speaking to prospective members in a language they understood. The focus on the poor and alcoholics, and the establishing of welfare bureaus and disaster relief resources, caused the earlier scornful attitude of observers to change to admiration. His works *In Darkest England* and *The Way Out*[46] contributed to this change in attitude regarding the Army.

Booth's chosen model for the organization of the Salvation Army was the British Army. With a general at the head (elected by the High Council since 1929, after William and then his son, Bromwell, occupied the position), the Army is divided into territories, districts, and corps, each with military-entitled leaders. Members sign the "articles of war," furloughs are granted, uniforms are worn by the officers, services are held in citadels, and the crest bears the words "Blood and Fire." Obedience is an important feature of the Salvation Army lifestyle, although Booth was often criticized for his heavy-handedness and for over-centralization of controls.

The *Orders and Regulations for the Salvation Army* of 1878[47] sets out in detail the pattern of life for a Salvationist. Although doctrine is given little formal attention, the Arminian emphasis on the universality of Christ's redemption, human freedom in responding to Christ, and the presence of the Spirit in an individual after conversion leading to trust in Christ are all fundamental. Their beliefs are set out in the eleven "articles of faith."[48]

Soon after the Salvation Army arrived in the United States, two divisions within the ranks occurred. The first was in 1884, when Thomas E. Moore, appointed leader by Booth and answerable only to him, sought to make the Army more democratic in style. The result was a distinctive body that, in 1913, took the name the "American Rescue Workers,"[49] a body that-continues to exist to this day. The second division happened in 1896, when Ballington Booth, William's son, was appointed leader of the American Salvationists and also attempted to democratize the Army. As a result, the Volunteers of America came into existence and continues to exist today. Both bodies follow the Salvation Army style of belief and worship, although the Volunteers of America, in contrast to Salvationist belief, has "sacramental observances and the ordination of its officers."[50]

Services, which are nonliturgical and largely informal and evangelical, comprise hymn singing led by a military-style band, free prayer and testimonies, readings from the Scriptures, and preaching.

It is difficult to discover the total number of people who belong to the Salvation Army because the *Salvation Army Year Book*, 1998, numbers people according to their ranking in the Army. For instance, senior soldiers exceed eight hundred thousand, and junior soldiers reach almost four hundred thousand. The total, given the several other categories, is about one million members. The international headquarters are located in London.[51]

Apart from exchanges that occur through the Conference of Secretaries of Christian World Communions, and local cooperative ventures, there are no formal ecumenical contacts between the Catholic Church and the Salvation Army.

Evangelicals

The term "Evangelical" was once applied to all the Protestant churches because of their common dependency on the Scriptures for their teachings. For a time, the name had a more limited applicability in Germany and Switzerland, being applied to the Lutherans to distinguish them from the Reformed.

Today, however, the term is descriptive of a Christian movement that traces its beginnings to Protestant revivals of the eighteenth and nineteenth centuries, especially those associated with Pietism. This latter placed great store on peoples' inner or subjective responses to religion rather than on dogmatic beliefs, their "experience" or conversion giving rise to a conviction that what had been received should be handed on. It had an impact on the Lutheran and Reformed traditions, and also within Anglicanism, where it expressed itself in Methodism, on the one hand, and as the evangelical or "low church" wing of Anglicanism on the other. In America, it was associated with the "Great Awakening" of American Protestantism.

Evangelicalism is hard to define because it is not just one identifiable body. Rather, it is manifold: some churches, old and new, call themselves "evangelical," sections within churches bear the title, and nondenominational bodies are labeled "evangelical." Thomas F. Stransky speaks of them this way:

> They come from within the mainline Churches (Episcopalian, Presbyterian, Methodist); those Reformation Churches with strict interpretations of their confessions (Missouri Synod Lutherans, Christian Reformed); the "peace" Churches (Brethren, Mennonite, Friends); the more conservative wing of the Restoration movement (Campbellites); the "Holiness" tradition (Wesleyan Methodist); Baptists; the fundamentalist groups, which now include those who gather around radio or TV preachers; Pentecostals; most black Churches; adherents of parachurch groups (the majority of U.S. Protestant mission organizations, InterVarsity Christian Fellowship, Campus Crusade for Christ, the Navigators, and so on). No wonder it is difficult to reach a description in which all the above would recognize themselves![52]

Given the breadth of this listing of "Evangelicals," the inevitable follow-up question must be, "What is it that so many share in common?"[53] Four features can be listed. The first, although not universally agreed on, is "evangelistic fundamentalism," marking them as the conservative wing of Protestantism. The second is their commitment to personal conversion—a born-again Christianity—which is, in fact, regarded as the point of entry into the church, baptism being relegated to a symbolic component in the total process. A side effect of this emphasis on the individual is a downplaying of a corporate church identity that has a magisterial or teaching role in the community. A third feature is their powerful dedication to Scripture, to its sufficiency, and to its literal interpretation, exclusive of other sources of truth, such as "tradition." A final identifying characteristic is the vigor they give to gospel communication, both in evangelism and in social work, the use of which other Christians sometimes question. Given that Catholics are numbered by some as among the unsaved, they are frequently the targets of evangelical proselytism.

The Evangelical churches make up the fastest growing branch of Christianity, their present total being three hundred million, second only to the Catholic Church in terms of numbers. The relationship, however, between these two dominant sections in the Christian world includes a tension, caused mainly by what Catholics regard as the aggressive tactics used by Evangelicals in drawing adherents from the Catholic Church. In 1993, a writer in *The Los Angeles Times* estimated that six hundred thousand Catholics in Brazil each year leave the Catholic Church, many finding their way into Evangelical churches. Twenty-five years ago, for example, Guatemala was ninety-seven percent Catholic; today, the percentage is below seventy, most of the departees having migrated into Evangelical churches.

Many movements throughout the world are Evangelical, including the Promise Keepers, founded in 1990 by former Catholic Bill McCartney,[54] World Vision, the Billy Graham Crusades,[55] the Christian Coalition, and others. The World Evangelical Fellowship was established in 1951 for the purpose of furthering, defending, and confirming the gospel and establishing fellowship in the gospel.

Evangelical–Roman Catholic Conversations

The first formal meeting of Pentecostals and Catholics was held in 1972, with a conversation on "mission" taking place between 1977 and 1984.[56] This conversation was prompted, in part, by a number of participants at the 1974 Congress on World Evangelization who sought greater understanding with Catholics. It was also prompted by Paul VI's 1975 Apostolic Exhortation, *Evangelii Nuntiandi* (On the Evangelization of the Modern World), which reveals how renewed Catholic thinking can readily meet evangelical thinking in a productive forum.

These words of Paul VI point to a common understanding that should be the basis of continuing fruitful discussions: "Evangelization would not be complete if it did not take account of the unceasing interplay of the Gospel and of man's concrete life, both personal and social"[57] (29).

Between 1991 and 1995, a further informal consultation took place, cosponsored by the PCPCU and the World Evangelical Fellowship (WEF). The discussions were back-grounded by a two-day meeting in 1990 on a book called *Roman Catholicism: A Contemporary Evangelical Perspective*, which Catholics regarded as an unfair document. These discussions gave way to a wider consultation on Revelation, Scripture and Tradition, and Justification by Faith. Father Avery Dulles presented a paper titled *Revelation as the Basis of Scripture and Tradition*, which was received positively by a representative of the Evangelical delegation.[58]

The 1997 discussion on the nature and mission of the church was held in Jerusalem. This discussion named points of common understanding and pinpointed subjects that needed exploration at future meetings of the WEF and the PCPCU. On the nature of the church, for example, the four marks of the church were seen as a good basis for further study, although the question was asked, "Are these marks or attributes descriptive of an ideal church or are they already present in someway in the existing churches?" Other interesting issues were raised at the meeting, and these are succinctly noted in the *Information Service* of the PCPCU.[59]

In addition to these conversations with "Evangelicals-proper," there have been ongoing discussions with the Pentecostals (discussed below) and with the Southern Baptist Convention since 1972. Further, local dialogues are in place, a particularly significant one being in the United States. This is well-documented in *Evangelicals and Catholics Together: Working Towards a Common Mission*.[60]

Finally, it should be observed that the Catholic Church regards commitment to a continuing dialogue with the Evangelicals as of great importance. From the Evangelicals, for example, Catholics can gain a greater appreciation for the importance of securely basing ongoing renewal in the Scriptures and how to recapture the call to live the church's missiononary vocation. Evangelicals can be led, for example, to appreciate the place of the church universal, to be less fundamentalist in their use of the Scriptures, and to enter into exchanges with the Catholic Church over the matter of proselytism.

Pentecostals

Pentecostalism traces its beginnings to the fundamentalist and holiness movements of the nineteenth century, including Wesleyanism, although the precise beginnings of the Pentecostal movement date from the start of the twentieth century. Charles Parham's 1901 Topeka Revival linked baptism in the Spirit with *glossolalia*, both of which remain a feature of Pentecostalism to this day. The movement's first great expansion is associated with the 1906 Azusa Street Revival in Los Angeles, led by black pastor William J. Seymour. Broadly speaking, the movement has developed along two paths.[61]

The first path, called Classical Pentecostalism, expresses itself in four main groups: Holiness churches, which add baptism in the Spirit as a third blessing after regeneration and sanctification (e.g. the Pentecostal Holiness Church); the "Two-stage Pentecostals," mostly of a reformed background, which teach baptism in the Spirit as a second blessing (e.g. Assemblies of God); the Oneness Churches, which reject the Trinity and baptize only in the name of Jesus (e.g. United Pentecostal Church); and those churches that have the office of apostle and prophet (e.g. Apostolic Church).

The second path is Neo-Pentecostalism or the Charismatic Movement, a renewal movement found primarily within the mainline churches and which gives particular emphasis to the gifts of the Spirit. It arose shortly after the Second World War, and has been significantly felt within the Catholic Church since 1967. In the United States at that time, a group of professors and students had a spiritual renewal that was accompanied by the experience of the charisms of the Spirit, some of which are listed in 1 Corinthians 12. It is estimated that today more than sixty million Catholics throughout the world have been baptized in the Holy Spirit.[62]

In addition to the characteristics held in common among Pentecostals, which can be gleaned from the above,

Pentecostalist churches generally feature acceptance of the Bible as the sole doctrinal authority, informal worship, congregational government, and vigorous missionary work. Some celebrate the Lord's Supper, although according to a wide variety of eucharistic theologies. Others have a wide range of ceremonies, including foot washing.

Although world conferences have taken place, the idea of a permanent world organization is rejected based on the notion that a "super church" that has visible bounds is contrary to the Pentecostalist preference for freedom in the Spirit. Besides, the differences among the churches are so great that it would be difficult to establish a cohesive international community. Few Pentecostal churches belong to the WCC, for instance, and most are opposed to involvement with the ecumenical movement.

Definite numbers are hard to come by, thus the more telling way to gauge the significance of Pentecostalism is by means of general percentages. Affiliated Christian church members worldwide are: Catholics, fifty-eight percent; Pentecostal/Charismatics, twenty-one percent; and all other Christians, twenty-one percent. The Pentecostal growth is phenomenal.[63]

Pentecostal–Roman Catholic Dialogue

The Pentecostal–Roman Catholic dialogue is conducted on behalf of the Catholic Church by the PCPCU and for the Pentecostals by some leaders of classical Pentecostal churches and various individuals from others. A point of great significance is the fact that this is a conversation between the world's largest Christian church, Catholicism, and the world's fastest growing Christian group, Pentecostalism.

The dialogue commenced in 1972.[64] At first it was a matter of coming to know one another. By the beginning of the second phase in 1977, however, important topics were being aired. These included Scripture and tradition, exegesis and biblical interpretation, faith and reason, healing and ministry in the church, and the Catholic understanding of Mary. The second phase examined the notion of *koinonia* and, among other things, surfaced a considerable convergence on baptism. The most recent phase, 1990–1997, addressed the deeply important subject of evangelism and evangelization, including the matter of proselytism, given expression in the 1998 document titled *Evangelization, Proselytism and Common Witness.*[65] The desired outcome is a growth in mutual trust, a lessening of competitiveness, and an increasing common witness. The fifth phase began in 1998.

Old Catholics

The Old Catholics, although continental, are considered here because of their relative recency and also because they and the Anglicans are in communion.[66]

The name "Old Catholic" was chosen by three groups of national churches as being descriptive of their intention to be the "original Catholicism." The first of these, sometimes called the "Church of Utrecht," began in 1724, when the papal handling of the Jansenist controversy led to the election of Cornelius Steenoven as archbishop of Utrecht, whom Rome regarded as unsuitable. He, and later his successor in 1725, were consecrated by the bishop of Babylon, Dominique Marie Varlet. Thus, apostolic succession was established in the Old Catholics, and has been maintained since.

The second group comprises German, Swiss, and Austrian churches that refused to accept the 1870 Vatican Council dogmas of papal infallibility and primacy, and were eventually excommunicated. These groups then looked to Utrecht "for support and leadership, and for episcopal orders in the establishment of their small churches."[67] The first German was consecrated in 1874, the first Swiss in 1876, and the first Austrian sometime later, apostolic succession coming through the Church of Utrecht.

The third group, of Slav origin, comprises Poles in the United States (1897) and Croats (1924), which gave rise to the creation of the Polish National Church in the United States. Today, this group makes up half of the five hundred thousand membership of the Old Catholic Church and also of the Yugoslav Old Catholic Church. A good and continuing dialogue has been taking place between the Polish National Catholic Church and the United States bishops' conference of the Catholic Church.[68] In 1965, the Philippine Independent Church entered into sacramental communion with the Old Catholics.

All these churches are united by their adherence to the 1889 Declaration of Utrecht. They recognize the first seven ecumenical councils and those doctrines in place before the east-west split in the eleventh century. The seven sacraments are part of Old Catholic life, as is apostolic succession, and the Real Presence of Christ in the Eucharist (although transubstantiation is denied). Auricular confession is not compulsory. Intercommunion is practiced with Evangelical-Lutheran Churches in Germany, and the Austrian, Swiss, and German Old Catholics agree to admit women to the priesthood. Clergy, including bishops, may marry.[69]

Old Catholics have long had close relations with Anglicans. The Bonn Agreement of 1931 established communion between the Anglican and Old Catholic Churches. Discussions with the patriarchs of Constantinople and Moscow have been held since the nineteenth century, a commission being set up in 1966 by the Pan-Orthodox Conference. An international Old Catholic congress has met regularly since 1890, the president of the conference being the archbishop of Utrecht. While there is no formal dialogue in place between the Old Catholics and the PCPCU at present, contacts between the two churches have increased and relations have greatly improved since the Second Vatican Council. Most of these fruitful contacts are taking place at the local level, as well as among theologians of the two traditions.[70]

◈ ◈ ◈

In bringing this chapter to a close, and in thinking about the content of chapters 5 and 6, we should be able to gauge something of the extent and nature of the divisiveness that has occurred in the western church since the sixteenth century. But what might have been interpreted as a bleak history, now reveals light and hope because of the great grace of the ecumenical movement. Christian communities are genuinely striving to mend Christianity's brokenness. What comes to mind is the Lund Principle,[71] which was first enunciated in 1952 and which should now be taken more seriously than ever before as signaling among the churches that they are ready to take concrete action in order to progress the journey toward a fullness of unity. Part of the text says:

> Should not our churches ask themselves whether they are showing sufficient eagerness to enter into conversation with other churches, and whether they should not act together in all matters except those in which deep differences of conviction compel them to act separately?

It is one thing to read these words as an invitation to sporadic cooperative efforts, such as during the Week of Prayer for Christian Unity; it is an altogether different matter to see the statement as referring to day-to-day cooperation, requiring permanent change. Parts IV and V of the *Directory for the Application of Principles and Norms on Ecumenism* explain how Catholics can and should become more ecumenically cooperative.

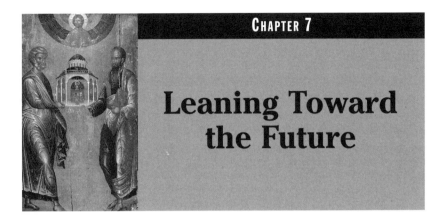

CHAPTER 7

Leaning Toward the Future

This final chapter concerns the future. We have briefly reviewed the accidents of history that caused divisiveness in the church. We saw how the ecumenical movement eventually brought the traditions face to face, challenging them to embark on the paths of dialogue. Against this background, questions inevitably arise. Has this spirit of ecumenism been thoroughly received by and into the contemporary church in a lasting way? Where are the dialogues leading, and what agencies are in place to keep the work alive? Even a cursory glance across the Christian world reveals that strategies are in place and agencies are at work, all aiming at the one goal: the unity of the church.

Other questions then follow. How will this goal of unity be achieved? Will unity first come about within traditions? Should it happen in stages? Will it possibly happen regionally? Will it begin to happen when one communion unites with another? Will all the problems have to be resolved before any effective reunion can be set in place?

The answers probably rest in saying "yes" to all of these, and to a range of similar questions, as long as the foundational structure is an acceptance of the biblical and patristic "ecclesiology of communion." This ecclesiology will allow particular ecclesial emphases, traditions, or "types" to have their places in the united church without compromising the essential unity that must characterize that one church. To spell this out further, the united church of tomorrow will not require the abolition or disappearance of distinctive churches, will be identified more in the form of "sister churches" along the lines of the *typoi* model, and will be served by ministers who are recognizable and acceptable across the Christian world.

Strategies for the Future

Stages of unity, then, must begin the process. Our historical overview acknowledged that among and within the various traditions, some enjoy greater levels of closeness. For instance, the Catholic Church and the Orthodox Church—because of the common apostolic succession, sacramental priesthood, and Eucharist—have an already high level of communion, and both experience varying degrees of communion with other churches. This is saying that these two traditions—all things being equal—have a greater theological, ecclesiological, and structural readiness for *communio* between them, than do either of them with churches that are connected with the Reformation.

Within the Reformed tradition, for example, where structures in most churches are nonepiscopal and liturgies are not given the same degree of prominence as in the Orthodox and Catholic traditions, one can identify other shared features. For instance, the centrality they give to the Scriptures and the insistence they place on the sovereignty of God and the Lordship of Jesus Christ. These Reformed preferences form a nucleus around which continuing growth in unity among the member churches can happen. Furthermore, the ongoing dialogue of churches of the Reformed tradition with the Catholic and the Orthodox Churches is likely to lead, in time, to a deepening ecclesial sense or awareness among them.

The fervent prayer and constant striving of Orthodox and Catholic people should be that unity will soon be achieved among their churches. The fruit of that prayer is the growing sense of agreement arising out of the dialogues, collaboration in certain social issues, and the annual pilgrimage exchanges by hierarchs (from east to west on the feast of Saints Peter and Paul on June 29, and from west to east on the feast of Saint Andrew on November 30). Beyond these positive moves, nothing more concrete has yet been achieved.

But members of the Anglican, Lutheran, Reformed, and some other Protestant Churches have already put in place certain strategies that they identify as stages in the process toward the fullness of unity. These strategies include the formation of "United and Uniting Churches."

United and Uniting Churches

We begin with a definition of terms. A "united church" is a distinctive church formed from two or more previously separate communities. A "uniting church" is either a union that is still being negotiated or is a title adopted by some united churches to signify that they consider their present state as transitional in the journey toward the fullness of ecclesial unity. An example of this latter is the Uniting Church in Australia formed in 1977, which today enjoys a membership of nearly two million people.[1] In both instances, there is an openness to other churches joining the unions.

A conservative estimate is that more than twenty million Christians belong to united and uniting churches, nineteen of which were formed between 1925 and 1945 and at least a score of them since the Second World War. The unions are not of international confessional bodies but are composed of smaller communities that are nationally or regionally situated, such as the Church of South India, formed in 1947, which is made up of Anglican, Methodist, and Reformed congregations. Often enough, doctrinal issues are not given a high profile before the forging of an actual union, the belief being that unity grows after, as well as before, the act of creating the union. In other words, the formal act of union is but a stage in a process. At the same time, it must be admitted that some unions have come about more out of expediency—that is, for survival's sake—and not because of a deeply felt response to the unity imperative. It also happens that a new creation comes about that leaves behind remnants of parent bodies that continue to exist as independent entities.

At the Sixth International Consultation of United and Uniting Churches in March 1995, the churches recognized themselves as having the witness task of being "a living challenge to other churches." They urged the WCC "to give a more prominent place to United and Uniting Churches and to church union negotiations and so, by keeping those constantly before its members, to encourage them to move towards visible unity."[2] The fact that the Catholic Church is officially represented at such consultations is a sign of her openness to learning from the experiences of these new foundations.

Beyond these concrete realizations of a certain kind of ecclesial unity, many other union programs have been and continue to be mooted. We briefly mention a few of them.

Consultation on Church Union (COCU): This began in 1962 and takes in nine United States churches whose aim is the establishing of a church that is catholic, evangelical, and reformed. The first plan of the 1960s, for an institutional merger, was displaced in the 1970s by a "covenanting" proposal. This latter, which continues to live, speaks not of organizational unity but of a communion of communions of the Episcopal and Presbyterian Churches, the International Council of Community Christian Churches, the Christian Methodist Episcopal Church, the United Church of Christ, the African Methodist Episcopal Church, the African Methodist Episcopal Zion Church, the Christian Church (Disciples of Christ), and the United Methodist Church. Given this composition, an episcopal ministry finds a place in the life of the communion, with joint ordinations of priests and pastors being an agreed practice.[3]

Should the plan meet with the approval of all the participants at their respective assemblies, the year 2000 is seen as a likely date for the inauguration of the new body.

The Porvoo Common Statement: This statement is between the Anglican Churches of England, Ireland, Scotland, and Wales with the Lutheran Churches of the Nordic and Baltic countries of Finland, Iceland, Norway, Sweden, Latvia, Estonia, and Lithuania. It proposes the establishing of a communion among them. The statement was unanimously agreed on in October 1992 and was presented to the participating churches for their approval.[4] By the end of 1996, ratification had been given by all, although Denmark did not join because it failed to secure synodal ratification.

One of the debated points in the common statement was the matter of the episcopate, which carries implications for many other union proposals throughout the Christian world. Although all the churches in this instance have maintained an episcopate, the Lutherans of Denmark, Norway, and Iceland had a break in the episcopal succession at the time of the Reformation. The fact that the Anglicans simply accepted the episcopate of these three countries without question gives a focus to the presently debated issue of the precise nature of apostolic succession. As Edward Yarnold says, "While apostolic succession is signified and focused in the succession of bishops, it also includes succession in faith and life and ministry, and therefore has other strands besides episcopal continuity."[5] In general, it would be true to say that while contemporary theology acknowledges that apostolicity belongs to the whole church, debate continues over whether or not bishops are simply a sign, and not also a means, of the church's apostolicity.[6] Much work has still to be done in clarifying this.

The appointment of an ecumenical bishop has been discussed by the Covenanted Churches in Wales, that is, by the Anglican, Baptist, Methodist, Presbyterian, and United Reformed Churches, even suggesting a beginning point of 1999. While the proposal has not been implemented, the thinking behind it is a way of enabling the covenanted Churches of Wales, through these emerging structures, to become familiar with a way of being the Church, that does not deny the past for each of them, and that does not require major changes to their inherited structures.'"[7] Scholars and church leaders have found problems in the proposal, yet it must be admitted that for the churches concerned, it is, in the words of Archbishop Robert Runcie, "ecumenism as a dimension of all that we do which releases energy through the sharing of resources."[8]

Two Catholic proposals: These come from Heinrich Fries and Karl Rahner on the one hand, and from Avery Dulles on the other. It is not possible to consider these proposals in detail, so a brief synopsis of each is offered. In justice to the authors, the reader is encouraged to refer to their texts for a more complete picture.

Fries and Rahner[9] pose the question, "whether a unity of faith and church could be achieved in the foreseeable future among the large Christian churches." Their answer is in the affirmative. Their eight theses include reference to the fundamental truths that must be acknowledged by all, especially as expressed in the Scriptures and in the two foundational creeds; a nonrejection of binding dogmas of partner churches; the kinds of ministry that will be necessary, including the papacy, the episcopacy, and the requirement that prayer and the laying on of hands be part of ordination rites; and finally, the right of partner churches to continue to exist with pulpit and altar fellowship happening among them.

Writers commenting on the Fries and Rahner proposal include Cardinal Ratzinger, who sees it as fundamentally wrong because he understands it as proposing a "negotiated" and "man-made" formula "that corresponds to neither the Catholic nor the Protestant understanding of the Church."[10] Avery Dulles considers their program as requiring too much haste, stating that "I am of the opinion that considerable time and effort will be needed to achieve the kind of doctrinal agreement needed for full communion between churches as widely separated as the Orthodox, Protestant, Anglican, and Roman Catholic. Such agreement must be accomplished, I believe, in stages."[11]

Dulles, in his own proposal, stresses that a level of communion already exists, stemming from baptism and agreement on basic Christian teaching. He further states that a measure of doctrinal accord is necessary, although he adds that complete agreement among the partners on every item will be unattainable and, in fact, unnecessary. He places importance on the hierarchy of truths and on a willingness among the churches to review and even reformulate doctrines that were articulated in times of polemic. Finally, Dulles stresses that identical formulations are not at all necessary; he suggests that there can be, at times, reasons for allowing another tradition to retain a belief that does not mean a great deal to the partner but does not contradict the body of Christian beliefs.

It would be easy enough to find fault with any of these suggestions and with others that are being proposed by various communities and theologians. Being content to rest in negatives is not at all productive, however. We need to be energized by the fact that Christian people are trying to discover appropriate unity formulae that should inspire us to seek to be equally creative.

The fact that people are big enough to think of possibilities is a healthy sign that the declared aim of ecumenism has become a reality in the hearts and minds of many Christians and their communities. It means that the ecumenical movement, according to John Hotchkin's analysis, has at least partially entered into its third stage.[12] The first stage was the pioneering and organizational stage dating from 1910 to the mid-sixties, with the entry of the Catholic Church into the movement. The second is the stage of the dialogues, to be reckoned from the sixties to the present, which must continue into the future. Hotchkin speaks of the third stage as "phased reconciliation," when churches are called to redefine their relationships. A very important aspect of this stage is a shared experience of the Christian life by one church with another, discovering that faith experiences can be differently perceived and named by each community or denomination. Bishop Peter Cullinane writes of it this way: "Something that has come to be understood in one community of Christians might not yet be fully appreciated by Christians in another denomination. Given the relationship between experiences and perception, a more shared experience of the faith could be necessary *so that* we can all eventually come to the same perceptions."[13]

Some Contemporary Problems

This section has considered examples of Christian denominations moving from theoretical positions into actual mergers, with proposals that are worthy of continued study. This new development, of course, surfaces yet again a set of problems that, according to the Catholic mind, cannot be swept aside. Some of these contemporary problems are now listed.

The nature of ecclesial communion: An important beginning point in every Catholic response to ecumenical initiatives is the nature of ecclesial communion. "Communion" requires "catholicity" and "catholicity" requires "communion," that is, the union of all the local churches, one with another and with the church of Rome. That is why Catholics have a hard time with the Anglican action when the churches of the British Isles are comfortable establishing a union with the Lutherans of Northern Europe without somehow involving the entire Anglican Communion.[14] This suggests that further work has to be done on the nature of the church and on defining of the nature of *communio.*

Ministry: The matter of ministry still requires a great deal of investigation. It is not just a matter of addressing what is widely considered to be an undeveloped theology of apostolic succession.[15] Rather, this area includes a returning to the question of the recognition or otherwise of the orders[16] of other Christian communities, and of reaching a more profound understanding of the role of women in the church, including the matter of the ordination of women.[17]

Many Christian leaders and theologians have taken seriously the acknowledgment by John Paul II that the effective functioning of the papacy in the united church requires an intensive contemporary consultation, even a redefining of the ministry.[18] What needs to happen next is the establishment of an ecumenical forum wherein theologians can scientifically address the entire subject.

Neoconservative movements: The presence of neoconservative movements, especially within the mainline churches, is without doubt antiecumenical. So as to reduce the spread and power of such influences, continuing education of the faithful, clerical and lay, has to be addressed.[19]

These are just some of problems that the churches have to face. Others have surfaced in the dialogues, for example, the matters of authority, the Eucharist, and Mary. What is different and special about today is the willingness to address the issues and to do so with good grace. Equally important is the establishment of the appropriate forums in which the continuing dialogues can occur and through which the churches will continue to be reminded of the need to press on in the work of securing unity.

Agencies Working for Unity

A further task is to consider some of those agencies charged with furthering the work of unity. Here, we look at the World Council of Churches, the Pontifical Council for Promoting Christian Unity, and the Joint Working Group.

The World Council of Churches: The World Council of Churches (WCC), with headquarters in the Ecumenical Center in Geneva, is a fellowship of more than three hundred member churches:

> ...who confess the Lord Jesus Christ as God and Savior according to the Scriptures and therefore seek to fulfill their common calling to the glory of the one God, Father, Son and Holy Spirit.[20]

The formal organization was founded in Amsterdam in 1948, but the vision of a "union of churches" goes back to the turn of the century. It was at Edinburgh in 1910, at a World Missionary Conference, that the need was expressed for greater cooperation among churches, especially in missionary places. The idea eventually took shape and was expressed principally through three movements whose titles reflect their concerns: the International Missionary Council (IMC) of 1921, concerned about Christian witness especially in non-Christian lands; the Life and Works Movement (L&W) of 1925, which was conscious of the social ills of the times and looked to practical ways of carrying out the Gospel injunctions; and the Faith and Order Movement (F&O) of 1927, which saw the need to address matters on the nature of the church, authority, doctrine, and worship.

The L&W and F&O combined in 1948 to become the World Council of Churches, being joined in 1961 by the IMC and, in 1971 by the World Council of Christian Education. In the late nineties, the council set about redesigning itself by replacing the former "units" with four clusters. Two of these are about communications and administrative matters; the third works under the title "Issues and themes"; and the fourth is called "Relations and constituencies."

Being a fellowship of churches, and not a church in its own right, the WCC has no legislative authority over its member churches. Nevertheless, the council does set certain criteria that churches must satisfy, including a minimum number of twenty-five thousand for a church to enjoy full membership of the council. Other criteria include active and financial support for the council's work.

As a servant of ecclesial unity, the WCC states its primary task to be the promotion of visible unity in fellowship and mission. Its long-term aim is to go out of business after securing what it set out to achieve, namely, Christian unity. Along the way, therefore, the council must not allow itself to be distracted from this primary goal. Although the Catholic Church is not a member of the WCC, it does cooperate with the council in many areas. We return to address some of these after first looking at the Pontifical Council for Promoting Christian Unity.

The Pontifical Council for Promoting Christian Unity: When this body first came to exist in 1960, it was called the "Secretariat for Promoting Christian Unity." As an agent of the Vatican Council, it was in contact with the leaders of other churches, seeking their suggestions for possible conciliar themes. It also invited the Christian World Communions to send observers to the council sessions.

During the Vatican Council deliberations, the secretariat was heavily involved in the preparation and subsequent promulgation of *Unitatis Redintegratio* (The Decree On Ecumenism), *Nostra Aetate* (The Declaration on the Relationship of the Church to Non-Christian Religions), *Dignitatis Humanae* (The Declaration on Religious Freedom), and in collaboration with the theological commission, *Dei Verbum* (The Dogmatic Constitution on Divine Revelation).

Since 1989, it has been known as the PCPCU and has taken on a double task. The first of these is the promotion within the Catholic Church of a correct interpretation and carrying out of the Catholic principles of ecumenism. To this end, it has produced the *Directory for the Application of the Principles and Norms of Ecumenism*, the latest revised edition being issued in 1993. Its second task includes working with the WCC and others at regional, national, and worldwide levels in the cause of Christian unity. This explains its dialogue work with the Orthodox Churches, the Anglican Communion, the Lutheran World Federation, the Alliance of Reformed Churches, the World Methodist Council, the Baptist World Alliance, and other churches and ecclesial communities.

The council's structures comprise an eastern section and a western section. The eastern section is concerned with the Orthodox Churches of the Eastern Orthodox tradition, the Oriental Orthodox Churches, and the Assyrian Church of the East. The western section deals with the churches and ecclesial communities that have come to exist since the sixteenth century. Two other tasks are to work with other organizations to spread the Bible and to promote Catholic-Orthodox student exchanges.

Closely associated with PCPCU, but distinct, is the Commission for Religious Relations with the Jews, established by Paul V1 in 1974. The cardinal president of PCPCU also presides over the Jewish Commission. A recent initiative of the commission was the document titled *We Remember: A Reflection on the Shoah.*[21]

The Joint Working Group: Since the Catholic Church is not a member of the WCC, a Joint Working Group (JWG) between the Catholic Church and the WCC was constituted in 1965. This group enables the two to cooperate in matters of study and other ventures, something that has happened increasingly over the more than thirty years of the group's life. The JWG is a consultative forum that reports back to its parent bodies: the WCC assembly and central committee and the PCPCU. Its co-secretaries are a staff member of the WCC and a staff member of the PCPCU.

Having established early on a broad agreement on the nature of ecumenism, and endorsing this with a commitment to serve the ecumenical movement, the JWG then undertook more specific tasks. These included a promotion of the Catholic Church's actual membership of the Faith and Order

Commission and a consultative relationship with other WCC bodies. The Catholic Church's full membership of the Faith and Order Commission began in 1968 and continues today. One of the major achievements of this commission is the document titled *Baptism, Eucharist and Ministry* (BEM) or, as it is sometimes called the Lima Document.

Beyond these tasks, the JWG has undertaken specific studies. These include *Catholicity and Apostolicity* (1968), *Common Witness and Proselytism* (1970), *Common Witness* (1980), *Hierarchy of Truths* (1990), and *The Church: Local and Universal* (1990).

During the 1990s, proselytism has been a matter of concern to the WCC. While it continues to produce documents on the subject (the latest being the 1997 *Towards Common Witness: A call to adopt responsible relationships in mission and to renounce proselytism*), the JWG has also addressed the subject in its 1995 statement titled *The Challenge of Proselytism and the Calling to Common Witness*. Other JWG topical reports of the 1990s are *The Ecumenical Dialogue on Moral Issues: Potential Sources of Common Witness or of Divisions* and *Ecumenical Formation: Ecumenical Reflections and Suggestions*.

Interreligious Dialogue[22]

By now it should be apparent that the Vatican Council called on the church to look beyond itself and to consider its relationship with other Christians. Such has been the main subject of this book. At the same time, the council called on Catholics to look to the whole world and to act responsibly in it. Within that world, there are many religions, although not Christian, which are of supreme importance to their millions of members. How, then, should the Catholic Church relate to these religions and to their individual members?

The strategy, if one would be bold enough to call it that, is to embark on another kind of dialogue with these peoples, not only with Jews but also with Muslims, Buddhists, Hindus, and the followers of Traditional Religion.[23]

The Aim of Interreligious Dialogue

The aim of interreligious dialogue is altogether different from the aims we recognized and named as integral to the Christian ecumenical movement. A starting point for understanding this interreligious dialogue is the realization that all people, not just Christians, ask fundamental questions about their origins and destinies, good and evil, suffering and happiness—and most of them turn to their religions to seek for answers. After all, only thirty-three percent of the total world population is Christian, thirty-seven percent of people being Muslims, Hindus, and Buddhists, with Jews making up half a percent of the total. These questions, common to all people, and the search for answers offer a good foundation for the sharing of ideas and cooperation in a range of ventures, either in a multireligious forum or in a bilateral setting.

The Catholic Understanding of Interreligious Dialogue[24]

It is helpful to realize that the Catholic Church's arrival at a desire for interreligious dialogue and cooperation is relatively recent, dating from the advent of *Nostra Aetate* (The Declaration on the Relationship of the Church to Non-Christian Religions) at the Second Vatican Council. Until this council, the church interpreted her "missionary" mandate principally in terms of working for the conversion of others so that they might enjoy the fruits of Christ's redemption as members of the church. The conciliar teaching alerted us to think in broader terms.

In the first instance, Vatican II faced up to the fact of religious pluralism in the world, in line with the figures listed above. Of course, the church holds firmly to the view that there is only one redeemer of people, Jesus Christ, but the same God who created all and who provides for all will have a means of extending salvation to members of other faiths, a means we may not fully comprehend. As Cardinal Arinze says, these religions "carry with them the echo of thousands of years of humanity looking for God ... It would be most unrealistic to ignore all this and live as if there were only one religion in the world."[25]

A subject much debated among modern theologians is the question of how these other religions actually mediate salvation to their members. It is not possible in this work to fairly present all the considerations of the discussions, although the reader is referred to the International Theological Commission's report, "Christianity and the World Religions," in order to briefly review the current thinking on the subject.[26]

A second conciliar teaching is the declaration "that the right to religious freedom has its foundation in the very dignity of the human person."[27] In such a statement, the church is not only addressing the world and its governments but is expressing the respect she has for others in their religious choices.

A third realization is that God's saving hand is at work wherever good is existing in the world. Without a doubt, immense goodness is to be found among the many religions of the world, so much so that in *NA* we read, "The Catholic Church rejects nothing which is true and holy in these religions."[28]

All of this means that the church has a task over and above caring for her own faithful and for those desirous of entering her. She also has the task of working with other Christian communities for the unity of the church. This additional task includes entering into dialogue with the world, particularly with other religions.

The Content of Interreligious Dialogue

Interreligious dialogue is a difficult but rewarding pursuit. Expressed ever so simply, this dialogue is two-pronged. On the one hand, it requires sharing information about our respective riches. This calls for respectfully listening to another's belief— an acquired art, indeed—and an honest presentation of one's own beliefs—which is equally demanding. On the other hand, there is the matter of discerning God's mysterious presence at work in these other religions, and of sensing the Divine presence that is in them for the enrichment of the members.

Such a dialogue builds needed bridges among peoples and, in fact, creates a special form of "communion." John Paul II made reference to this during the 1986 International Year for Peace when he and other religious leaders met in Assisi for prayer. His concluding words were:

The form and content of our prayers are very different, as we have seen, and there can be no question of reducing them to a kind of common denominator. Yet, in this very difference we have perhaps discovered anew that, regarding the problem of peace and its relation to religious commitment, *there is something which binds us together.*[29]

It is worth noting here that the spirit of Assisi has been taken into the wider world. For example, since Assisi, the Rome-founded Saint Egidio community annually organizes prayer and dialogue occasions in a number of cities around the world. The annual interfaith pilgrimage for peace, held in London since 1986, is another example. Interfaith organizations now exist, including the World Congress of Faiths, the Temple of Understanding, and the World Conference on Religion and Peace, the latter being supported by the PCID.

Dialogue, in other words, helps us discover, at the deepest level, the unity that already exists in humankind: our one single origin and our common goal. Four forms of dialogue are listed in the PCID document titled *Dialogue and Proclamation.*[30] The first of these is the "dialogue of life," which includes all the informal contacts among neighbors who are from different religions. *NA* provides the backing for such a dialogue: "Let Christians, while witnessing to their own faith and way of life acknowledge, preserve and encourage the spiritual and moral truths found among men" (2).

The second form is the "dialogue of action," when Christians, with other people, cooperate in projects for the sake of human development and for the liberation of people. During his address at Assisi, John Paul II referred to this kind of activity: "Either we learn to walk together in peace and harmony, or we drift apart and ruin ourselves and others."[31]

The "dialogue of theological exchange" is the third form suggested by the pontifical council. In this instance, experts exchange information about their respective heritages, detecting as they go what is shared in common.

The "dialogue of religious experience" is the final form, when people who are deeply committed to their own traditions feel confident enough to share their spiritual experiences, including their search for God or the Absolute, their ways of prayer, and their beliefs.

Given these four forms of dialogue, Raimundo Panikkar's remark[32] expresses something of the beauty that can be achieved by one who approaches others in the right frame of mind: "I 'left' as a Christian; I 'found' myself as a Hindu; and I 'returned' as a Buddhist, without having ceased to be a Christian."

Some of the "Formal" Interreligious Dialogues

Some dialogues are multireligious, such as those that have happened in India, Malaysia, Mauritius, and Great Britain. Others are one on one, including discussions between the PCID and Buddhist representatives. Even more common are the local dialogues that are in place, for example between Catholics and Muslims in several countries.

Jews: There is a dialogue with the Jewish community that is conducted by the Catholic-Jewish International Liaison Committee (ILC). This committee, which gives high priority to education and cooperation in local situations, has also had discussions on the family, ecology, human rights, and the fights against anti-Semitism, racism, and xenophobia. These ongoing theological dialogues will lead to a better appreciation of the common rich heritage that belongs to Jews and Christians.[33]

Muslims: Too often, relations with the Muslim world are not given good press because of the focus on the tension points where fundamentalism in religion segregates people into bitter camps.[34] But given the great mobility of people in these times, and the fact that people of different faiths live in the same neighborhoods, we should be discovering that the "dialogue of life," spoken about earlier, is of growing importance. Given a healthy communication at this level, more organized dialogues can take up discussions on our common heritage, which includes our monotheistic foundations, our connection with Abraham, the fact that both religions accept divine revelation and acknowledge Jesus and Mary, and that we have common concerns in ethical matters. Dialogues are in place in Africa,

Asia, and the United States; pastoral letters have been written; colloquia have been held; and Islamic studies have been presented in Catholic institutions. It is now a matter of intensifying these fruitful contacts.

Buddhists: Establishing international contacts with Buddhism has not always been easy, due mainly to political complications in the countries where Buddhists have a presence. Nevertheless, the PCID has had some discussions, for example, with Japanese schools of Mahayana Buddhism, which see in Buddha a certain deification. While Buddhists generally choose not to speak about God, they do enter into discussions on meditation and the mystics and on moral and social issues. The Asian Bishops' Conference sponsored a dialogue in Thailand on the differences and similarities between Buddhists and Christians on social and personal disharmony. Besides, monastic exchanges have been taking place for quite some time. For example, the Catholic Focolare Movement has had a number of exchanges with its lay equivalent in Buddhism, the Japanese Risso Kosei-Kai. July 1996 saw a five-day meeting of nearly fifty Buddhist and Christian monks and nuns at the Gethsemani Trappist monastery. The rich dialogue that took place there is fully reported in the 1998 publication *The Gethsemani Encounter.*[35]

On May 11, 1998, Cardinal Arinze, the president of the Pontifical Council for Inter-religious Dialogue, addressed a message to Buddhist friends on the occasion of *Vesakh,* which celebrates important events in the life of Buddha. In line with what is said above about a common meeting ground for Christians and Buddhists, the cardinal noted that the "ongoing dialogue between Buddhists and Christians is distinguished by efforts to meet at the level of religious experience." Another comment the cardinal made is worth quoting in full, since it does suggest to us ideas and words that all of us can employ as we place ourselves on the path of interreligious dialogue. The cardinal first acknowledges that hope of new life is the source of our dialogue. He then continues:

> People of hope are, at the same time, realists who do not
> close their eyes to reality with all its positive and nega-

tive aspects. We cannot turn a blind eye to the dramatic crises of our world: the wars between different countries, civil wars, terrorism in all its forms, injustice which is forever widening the gap between rich and poor, hunger, the lack of shelter, unemployment—especially among the youth, globalization without solidarity, the heavy burden of external debt, the problems of drugs, immorality, abortion. The list could be extended. Nevertheless the small lamp of hope must always remain alight, shining on the paths leading humanity to a better future.

We Christians and Buddhists, embarked on our respective spiritual paths, can work together to give increased hope to humanity. Yet first we must accept our differences and show each other mutual respect and true love.[36]

Hindus: Hinduism is less a single religion and more a cluster of philosophical, ascetical, and popular groupings. This means that dialogues need to be very localized, individual with individual. Nevertheless, a formal dialogue of Catholics, other Christians, and Hindus did take place in India, centering on "our spiritual heritage and our commitment to harmony and integration—the human community." There are other parallels that suggest themselves for fruitful exchanges: the common valuing of meditation, nonviolence for Hindus alongside Christian attitudes to peace, Christian grace and Hindu devotionalism, celebrations of religious initiation, and marriage and other festivals.

In an open letter written in anticipation of the October 1998 Hindu feast of Diwali, their new year, Cardinal Arinze asked for a dialogue between Hindus and Christians in order to "render us more credible as a clear sign of hope for the human family." The cardinal referred to modern-day problems but added, "The lamp of hope must always remain alight, indicating the path to a better future."[37]

Finally, it has to be noted that this brief consideration of inter-religious dialogues is far from an exhaustive study of the subject. The dialogues and dialogue partners mentioned are by way of example only. There are others, and consideration of them all—including what can and should be taking place with members of Traditional Religion—is beyond the scope of this work. Nevertheless, as we survey the world scene and its range of religions, we should consider our relationship with them not simply in terms of what they can learn or take from us but what we can learn from them as well. That is what the bishops of Malaysia, Singapore, and Brunei said in Rome to the 1998 Synod for Asia:

> From Muslims the Church can learn about prayer, fasting and almsgiving. From Hindus the Church can learn about meditation and contemplation. From Buddhists the Church can learn about detachment from material goods and respect for life. From Confucianism the Church can learn about filial piety and respect for elders. From Taoism the Church can learn about simplicity and humility. From animists the Church can learn about reverence and respect for nature and gratitude for harvests. The Church can learn from the rich symbolism and rites existing in their diversity of worship. The Church can, like the Asian religions, learn to be more open, receptive, sensitive, tolerant, and forgiving in the midst of a plurality of religions.[38]

It is qualities such as these that are to characterize our attitudes and our dealings with all peoples, Christians as well as members of other religions. In so acting we are becoming, each in our own way, conquerors of the world's divisions.

Endnotes

Foreword

1   See for example the work of J.M.R. TILLARD, L'Église locale :
     ecclésiologie de communion et catholicité, Cogitatio Fidei, 191
     (Paris : Cerf, 1995); J. FONTBONA I MISSÉ, *Comunión y sinodal-
     idad : la eclesiología eucarística después e N. Afanasiev en I.
     Zizioulas y J.M.R. Tillard,* Collectània Sant Pacià, 52 (Barcelona:
     Herder, 1994), J. RIGAL, *L'ecclésiologie de communion: son évo-
     lution historique et ses fondements,* Cogitatio Fidei, 202 (Paris:
     Cerf, 1997); J.A. KOMONCHAK, "Concepts of Communion: Past
     and Present," *Cristianesimo nella storia* 16 (1995) 321–340.

Chapter 1

1   Father Paul Wattson (1863–1940) was an Episcopal priest and
     co-founder, with Mother Lurana White (1870–1935), of a
     Franciscan religious community called the Society of the
     Atonement. In 1909, they and the other members of the society,
     men and women, became Catholics. Such is one of the first
     examples of corporate reunion after the Reformation. Today,
     an important work of theirs is the promotion of Christian
     unity. The headquarters are still in Graymoor.

2   Another of Abbé Couturier's (1881–1953) initiatives was the
     founding of the Groupe de Dombes in 1937, which continues to
     meet annually at the Cistercian Abbey of Les Dombes, 40 km
     NE of Lyon. Comprised of Catholic and Protestant friends, the
     group is convinced that reconciliation is achievable only as
     the result of a conversion process—conversion to one another,
     and together unto God. Their publications continue to influ-
     ence the direction of the ecumenical movement.

3   *Unitatis Redintegratio, The Documents of Vatican II.* Walter M.
     Abbott ed. London: Geoffrey Chapman, 1966: no.8

4   John Paul II. *Orientale Lumen* (1995) Boston: Pauline Books and
     Media, 1995

5   John Paul II. *Ut Unum Sint* (1995) Vatican: Libreria Editrice
     Vaticana, 1995

6   *Directory for the Application of Principles and Norms on
     Ecumenism.* Vatican City: PCPCU, 1993

7   Raymond E. Brown. *The Churches the Apostles Left Behind.*
     London: Chapman, 1984

8   *Unity and Diversity in the Church.* Pontifical Biblical
     Commission. Vatican: Libreria Editrice Vaticana: 1988: 5

9   See Eusebius. *The History of the Church from Christ to
     Constantine.* G. A. Williamson tr. New York: NY University
     Press, 1966: (4.23) 183. Here, and elsewhere in his text,
     Eusebius offers numerous examples of letters written by bish-
     ops to their colleagues and carried by a *frumentarius* or couri-
     er. These letters were understood as being testimonies to their
     mutual communion.

10   Frederick M. Bliss. *Understanding Reception: A Backdrop to Its
     Ecumenical Use.* Marquette: Marquette University Press, 1993:
     34–42

11   "The First Letter of Clement of Rome" in *Message of the Fathers
     of the Church.* Robert B. Eno ed. Wilmington: Michael Glazier
     Inc., 1984: 36

12   Canon 6 of the First Council of Nicaea in *Decrees of the
     Ecumenical Councils*, Vol 1. Norman P. Tanner ed. London:
     Sheed and Ward, 1990: 8–9

13   G. R. Evans. *The Church and the Churches.* Cambridge:
     Cambridge University Press, 1994: 200

14   Yves Congar. *Power and Poverty in the Church.* Jennifer
     Nicholson tr. London: Chapman, 1965: 34–38

15   Robert F. Taft. *Beyond East and West: Problems in Liturgical
     Understanding.* Rome: Edizioni Orientalia Christiana, 1997: 203

16   Eric G. Jay. *The Church*. Vol. 1. London, SPCK, 1977: 157

17   Originally the "Byzantine rite" referred to that ecclesial way of
     life which was limited to the church of Constantinople; today it
     more strictly refers to the system of worship used by the Greek
     and Russian and some Eastern-rite Catholic churches.

18   Jay. *The Church:* 142

19   Herman Wegman. *Christian Worship in East and West: A Study
     Guide to Liturgical History.* Gordon W. Lathrop tr. New York:
     Pueblo, 1976: 57

20   Norbert Brox. *A History of the Early Church.* John Bowden tr.
     London: SCM, 1994: 86–87

21   Joseph Ratzinger. "Primacy and Episcopacy" in *Theology Digest*,
     March 1971: 204

22   *UUS:* no. 96

23   Ratzinger. "Primacy and episcopacy" in *Theology Digest*, March
     1971: 206

24   Bede. *The Ecclesiastical History of the English People*. Judith
     McClure and Roger Collins eds. Oxford: Oxford University
     Press, 1994: 1, 27, 2

25   Jan Cardinal Willebrands. "Cardinal Willebrands' Address in
     Cambridge, England. January 18, 1970" in *Called to Full Unity:
     Documents on Anglican–Roman Catholic Relations 1966–1983*.
     Joseph W. Witmer and J. Robert Wright eds. Washington:
     United States Catholic Conference, 1986: 52

26   Yves Congar. *Diversity and Communion*. John Bowden. tr.
     London: Chapman, 1966: 92

27   "Look at it our way: Asian bishops respond to Rome" in *The
     Tablet,* May 2, 1998: 571

28   *UUS:* no. 102

29   William J. Bausch. *Pilgrim Church.* Mystic: Twenty-Third
     Publications, 1989: 200

30   Jay. *The Church:* 204

31   Richard McBrien. *Catholicism.* Third ed. London: Geoffrey
     Chapman, 1994: 748

32   Patrick Granfield. *The Limits of the Papacy.* London: Darton,
     Longman and Todd, 1987: 79

33   Jay. *The Church:* 103

34   Granfield: See chapter 4 for a presentation of this subject.

35   Ernst Niermann. "The Layman in the Church" in *Sacramentum
     Mund: An Encyclopedia of Theology.* Karl Rahner et al. eds. vol
     3. "Laity." Bangalore: Theological Publications in India: 1968.
     See also Faivre, Alexandre. *The Emergence of the Laity in the
     Early Church.* New York: Paulist, 1990

36   Congar. *Power and Poverty in the Church:* 64

37   *The Church and the Reconstruction of the Modern World: The
     Social Encyclicals of Pius XI.* Terence P. McLaughlin ed. New
     York: Image Books, 1957: 303

38   *UUS:* no. 88

39   *UUS:* no. 94

40   Congar. *Power and Poverty in the Church*: 53

41   Giles of Rome. "De eccl. Potest." 1,iii,c.12 as quoted in Yves
     Congar. *Lay People in the Church.* Donald Attwater tr. London:
     Chapman, 1959: 42

42 Robert Bellarmine. "De controversiis christianae fidei," in *Opera omnia*, 12 vols. Justinus Fevre. Paris: L. Vives, 1870–1874

43 Karl Rahner. "Theological Interpretation of Vatican II," in *Theological Investigations* 20, Edward Quinn tr. London: Darton, Longman and Todd, 1981: 82ff

44 Jacques Dupuis. *Toward a Christian Theology of Religious Pluralism.* New York: Orbis Books, 1997: 86

45 Origen. "Hom on Joshua" III, 5 as quoted in Eric G Jay. ibid: 64. See also *Omelie sui Salmi.* E. Prinzivalli, ed. Series: Biblioteca Patristica. Firenze: Nardini Editore 1991: Psalmo 36, II, 1

46 Francis A. Sullivan. *Salvation Outside the Church?* London: Geoffrey Chapman, 1992: 18–39

47 Council of Basle-Ferrara-Florence-Rome. *Decree for the Jacobites.* DS 1351

48 Pius XII. *Mystici Corporis Christi.* London: CTS, 1964

49 Joseph A. Komonchak. *Modernity and the Construction of Roman Catholicism.* Paper presented to the American Academy of Religion: Seminar on Roman Catholic Modernism: 1994

50 All these encyclicals of Leo XIII can be found in *The Great Encyclical Letters of Leo XIII.* New York: Benziger Brothers, 1903

51 It is the view of at least one contemporary writer that Rome continues to emphasize "its political sovereignty." John Paul II "has never ceased to put the Church forward as the fount of civilization, the mediator of ethics that converge around fundamental human rights and values, in the face of the drift of secularized society and the inadequacy of its model." Giancarlo Zizola. "The power of the Pope: 1" in *The Tablet.* 17 October 1998: 1352–1353

52 Pius XI. "Mortalium Animos" (1928) in *Selected Papal Encyclicals and Letters 1928–1932*. London: CTS, 1933: 20–21

53 Herbert Alphonso. See footnote 3 in "The Idea of Holiness in Christianity" in *Pro Dialogo*. Pontificium Consilium Pro Dialogo Inter Religiones: 92, 1996/2: 243

54 George H. Tavard. *The Church, Community of Salvation*. Collegeville: Glazier, 1992: 172ff

55 Thomas à Kempis. *The Imitation of Christ*. New Delhi: St. Paul Publication, 1991

56 Reginald Garrigou-Lagrange. *The Three Ages of the Interior Life*. Vol. 1 St. Louis: Herder, 1947–48: 3–4

57 Teilhard de Chardin. *Le Milieu Divin*. London: Collins, 1960: 101

58 de Chardin. *Le Milieu Divin:* 104–105

59 Thomas Merton. *Contemplation in a World of Action*. London: George Allen and Unwin, 1971: 179–180

60 Merton. *Contemplation in a World of Action:* 186–187

Chapter 2

1 Martha Driscoll. "Maria Gabriella Sagheddu" in *Ecumenical Pilgrims: Profiles of Pioneers in Christian Reconciliation.* Ion Bria and Dagmar Heller eds. Geneva: WCC Publications, 1995: 207–211

2 *UUS:* no. 3 and footnote 50

3 Emmanuel Lanne. "Dom Lambert Beauduin" in *Ecumenical Pilgrims.* op cit. 28

4 Lanne: 29

5 Lanne: 27

6   Quoted in Canon Roger Aubert's text: *Cardinal Mercier: A Churchman Ahead of His Time*. Francis J. Thomson ed. This booklet was produced with the support of the Generale Bank, Brussels: 20

7   Roger. *Cardinal Mercier:* 21

8   Roger. *Cardinal Mercier:* 27–28

9   Stjepan Schmidt. "Augustin Cardinal Bea" in *Ecumenical Pilgrims:* 22–26

10   John Henry Newman. *On Consulting the Faithful in Matters of Doctrine*. John Coulson ed. London: Collins, 1986

11   John Henry Newman. *An Essay on the Development of Christian Doctrine*. London: Sheed and Ward: 1960. See also "An Unpublished Paper by Cardinal Newman on the Development of Doctrine" in *Gregorianum:* 39, 1958: 589–596

12   *Mysterium Ecclesiae*. "Declaration in Defense of the Catholic Doctrine of the Church Against Certain Errors of the Present Day." Congregation for the Doctrine of the Faith, 1973, in *Doctrine and Life,* August 1973: 447–459

13   *A History of the Ecumenical Movement*. Vol. 1, Ruth Rouse and Stephen Charles Neill eds. Geneva: WCC, 3rd ed .1986: 684ff

14   As quoted in "The Response" to *Dignitatis Humanae* in *The Documents of Vatican II*. Walter M. Abbott ed. London: Geoffrey Chapman, 1966

15   Karl Rahner. *Mission and Grace*. Vol. 1, Cecily Hastings tr. London: Sheed and Ward, 1963: 9

16   Karl Rahner. *Free Speech in the Church*. London: Sheed and Ward, 1959: 25

17   Leon-Joseph Cardinal Suenens. *Coresponsibility in the Church*. Francis Martin tr. London: Burns and Oates, 1968: 13

18   The condemnations were articulated in three documents: the decree *Lamentabili* (1907) of the Holy Office, the encyclical of Pius X, *Pascendi* (1907), and the "Oath Against Modernism" (1910)

19   Raymond E. Brown. *The Critical Meaning of the Bible.* New York: Paulist, 1981: ix

20   John Paul II. *Gift and Mystery.* Nairobi: Paulines Publications Africa, 1996

21   Avery Dulles. Introduction to *Lumen Gentium* in *The Documents of Vatican II:* 10

22   See footnote 27 in *Lumen Gentium. The Documents of Vatican II.* ibid: 24–25

23   John E. Linnan. "Declaration on Religious Liberty" in *Vatican II and Its Documents. An American Reappraisal.* Timothy E. O'Connell ed. Collegeville: The Liturgical Press, 1986: 176

24   *AAS:* 42, 1950: 142–147

25   For a very readable account of the beginnings of the secretariat, see Thomas Stransky's article "The Foundation of the Secretariat for Promoting Christian Unity" in *Vatican II by Those Who Were There.* Alberic Stacpoole ed. London: Geoffrey Chapman, 1986: 62–87.

26   Cardinale Giovanni Battista Montini. *"Il mistero della Chiesa nella luce di S.Ambrogio"* in *OR*: December 10–11, 1962: 6

27   Cardinale Giovanni Battista Montini. *"Discorsi al Clero"* (Milan 1963, 78–80) quoted by M. D. Chenu in *Peuple de Dieu dans le monde.* Paris: Editions du Cerf, 1966: 12–13, no. 1

28   Karl Rahner. "Theological Interpretations of Vatican II" in *Theological Investigations 20.* London: 1981: 82f

29   "Message to Humanity" in *The Documents of Vatican II:* 3

Chapter 3

1   A fuller listing of official Catholic documentation on ecumenism is provided in footnote 3 of the 1993 *Directory for
the Application of Principles and Norms on Ecumenism.*
Vatican City: PCPCU, 1993

2   William Johnston. *Letters to Contemplatives.* New York: Orbis
Books, 1991: 22

3   See also the chapter "Inter–religious Dialogue" in his earlier
book, *The Mirror Mind: Spirituality and Transformation.* San
Francisco: Harper and Row Publishers, 1981

4   See especially "Introduction" to *Churches Respond to BEM:
Official Responses to the "Baptism, Eucharist, and Ministry."*
Vol. 1. Max Thurian ed. Geneva: WCC, F&O Paper 129, 1986

5   In *Apostolic Faith Today: A Handbook for Study.* Hans-Georg
Link ed. Geneva: WCC, F &O Paper 124, 1985

6   Gunther Gassmann, compiler. Geneva: WCC, F&O Paper 156,
1991

7   Alan D. Falconer, compiler. Geneva: WCC, F&O Paper 179, 1997

8   According to Schuyler Brown, the word *koinonia* in the New
Testament is never attributed to the church as such, although
it is used as descriptive of Christian behavior. Only indirectly,
then, does it connect with ecclesiology. "*Koinonia* as the Basis
of New Testament Ecclesiology?" in *One in Christ:* 12, 1976:
157–67

9   *Towards Koinonia in Faith, Life and Witness—a discussion
paper.* Geneva: WCC, F&O Paper 161, 1993: no. 21

10   "Letter to the Bishops of the Catholic Church on Some Aspects
of the Church Understood as Communion" in *Origins:* 25, 1992:
no. 1

11   nos. 13–17

12   *Unity and Diversity in the Church.* Vatican: Libreria Editrice
     Vaticana, 1991: 17

13   Saint Augustine. *Against Cresconius,* III, 35, 39, PL 43, 517

14   Werner Küppers. "Reception, Prolegomena to a Systematic
     Study" in *Councils and the Ecumenical Movement.* Geneva:
     WCC, 1968

15   Ludwig Hertling. *Communio.* Church and Papacy in Early
     Christianity. Jared Wicks tr. Chicago: Loyola University Press,
     1972: 41

16   Eusebius. *The History of the Church from Christ to Constantine.*
     G. A. Williamson tr. New York: New York University Press, 1966:
     (4.23) 183

17   Eusebius. *The History of the Church from Christ to Constantine:*
     (7. 30) 315

18   "Irenaeus Against Heresies" (1, 10, 2) in *The Writings of
     Irenaeus.* A. Roberts and W. H. Rambault tr. vol. 1. Edinburgh:
     T and T Clark, 1869: 43

19   John A. Saliba. *Perspectives on New Religious Movements.*
     London: Geoffrey Chapman, 1995: 39. See endnote 9 of chapter
     2 in Saliba for the names of scholars suggesting a revival of
     Gnosticism in a new form.

20   "The Martyrdom of Saint Polycarp" (Introduction and 8) in
     Ancient Christian Writings. James A. Fleist tr. Cork: Mercier
     Press, 1948: 85–102

21   Eric G. Jay. *The Church.* Vol. 1. London: SPCK, 1977: 67–74

22   Saint Jerome. *Adv. Lucif.* 19

23   David Christie-Murray. *A History of Heresy.* Oxford: Oxford
     University Press, 1976 and 1989: 47–48, where the Caesaraen

and Nicaean-Constantinopolitan creeds are printed side by side

24   *OR:* November 16, 1994: Sunday *Angelus* address of November 13

25   *AAS:* 8, 1995: 686

26   *OR:* November 16, 1994

27   The General Council of Chalcedon in *The Christian Faith.* J. Neuner and J. Dupuis eds. 5th ed. New York: Alba House, 1990: no. 613

28   *AAS:* 11, 1971: 814

29   *AAS:* 6, 1973: 299

30   Ronald G. Roberson. *The Eastern Christian Churches: A Brief Survey.* 5th revised edition. Rome: Edizioni Orientalia Christiana, 1995: 222

31   Roberson. *The Eastern Christian Churches:* 21–37

Chapter 4

1   Stephen Happel. "Symbol" in *The New Dictionary of Theology.* Joseph A. Komonchak, Mary Collins, Dermot A. Lane eds. Dublin: Gill and Macmillan, 1987: 1002

2   Paul VI. *Anno Ineunte.* July 25, 1967. This Brief was handed by Paul VI to Ecumenical Patriarch Athenagoras after Bishop Willebrands had read it in the Latin Cathedral of the Holy Spirit, at the end of a joint prayer service. *Towards The Healing of Schism: The Sees of Rome and Constantinople. (Public statements and correspondence between the Holy See and the Ecumenical Patriarchate 1958–1984).* E. J. Stormon ed. New York: Paulist, 1987: 161–163

3   *Anno Ineunte:* 162

4 Yves Congar. *Diversity and Communion*. John Bowden tr. London: SCM, 1984: 89

5 See especially no. 6 of *Lumen Gentium*, which uses a number of biblical metaphors to point to the inner nature of the church.

6 See Gérard Philips. "History of the Constitution" in *Commentary on the Documents of Vatican II*. Vol. I. London: Burns and Oates, 1967: 105–137

7 *LG:* 8

8 See Francis A. Sullivan. "The Significance of Vatican II's Decision to Say of the Church of Christ not that it 'Is' but that it 'Subsists In' the Roman Catholic Church." *Bulletin/Centro Pro Unione*: 29, 1986: 3–8

9 *UR:* 3

10 A useful overview of the Orthodox Church is offered in *The Orthodox Church: Its Past and Its Role in the World Today* by John Meyendorff, as revised and expanded by Nicholas Lossky. Crestwood: St. Vladimir's Seminary Press, 1981. Fourth revised edition, 1996

11 There are fifteen autocephalous or "self-headed" churches in the Orthodox world. They comprise the four ancient Eastern patriarchates of Constantinople, Alexandria, Antioch, and Jerusalem as well as eleven others that have come to exist over time. They are self-governing churches that are not subject to any authority beyond themselves; nor do they claim any jurisdiction over other autocephalous sister churches. Each such church sees itself as a microcosm of the whole church, being a sacramental and complete community. Autocephalous churches are distinct from "autonomous" churches which are self-governing, although without full independence.

12 Timothy Ware. *The Orthodox Church*. London: Penguin Books, 1993: 29–30

13 Paul McPartlan. "The Greatest Task" in *Priests and People:* 1, January 1996: 5

14 From notes taken at the address given by J. D. Zizioulas at the Pontifical University of Saint Thomas, Rome, April 21, 1998: "The *Filioque* Issue and Its Consequences for Ecclesiology"

15 "The Greek and Latin Traditions Regarding the Procession of the Holy Spirit" in *OR:* September 20, 1995

16 *OR.* July 5, 1995: 6

17 Yves Congar. *After Nine Hundred Years: The Background of the Schism Between the Eastern and Western Churches.* Westport: Greenwood Press, 1959: 29–31

18 Congar. *After Nine Hundred Years*: 38–44

19 John Paul II. "We Cannot Remain Separated." Papal homily for the Feasts of Saints Peter and Paul in *Catholic International:* November 1995: 414

20 Eric G. Jay. *The Church.* Vol. 1. London: SPCK, 1977: 144–145

21 Congar. *After Nine Hundred Years:* 23–27

22 Carl Andresen. "History of the Medieval Councils in the West" in *The Councils of the Church: History and Analysis.* Philadelphia: Fortress Press, 1966: 165

23 Francis Dvornik. *The General Councils of the Church.* London: Burns and Oates, 1961: 74–80

24 Ronald G. Roberson. *The Eastern Christian Churches: A Brief Survey.* 5th edition. Rome: Edizione Orientalia Christiana, 1985: 169–170

25 "Decree on Eastern Catholic Churches" in *The Documents of Vatican II.* Walter M. Abbott ed. London: Geoffrey Chapman, 1966: no. 24

26 Roberson. *The Eastern Christian Churches:* 171–172

27 *The Tablet,* January 20, 1990, reports on how the Byzantine-rite Catholic Church was forcibly absorbed into the Orthodox Church in 1948. See also Roberson: 173–177

28 *Origins:* 10, August 12, 1993: 166–169

29 Bishop Vsevolod of Scopelos. "Toward Reconciliation of the Catholic Church and the Orthodox Church" in *Eastern Churches Journal,* January 1995: 87–104

30 See the Documentation Supplement: "The Balamand Report: Questions and Answers" in *Information Service,* PCPCU: 1996/IV: 169–172

31 Ware: 3–5. The present patriarch is Patriarch Bartholomew. He is the 270th successor of the apostle Saint Andrew and has been in office since 1991

32 "Encyclical of the Ecumenical Patriarchate, 1920" in *The Ecumenical Review:* January 1959: 79

33 "Encyclical of the Ecumenical Patriarchate, 1920": 80

34 Theodore Stylianopoulos. "The Question of the Reception of BEM in the Orthodox Church in the Light of its Ecumenical Commitment" in *Orthodox Perspectives on Baptism, Eucharist, and Ministry.* Gennadios Limouris and Nomikos Michael Vaporis eds. F&O Paper 128. Brookline: Holy Cross Orthodox Press, 1985: 128

35 See "Mysterium Ecclesiae," Declaration on Defense of the Catholic Doctrine on the Church Against Certain Errors of the Present Day—The Sacred Congregation for the Doctrine of the Faith. *Doctrine and Life:* 23, 1973: 447–459

36 *Origins:* 10, August 12, 1993: 167

37 Paul VI. "Address of welcome in reply by Patriarch Athenagoras," July 25, 1967 in *Towards the Healing of Schism:* 171

38 *Towards the Healing of Schism:* 172–173

39 *Towards the Healing of Schism:* See endnote 2 of this chapter for the full reference to this text.

40 Yves Congar. *Diversity and Communion.* John Bowden tr. London: SCM, 1984: 87

41 Congar. *Diversity and Communion:* 87

42 Congar. *Diversity and Communion:* 87

43 *Towards the Healing of Schism:* 49

44 *Towards the Healing of Schism:* 52

45 Congar. *Diversity and Communion:* 88

46 Cardinal Willebrands in *Doing the Truth in Charity.* New York: Paulist, 1982: 227

47 *The Quest for Unity: Orthodox and Catholics in Dialogue.* John Borelli and John H. Erickson eds. Crestwood: St. Vladimir's Seminary Press, 1996: 53–64

48 "An Agreed Statement on the Lima Document: Baptism, Eucharist, and Ministry. U.S. Theological Consultation, 1984" in *The Quest for Unity:* 71

49 "Faith, Sacraments, and the Unity of the Church" in *The Quest for Unity:* 93–104

50 *The Quest for Unity:* 166

51 See a paper report on why "the dialogue stalled" in *The Tablet.* February 14, 1998: 223–224

52   In 1989, Edward Idriss Cardinal Cassidy was appointed the
      third president of the PCPCU, following Augustin Cardinal
      Bea, the founding president, and his successor, Jan Cardinal
      Willebrands.

53   *Briefing:* June 19, 1997: 20

54   *Catholic International:* 9, September 1995: 413

Chapter 5

1   *Catechism of the Catholic Church.* Washington: United States
      Catholic Conference, 1994: nos. 811– 812

2   A handy approach to understanding the "degrees of being
      church" is by reflecting on the three "polities" of church organ-
      ization. The first is *episcopal polity*, which stresses the impor-
      tance of bishops in terms of church continuity and doctrinal
      and liturgical decisions. Episcopal churches include the
      Catholic, Orthodox, and Anglican Churches. The second is
      presbyterian polity, which means that government is in the
      hands of elders who may be ordained and who have oversight
      of the church. The third is *congregationalist polity*, which
      places great stress on the primacy and sufficiency of the local
      congregation. Baptists, Congregationalists, and Disciples of
      Christ follow this third form of government. See Bernard
      Leeming. *The Vatican Council and Christian Unity.* London:
      Darton, Longman and Todd, 1966: 38–42

3   Francis A Sullivan. *The Church We Believe In.* New York:
      Paulist, 1988: 59–61

4   Owen Chadwick. *The Reformation.* Middlesex: Penguin, 1964,
      1985. See Chapter 1 "The Cry for Reformation."

5   Eric G. Jay. *The Church.* Vol. 1. London: SPCK, 1977: 107

6   Jay: *The Church:* Vol. 1, 127–128

7   Jay: *The Church:* Vol. 1, 128–129

8   Jay: *The Church:* Vol. 1, 130–132

9   Jay: *The Church:* Vol. 1, 132–136

10   Jay: *The Church:* Vol. 1, 135–136

11   John A. Saliba. *Perspectives on New Religious Movements.* London: Geoffrey Chapman, 1995: 41–43

12   Timothy George. *Theology of the Reformers.* Nashville: Broadman Press, 1988: 37–38

13   George: *Theology of the Reformers:* 38

14   Jay: *The Church:* 125

15   "Ratzinger, The Ecumenical Prefect" in *30 Days:* February 1993: 69

16   "The Papacy in Discussion: Expectations and Perspectives for the Third Millennium." *Sant' Anselmo Forum.* December 1966: 10. Also in *One in Christ:* 4, 1997: 283–289

17   *The Tablet.* August 30, 1997: 1109

18   "Al Sinodo delle Chiese Valdesi e Metodiste d'Italia per la prima volta la voce di un Vescovo Cattolico" in *Radiogiornale.* Giovedi 28 agosto 1997

19   George: *Theology of the Reformers:* 31

20   Cited in George: *Theology of the Reformers:* 32

21   See Patrick Granfield. *The Limits of the Papacy.* London: Darton, Longman and Todd: 1987 where he lists the twenty-seven propositions of Gregory VII: 34–35

22   Granfield: *The Limits of the Papacy:* 35

23   "Unam Sanctam" in *The Christian Faith: Doctrinal Documents of the Catholic Church*. Fifth Revised Edition. J. Neuner and J. Dupuis eds. New York: Alba House, 1990: no. 875

24   Granfield: *The Limits of the Papacy:* 36

25   George: *Theology of the Reformers:* 33–34

26   Chadwick: *The Reformation:* 26–27

27   Peter C. Hodgson. *Revisioning the Church: Ecclesial Freedom in the New Paradigm*. Philadelphia: Fortress Press, 1988: 44

28   Chadwick: *The Reformation:* 45–46

29   Jay: *The Church:* Vol. 1, 162–163

30   Nominalism is a philosophical theory associated with William of Ockham. In reacting against scholastic metaphysics, the theory maintained that universal concepts, such as goodness and truth, are merely names and in no way match objective reality. Only individual things exist.

31   Jay: *The Church:* Vol. 1, 163–164

32   Jay: *The Church:* Vol. 1, 165–166

33   *Handbook Member Churches: World Council of Churches*. Hans J. van der Bent ed. Geneva: WCC, 1985:21

34   Figures from *Lutheran World Information*. 1: January 12, 1995

35   *Constitution of the Lutheran World Federation*, adopted by the LWF Eighth Assembly, Curitiba, Brazil: January–February 1990: III, J2

36   These are the words of Professor Harding Meyer who has, for many years, participated in the dialogue of the Joint International Lutheran–Catholic Commission. The words are

recorded in "The Lutheran/Catholic Dialogue" in *Information Service*. Vatican City: PCPCU: 91, 1996/I–II: 31.

37 See "The Lutheran/Catholic Dialogue" in *Information Service:* 30–36

38 As quoted in René Girault. *One Lord, One Faith, One Church: New Perspectives in Ecumenism*. Susan Leslie tr. Middlegreen: St. Pauls, 1993: 102

39 "Report of the Third Phase of Lutheran/Roman Catholic International Dialogue" in *Information Service*. Vatican City: PCPCU: 86, 1994/II–III: 159

40 Useful commentaries on the third phase, by Theodore Schneider and Heinz-Albert Raem, accompany the official report in PCPCU *Information Service*. 86: 1994/II–III:182–197

41 "Joint Declaration on the Doctrine of Justification" in *Origins*, 8: July 16, 1998: 120–127. In the same number can be found the statement at the June 25, 1998, press conference given by Cardinal Cassidy, and the official Catholic response to the Joint Declaration as prepared by the Congregation for the Doctrine of the Faith and PCPCU.

42 Reports on the meetings of the fourth phase will continue to be published in the *Information Service* of the PCPCU.

43 Chadwick: *The Reformation:* 78–79

44 Chadwick: *The Reformation:* 80

45 Alister E. McGrath. *Reformation Thought: An Introduction*. Oxford: Blackwell, 1988, 1993: 8–9

46 John Calvin. *Institutes of the Christian Religion*. Two volumes. John T. McNeill ed. Ford Lewis Battles tr. Philadelphia: The Westminster Press, 1960

47   Calvin. *Institutes:* IV.I.4: 1016

48   Chadwick: *The Reformation:* 88–92

49   Calvin: *Institutes:* IV.19.28: 1476

50   McGrath: *Reformation Thought:* 123–131

51   *Handbook Member Churches. WCC:* 24–25

52   PCPCU *Information Service.* 91: 1996/I–II: 35

53   McGrath: 6. He explains that the term *magisterial Reformation* "draws attention to the manner in which the mainstream reformers related to secular authorities, such as princes, magistrates, or city councils. Whereas the *radical reformers* regarded such authorities as having no rights within the church, the mainstream reformers argued that the church was, at least to some extent, subject to the secular agencies of government."

54   McGrath: *Reformation Thought:* 10

55   *Integrierte Gemeinde* began in Munich after the Second World War, when a group of Catholics expressed concern at the apparent ineffectiveness of the church during the war years. Hence, they began a modest attempt at a living answer by establishing a form of community life aimed at a re-creation or renewal of Christianity.

56   "Steps toward Reconciliation" in *The Plough.* Summer 1995, 45: 23

57   *Handbook Member Churches. WCC:* 21–22. See also Mennonite World Handbook. Diether Götz Lichdi ed. Carol Stream, Illinois: MWC, 1990

58   PCPCU *Information Service.* 94, 1997/1:37

59   Message in the *1997–98 Program of "Catholic and Anabaptists in Conversation about Spirituality,"* Elizabethtown College, Penn.

For an extended discussion on Mennonite–Catholic dialogues, See Ivan J. Kauffman in *One in Christ,* 3: 1998: 220–246

60   *Handbook Member Churches. WCC:* 18–19

61   Walter B. Shurden. *The Baptist Identity: Four Fragile Freedoms.* See especially Appendix I: "Towards a Baptist Identity," and Appendix II: "Baptist Distinctives and Diversities." Macon: Smyth and Helwys Publishing, 1993

62   "The Baptists of the future" in *The Tablet.* May 12, 1990: 600

63   "An Agreed Statement from the Southern Baptist–Roman Catholic Scholars' Conversations" in *Origins,* 10: July 20, 1989: 166–168

64   PCPCU *Information Service.* 78, 1991/III–IV: 164–166

65   PCPCU *Information Service.* 91, 1996/I–II: 37–39

66   PCPCU *Information Service.* 91: 39

67   *Handbook Member Churches. WCC:* 19–20

68   PCPCU *Information Service.* 49, 1982/II–III: 65–73

69   PCPCU *Information Service.* 84, 1993/III–IV: 162–169

70   PCPCU *Information Service.* 91, 1996/I–II: 41–42

71   McGrath: *Reformation Thought:* 11

72   Chadwick: *The Reformation:* 22

73   Jay: *The Church:* Vol. 1, 195–202

74   Jay: *The Church:* Vol. 1, 196

75   Robert Bellarmine. "De controversiis fidei" in *Opera omnia,* 12 vols. Justinus Fevre. Paris: L. Vivès, 1870–1874: IV. iii, 2

76   Jay: *The Church:* Vol. 1, 202–204

Chapter 6

1   Paul A. Crow, Jr. "Reflections on Models of Christian Unity" in *Living Today Towards Visible Unity.* Thomas F. Best ed. Geneva: WCC, 1988: 21–25

2   Jude D. Weisenbeck. *Conciliar Fellowship and the Unity of the Church.* Rome: Universitas A.S. Thoma Aq. in Urbe, 1986: 67–71

3   Hervé Legrand. "Uniatism and Catholic-Orthodox dialogue" in *Theology Digest,* 42: February 1995: 131

4   Yves Congar. *Diversity and Communion.* John Bowden tr. London: SCM, 1984: 152

5   Crow: 32; Weisenbeck: 101–103

6   Emmanuel Lanne. "Pluralism and Unity. The Possibility of a Variety of Typologies Within the Same Ecclesial Allegiance" in *One in Christ:* 2, 1970: 430–451

7   Jan Cardinal Willebrands. "Cardinal Willebrand's Address in Cambridge. January 18, 1970" in *Called to Full Unity: Documents on Anglican–Roman Catholic Relations 1966–1983.* Joseph W. Witmer and J. Robert Wright eds. Washington: United States Catholic Conference, 1986: 51

8   Willebrands: 51

9   *Towards Koinonia in Faith, Life and Witness.* Fifth World Conference on Faith and Order. Santiago de Compostela 1993. Geneva: WCC, F&O Paper 161

10   Congar: *Diversity and Communion.* 126–133

11   G. H. Tavard. " 'Hierarchia Veritatum': A Preliminary Investigation" in *Theological Studies,* 32, 1971: 278

12 To this end, the Joint Working Group commissioned and received an ecumenical study of "The Notion of Hierarchy of Truths—An Ecumenical Interpretation," a copy of which can be found in *Deepening Communion: International Ecumenical Documents with Roman Catholic Participation*. William G. Rusch and Jeffrey Gros eds. Washington: United States Catholic Conference, 1998: 561–570

13 Owen Chadwick. *The Reformation*. Middlesex: Penguin, 1964, 1985: 97–99

14 The two sets of words from the prayer books are quoted in Chadwick: 121

15 Ernest C. Messenger. *The Reformation, The Mass and the Priesthood*. London: Longmans, Green and Co., 1936. Vol. I: "The Revolt From the Mediaeval Church": 530–531. The "Black Rubric" was added to the prayer book of 1552 at the last moment, was removed in 1559, and after a slight revision was restored in 1662.

16 Congar: *Diversity and Communion*. 115

17 Paul Avis. "Keeping Faith with Anglicanism" in *The Future of Anglicanism*. Robert Hannaford ed. Leominster: Gracewing, 1996: 8–10. Avis offers a brief treatment of Anglican confessional identity based on the 1930 Lambeth Conference definition of the Anglican Communion.

18 Jean Tillard. "The Lesson for Ecumenism of Lambeth 1988" in *The Ecumenical Society of the Blessed Virgin Mary,* January 1998: 10–11

19 Information from *The Anglican Communion*. London: The Anglican Communion Secretariat. The number of self-governing churches is likely to increase in the next few years.

20 *Handbook Member Churches: World Council of Churches:* Ans J. van der Bent ed. Geneva: WCC, 1985: 17–18

21   See Gillian R. Evans. "The Problem of Authority" in *The Future of Anglicanism*

22   *Called to Full Unity: Documents on Anglican–Roman Catholic Relations 1966–1983.* Joseph W. Witmer and J. Robert Wright eds. United States Catholic Conference, Washington, 1986: 3–4

23   "The Malta Report" in *Called to Full Unity:* 4

24   Preface to The Final Report in *Called to Full Unity:* 229

25   ibid: 232

26   *Common Witness To the Gospel: Documents on Anglican–Roman Catholic Relations 1983–1995.* Jeffrey Gros, E. Rozanne Elder, Ellen K. Wondra eds. United States Catholic Conference, Washington, 1997: 66

27   *Common Witness:* 69

28   *Common Witness:* 121

29   Margaret Hebblethwaite. "Laity at the head of the Anglican table?" in *The Tablet*, March 26, 1994: 382–384

30   "Salvation and the Church" in *Common Witness:* 30–42

31   "Life in Christ: Morals, Communion, and the Church" in *Common Witness:* 186

32   See *Called to Full Unity* for an explanation of a "Covenant Relationship": 95–97. Among other things it says that "A 'Covenant Relationship' is an agreement between two communities—e.g., a Roman Catholic parish and a parish or congregation of a non-Roman Catholic church—in which the members of these communities commit themselves to pray for each other, and together; to cooperate in whatever ways they determine are mutually desirable; and to come to know and to support one another in the LORD."

33   Bernard Barlow. *A Brother Knocking at the Door: The Malines Conversations 1921–1925*. Norwich: The Canterbury Press, 1996

34   See Henry D. Rack. *Reasonably Enthusiast: John Wesley and the Rise of Methodism*. London: Epworth, 1989 for a lengthy study of a man whose life "had been full of controversy": xi

35   Maldwyn Edwards. "John Wesley" in *A History of the Methodist Church in Great Britain*. Vol I. Rupert Davies and Gordon Rupp eds. London: Epworth Press, 1965: 44

36   John Wesley. *Journal*, May 24, 1738 as recorded by Edwards: 50

37   James Haskins. *The Methodists*. New York: Hippocrene Books, 1992: 71

38   *Handbook Member Churches. WCC:* 22–23

39   Rupert Davies. "The People Called Methodists. 1. 'Our Doctrines'" in *A History of the Methodist Church*. ibid: 166

40   David Carter. "Catholics, Methodists and Reception" in *One in Christ:* 3, 1992: 242–243

41   George H. Tavard. "The Dialogue Between Methodists and Catholics" in *One in Christ:* 2, 1994: 176

42   "Holiness: an important factor in ecumenism" in *OR:* April 1, 1992: 3

43   David Carter. "A Methodist Reaction to *Ut Unum Sint*" in *One in Christ:* 2, 1997: 125–137

44   Clifford W. Kew. *The Salvation Army*. Exeter: The Religious Education Press, 1977: 32

45   Bernard Leeming. *The Vatican Council and Christian Unity*. London: Darton, Longman and Todd, 1966: 84

46   William Booth. *In Darkest England* and *The Way Out.* London: International Headquarters of the Salvation Army: 1890

47   William Booth. *Orders and Regulations for the Salvation Army.* London: International Headquarters of the Salvation Army: 1878

48   Kew: *The Salvation Army.* Exeter. 30–31

49   E. H. McKinley. *Marching to Glory. The History of the Salvation Army in the United States, 1880–1992.* Second Edition. Grand Rapids: William B Eerdmans, 1995: 297–298. See also p 30

50   McKinley. *Marching to Glory:* 102

51   A contemporary statement on the Salvation Army is found in a one-hundred-page book titled *Marching On! The Salvation Army. Its origin and development.* First published in 1927, it has been revised in successive editions, the latest being in 1990 by Malcom Bale. London: International Headquarters of The Salvation Army: 1990

52   Thomas F. Stransky. "A Look at Evangelical Protestantism" in *Theology, News and Notes:* 35, March 1988: 24

53   Thomas F. Stransky. "A Catholic looks at evangelical Protestants" in *Priests and People*, January 1998: 3–8

54   Thomas P Rausch. "Catholic-Evangelical Relations: Signs of Progress" in *One in Christ:* 1, 1996: 46

55   Stransky: "A Catholic looks at evangelical Protestants": 6

56   Rausch. "Catholic-Evangelical Relations: Signs of Progress": 40

57   Paul VI. *Evangelii Nuntiandi.* London: Catholic Truth Society, 1975: 29

58   "Relationships with Evangelicals" in *Information Service:* PCPCU, 91, 1996/I–II: 45

59   PCPCU *Information Service*. 96, 1997/IV: 137–138

60   *Evangelicals and Catholics Together: Working Towards a Common Mission*. Charles Colson and Richard Neuhaus eds. London: Hodder and Stoughton, 1996

61   Paul D. Lee. *Pneumatological Ecclesiology in the Roman Catholic–Pentecostal Dialogue*. Romae: Dissertatio ad Lauream in Facultate S. Theologiae Apud Pontificiam Universitatem S. Thomae in Urbe, 1994: 18–19

62   *Toward a New Pentecost for a New Evangelization: Malines Document I*. Kilian McDonnell ed. Collegeville: The Liturgical Press, 1993: 1

63   Kilian McDonnell. "Improbably Conversations: The Classical Pentecostal–Roman Catholic International Dialogue" in *One in Christ*: 1, 1995: 21–22

64   "The Pentecostal–Roman Catholic Dialogue" in *Information Service:* PCPCU, 91, 1996/I–II: 42–44

65   *Evangelization, Proselytism and Common Witness*. The Report from the Fourth Phase of the International Dialogue 1990–1997 Between the Roman Catholic Church and Some Classical Pentecostal Churches and Leaders. PCPCU *Information Service:* 97, 1998/I–II: 38–56

66   *Old Catholics and Anglicans 1931–1981*. Gordon Huelin ed. Oxford: OUP, 1983

67   John Gibraltar. "Foreword" in *Old Catholics and Anglicans 1931–1981:* vi

68   *Journeying Together in Christ: The Report of the Polish National Catholic–Roman Catholic Dialogue*. Stanislaus J. Brzana and Anthony M. Rysz eds. Washington: Bishops' Committee for Ecumenical and Irreligious Affairs, 1990

69   *Handbook Member Churches. WCC:* 23

70 *Old Catholics and Anglicans:* 157–161. This passage offers a good summary of relations between Old Catholics and Roman Catholics, most especially on aspects of the improving relations between the two.

71 Morris West. "Lund Principle" in *Dictionary of the Ecumenical Movement.* Nicholas Lossky et al. eds. Geneva: WCC Publications, 1991: 633–634

Chapter 7

1 Thomas F. Best. "Introduction: United Churches and the Ecumenical Movement" in *Called to be One: United Churches and the Ecumenical Movement.* Michael Kinnamon and Thomas F. Best eds. Geneva: WCC, F&O paper 127. Geneva: 1985: vii–xi

2 *Built Together: The Present Vocation of United and Uniting Churches.* Thomas F. Best ed. Geneva: WCC, F&O paper 174. Geneva: 1996: 174

3 Gerald F. Moede. "Consultation on Church Union" in *Dictionary of the Ecumenical Movement.* Nicholas F Lossky et al. eds.

4 *Conversations Between the British and Irish Anglican Churches and the Nordic and Baltic Lutheran Churches: The Porvoo Common Statement.* London: The Council for Christian Unity of the General Synod of the Church of England. Occasional Paper No 3: 1993

5 Edward Yarnold. "Flawed route to unity" in *The Tablet:* November 30, 1996: 1598

6 Walter Kasper. "Apostolic Succession in Episcopacy in an Ecumenical Context" in *The Bicentennial Lecture.* Rudi Ruckmann ed. Baltimore: St Mary's Seminary and University, 1991: 1

7 Colin Davey. "Recent Ecumenical Developments" in *One in Christ:* 3, 1997: 267

8   Davey. "Recent Ecumenical Developments": 270

9   H. Fries and K. Rahner. *Unity of the Churches: An Actual Possibility.* New York: Paulist: 1985: 7–10

10 Cardinal Joseph Ratzinger. *Church, Ecumenism and Politics.* New York, Crossroads, 1988: 135

11 Avery Dulles. "Paths to Doctrinal Agreement: Ten Theses" in *Theological Studies:* January 1986: 46

12 John Hotchkin. "The Ecumenical Movement's Third Stage" in *Origins:* 21, 1995: 354–361

13 Peter J. Cullinane. *One Lord, Faith, Baptism. Praying and Working for Christian Unity.* Palmerston North: Chancery Office, 1989: 42–43

14 Yarnold: "Flawed route to unity": 1598

15 A great deal of discussion is now happening on the matter of apostolic succession. One contribution, among the many, is entitled *Apostolicity and Succession.* House of Bishops Occasional Paper. London: General Synod of the Church of England: 1994

16 Edward Yarnold. "*Apostolicae Curae:* past and future processes" in *The Month:* November 1996: 430–434

17 So much is being written on this subject, and so much more thought has to go into the broader subject of "ministry" and the place of women in it. One contribution of a few years back on the matter of ordination of women was offered by Kenneth Untener: "Forum: The Ordination of Women: Can the Horizons Widen?" in *Worship:* January 1991: 50–59. An important contribution to this study is Hervé Legrand's "Traditio perpetuo servata? The Non-ordination of Women: Tradition or Simply an Historical Fact?" *Worship,* 65, 1991: 482–508

18   *UUS:* 96. Some responses to John Paul II's invitation include: *May They All Be One*: A Response of the House of Bishops of the Church of England to *Ut Unum Sint*. House of Bishops Occasional Paper. London: General Synod of the Church of England: 1997. Many other churches have made contributions. See for example, the international symposium held in Rome on the occasion of the 100th anniversary of the foundation of the Society of the Atonement. *The Petrine Ministry and the Unity of the Church.* James F. Puglisi ed. Collegeville: Liturgical Press, 1999. The CDF sponsored a similar symposium but among Catholic theologians. See *Il Primato del Successore di Pietro. Atti del simposio teologico, Roma dicembre 1996.* Vatican City: Libreria Editrice Vaticano, 1998

19   Thomas P. Rausch. "The Third Stage of the Ecumenical Movement: Is the Catholic Church Ready?" in *Ecumenical Trends:* October 1997: 145–151

20   "Constitution of the World Council of Churches" in *Handbook Member Churches: World Council of Churches.* Ans J. van der Bent ed. Geneva: WCC, 1985: 269

21   *We Remember: A Reflection on the Shoah.* Vatican City: Libreria Editrice Vaticana: 1998

22   A very useful reference text on this subject is *Inter-religious Dialogue: The Official Teaching of the Catholic Church (1963–1995).* Francesco Gioia ed. Boston: Pauline Books and Media. English edition: 1997

23   See *Christianity and the World Religions* of the International Theological Commission. Vatican City: Libreria Editrice Vaticana, 1997

24   See Jacques Dupuis. *Toward a Christian Theology of Religious Pluralism.* New York: Orbis Books, 1997

25   Francis Cardinal Arinze. *Meeting Other Believers.* Leominster: Gracewing, 1997: 8–9

26   *Origins:* 10, 1997

27   *DH:* no. 2

28   *NA:* no. 2

29   Pontifical Commission *Justitia et Pax*, Assisi. World Day of
     Prayer for Peace. Vatican City: Polygot Press, 1987

30   Bulletin 77: Vatican City, 1991

31   "We will seek to be peacemakers in thought and deed!" in *OR:*
     November 3, 1986: 3

32   Raimundo Panikkar. *The Intra-Religious Dialogue.* New York:
     Paulist, 1978: 19. (Nowadays he spells his first name
     "Raimon.")

33   *Vision of the Other: Jewish and Christian Theologians Assess the
     Dialogue.* Eugene J. Fisher. ed. New York: Paulist, 1994. See
     also Johannes Cardinal Willebrands. *Church and Jewish People.*
     New Considerations. New York: Paulist, 1992

34   Nevertheless, there are Christian voices that recognize prob-
     lems in Islamic-Christian relations that arise not solely from
     fundamentalist groups. Bishop Joseph Coutts of Hyderabad,
     Pakistan, says that "Islam cannot and should not be put in the
     same category as Hinduism, Buddhism, Shintoism, etc. Islam is
     very different. It is a force, a religio-political force with expan-
     sionist tendencies that have special consequences for the
     Church in Asia…While continuing to dialogue with Islam with
     Christian love and understanding, we should not fail to speak
     out and condemn the rising tide of intolerant, militant and
     oppressive Islam that is making many Asian Churches suffer."
     OR: May 20, 1998: 11

35   *The Gethsemani Encounter: A Dialogue on the Spiritual Life by
     Buddhist and Christian Monastics.* Donald W. Mitchell and James
     A. Wiseman, eds. New York: Continuum, 1998

36   Francis Cardinal Arinze. "Together in hope" in *Briefing*, 5, May 21, 1998: 37

37   As reported in *The Tablet:* October 10, 1998: 1336

38   "Look at it our way: Asian bishops respond to Rome" in *The Tablet:* May 2, 1998: 571

Index

Ad Gentes, 48
Albigensians, 104–105
Alexander III, 105, 107
Alexandria, 6, 80
Amish, 130–131
Amman, Jacob, 130
Anabaptists, 127 ff
Anglican Communion, 10, 33,
    154–155
    Anglican-RC dialogue, (ARCIC
      I & II), 148, 156–160
Anno Ineunte, 74, 75
Antioch, 6, 62, 80, 89
Apostolic succession, 84, 93,
    96, 101, 116, 175–176, 180,
    183, 186
Apostolicam Actuositatem, 16
Arius/Arianism, 65–66
Arinze, Cardinal Francis, 195–196
Arminius, Jacobus/Arminianism,
    132, 160, 163
Assyrian Church of the East,
    67–68
    Assyrian Church-RC dialogue,
      68–69
Athanasius of Alexandria, 4, 66
Athenagoras I, Patriarch, 74, 83,
    94–95
Augsburg Confession, 113, 139
Augustine of Canterbury, 10
Augustine of Hippo, 4, 20,
    112, 121
Autocephalous churches, 79,
    90, 210

Balamand Statement, 88–89, 93

Baptism, Eucharist, Ministry
    (BEM), 96, 190
Baptists, 115, 132–134
    Baptist-RC dialogue, 132 ff
Bartholomew I, Patriarch, 81, 98
Basil of Caesarea, 4, 61
Bea, Cardinal Augustin, 35–36,
    50, 94
Beauduin, Lambert, 34–35
Bede, Venerable, 10
Believer's Baptism, 126, 129, 132
Bellarmine, Robert, 13, 17, 22,
    46, 139–140
Benedict VIII, 81
Benedict XV, 33
Bernard of Clairvaux, 102
Biblical Movement, 40–41
Black Rubric, 151–152
Boleyn, Anne, 149
Boniface VIII, 12, 21, 103, 108
Book of Common Prayer,
    150–151, 153
Booth, William, 167–169
Borromeo, Charles, 139
Brown, Raymond, 3, 40
Bruderhof, 128
Bucer, Martin, 119–120, 150
Buddhism, 50, 195–196
Byzantine Rite, 7, 200

Calvin, Jean, 110, 119, 120–123
Calvinism, (see Reformed
    Churches)
Campbell, Thomas and
    Alexander, 135, 137

Cassidy, Cardinal Edward, 97, 129, 158, 214
Cathari, (see Albigensians)
Catherine of Aragon, 149
Catholic Action, 16
Cerularius, Patriarch Michael, 83
Chalcedon, Council of, 7, 69–71
Chaldean Churches, 54
Charismatic movement, 44
Charlemagne, 80–81
Chenu, Marie-Dominique, 37
Christian Church, 135–136
    Christian Church-RC
      dialogue, 136–137
Chrysostom, John, 20
Church of the elect, 103
Clement of Rome, 4, 12, 62
Clement VI, 108
Clement VII, 149
College of bishops, 14–15
Communio, (see *Koinonia*)
Communion of churches, 4
Conciliarism, 108–109
Conciliar Fellowship, 145
Congar, Yves, 10, 15, 16–17, 37–38, 74–75, 82, 144
Constans II, 78
Constantine, 5, 7, 8, 65–66
Constance, Council of, 104, 109
Constantinople, 6, 7, 8, 81, 83, 90
    Council of, 66, 82
    Encyclical of, 91
Consultation on Church Union (COCU), 182
Couturier, Paul-Iréné, 1, 199
Covenanted Churches in Wales, 183
Coverdale, Miles, 150
Cranmer, Thomas, 149–151
Cromwell, Thomas, 149

Crusades, 83–84
Culture, Catholic, 24–28
Curialism, 108
Cyprian of Carthage, 20, 22, 64
Cyril of Alexandria, 67, 70

Damasus I, 12
Danielou, Jean, 41
Dante Alighieri, 103
de Chardin, Teilhard, 27–28, 37
De Ecclesia, 75–76
de Lubac, Henri, 37, 41
Dei Verbum, 45, 188
Dialogues, 55–57
    Bilateral, 56–57
    Multilateral, 56
    of charity, 93–94
    of doctrine, 95–97
Dictatus papae, 12, 108
Dignitatis Humanae, 48, 188
Dimitrios I, Patriarch, 95
Dinkha IV, Mar, 68–69
Diocletian, Emperor, 8, 79
Dionysius of Alexandria, 61–62
Directories on Ecumenism, 2, 54, 58, 177, 189
Disciples of Christ, (see Christian Church)
Divino Afflante Spiritu, 45
Doctrine of the Faith, Congregation of (CDF), 159
Donatists, 4, 20
Dulles, Avery, 46, 184–185

Eastern Catholic Churches, 86–89
Eastern Orthodox Church, (see Orthodox Church)
Ecclesia Catholica, 49
Ecumenical Movement, 1, 26, 43–44, 53–54, 100 ff, 185

Edward VI, 150
Elizabeth I, 151–152
England, Church of, 149
Ephesus, Council of, 66–67
Episcopacy, 14–15
Episcopal Church, (see Anglican
    Communion)
Episcopal visitors, 155
Erasmus, Desiderius, 110
Eucharist
    Increasing consensus, 116,
        157
    Inter-communion, 116, 148
    Liturgy, 34, 41
    Problems, 66, 120, 129, 131,
        136, 150, 152, 158, 174
    Shared belief with RC Church,
        95, 97, 101, 176, 180
Eugene IV, 85
Eugenius IV, 109
Eusebius, 62
Eutyches, 69-70
Evangelicals, 169–171
    Evangelical-RC dialogue,
        171–173
Evangelii Nuntiandii, 171–172
Execrabilis, 109

Faith and Order (F&O), 26, 43,
    56, 58, 146, 187, 189–190
Filioque, 67, 81–82, 84–85
Florence, Council of, 21–22, 78,
    85–86, 109
Fox, George, 131
Frequens, 109
Friends, Society of, 131–132, 167

Garrigou-Lagrange, Reginald, 27
Gaudium et Spes, 39, 47–48
Gelasius I, 108

Giles of Rome, 17
Glossolalia, 173
Gnosticism, 63–64
Great Schism, 109
Grebel, Conrad, 126
Gregory I, 10, 12
Gregory VII, 12, 14, 108
Gregory X, 84
Group de Dombes, 199
Guardini, Romano, 37

Halifax, Lord, 34, 160
Heidelberg Catechism, 121
Henry VIII, 149
Hertling, Ludwig, 60
Hierarchy of Truths, 146–148
Hincmar of Rheims, 14
Hinduism, 50, 196
Hooker, Richard, 152–153
Humani Generis, 75
Humbert, Cardinal, 83
Hus, John, 106–107
Hutter, Jakob, 127
Hutterites, 127–129

Ignatius of Antioch, 19
Imitation of Christ, 26–27
Imperfect communion, 100 ff
Indulgences, 111
Innocent I, 12
Innocent III, 21, 83, 104, 108
Inscrutabili Dei Consilio, 24
Integrietre Gemeinde, 128
Interreligious Dialogue, 190 ff
Invisible Church, 103–105, 112,
    121
Irenaeus, St, 63
Irénikon, 35
Islam, 50, 80–81, 86,
    194–195, 229

James of Viterbo, 17
Jerome, St, 4, 65
Jerusalem, 6, 80
Jewel, John, 152
Jews, 189, 194
John of Paris, 103
John XXIII, 49, 52, 156
John Paul II, 2, 9, 42, 47–48, 67–68,
    82, 95–97, 107, 192–193
Johnston, William, 55
Joint Working Group (JWG), 189
Justification, 112, 118

à Kempis, Thomas, 26–27
Knox, John, 123
Koinonia, 15, 58 ff, 79, 90, 96,
    145–146, 157, 174, 180, 186, 207
Komonchak, Joseph, 24
Küppers, Werner, 61

Laetentur coeli, 78, 85
Laity, 15–16
    Lay Movement, 42
Lambeth Conference, 154, 157
Lateran Council, third, 105
Lateran Council, fourth, 21
League of Churches, 92
Leo I, 12
Leo III, 12, 80
Leo IX, 83
Leo X, 110
Leo XIII, 24–25
Letters of communion, 4
Leuenberg Concord, 123
Liberalism, 24–25, 43
Life and Works, 43
Lima Document (see Baptism,
    Eucharist, Ministry: BEM)
Liturgical Movement, 34, 41

Local Church, 3, 5, 9, 60 ff, 79–80
Lumen Gentium: 45–47, 53,
    76–77, 140
Lund Principle, 176–177
Luther, Martin, 103, 104, 110,
    111 ff, 116, 119
Lutheranism, 114–115, 150,
    Lutheran-RC dialogue, 115–119
Lyons, Council of, 84–85

Malines Conversation, 34, 160
Manichaean dualism, 104
Marian dogmas, 147–148
Marks of the Church, 99
Martin I, 78–79
Martin V, 109
Mary Stuart, 152
Mary Tudor, 151
Mediator Dei, 41
Melanchthon, Philip, 111, 113,
    120
Menno Simons, 129
Mennonites, 115, 129–130
    Mennonite-RC dialogue, 130
Mercier, Dèsirè, 33–34, 160
Merton, Thomas, 28
Methodists, 107, 160–164
    Methodist-RC dialogue,
    164–166
Metropolitans, 6
Miller, William, 135
Ministry, 186
Models of Church, 8–9, 143–146
Monophysitism, 69–71
Montanism, 63
Mortalium Animos, 25–26, 35, 49
Murray, John Courtney, 38
Mystici Corporis Christi, 22, 46,
    75, 103–104, 140

Neoconservatism, 186
Nestorius/Nestorianism, 66–67
Newman, John Henry, 36–37
Nicaea, Council of 6, 14, 65–67
Nicholas I, 82
Nominalism, 112
Non abbiamo bisogno, 16
Non-Chalcedonian Churches
    (see Oriental Orthodox
    Churches)
Nostra Aetate, 36, 45, 50, 54,
    188, 191
Nouwen, Henri, 130
Novationists, 20

Old Catholics, 175–176
Oriental Orthodox Churches,
    70–71
Orientale Lumen, 2, 54
Orientalium Ecclesiarum, 54, 87
Origen, 20
Orthodox Church, 2, 101, 180
    Orthodox-RC dialogue, 88,
    91–97
Oxford Movement, 155

Pacem in Terris, 52
Pan-Orthodox Conferences, 92, 93
Parham, Charles, 44
Parker, Michael, 152–153
Patriarchs/Patriarchates, 6, 7, 8,
    9, 11, 90, 94
Patristic
    movement, 41–42
    period, 4
Paul VI, 47, 51, 70–71, 74, 83,
    94–95, 156, 172, 189
Paul of Samosata, 62–63
Pelagians, 20–21
Penn, William, 132

Pentarchy, 7
Pentecostals, 44, 173–174
    Pentecostal-RC dialogue,
    174–175
Photius, Patriarch, 82
Pian popes, 13
Pietism, 43
Pius II, 109
Pius V, 152
Pius IX, 25
Pius X, 24
Pius XI, 16, 24–26, 35
Pius XII, 22–24, 41, 45, 75, 140
Polycarp, St, 64
Pontifical Biblical Commission
    (PBC), 4
Pontifical Council for Christian
    Unity (PCPCU), 2, 81,
    105–106, 115, 130, 158, 172,
    174, 188–189, 206
Pontifical Council for
    Interreligious Dialogue
    (PCID), 50, 193 ff
Portal, Fernand, 34, 160
Porvoo Common Statement,
    182–183
Preparatory Theological
    Commission, 76, 77
Presbyterianism (see Reformed)
Primacy, papal, 7, 12–17, 186
Proselytism, 35, 88, 134, 171, 175

Quakers (see Friends, Society of)

Rahner, Karl, 18, 38–39, 184
Ramsey, Archbishop Michael, 156
Ratzinger, Cardinal Joseph, 8, 9,
    11, 106, 128, 184
Reception, 4–5
Reconciled Diversity, 144

Redemptoris Missio, 44
Reformation,
    Catholic, 138 ff
    Churches, 9, 10
    Magisterial, 111 ff, 119 ff, 126,
        217
    Protestant, 13, 86, 101 ff
    Radical, 125 ff, 218
Reformed Churches, 105, 119–
    124, 150, 160, 180
    Reformed-RC dialogue,
        124–126
Ricca, Paolo, 106–107
Rites, 6–7, 87, 200
Roberson, Ronald G, 71, 86
Rome, bishop of, 8, 9
Royal Supremacy, 149, 152

Sacrosancta, 109
Sacrosanctum Concilium, 41
Sagheddu, Blessed Maria
    Gabriella, 32–33
Salvation, 19–23, 111–112,
    122–123, 158–159
Salvation Army, 167–169
Santa Sophia, 83
Schleitheim Confession, 127
Schwenckfeld, Caspar, 131
Secretariat for Promoting
    Christian Unity (SPCU), 36,
    49, 54
Seventh-Day Adventists, 115, 135
Seymour, William, 44
Reconciled Diversity, 144
Siricius I, 12
Sister Churches, 74–75, 94–95,
    101, 180
Sixtus V, 13
Shenouda III, Coptic pope, 71
Smyth, John, 132

Social Creed, 164
Sola fide, 112
Sola gratia, 112
Sola scriptura, 112, 127
Sources Chretiennes, 41
South India, Church of, 181
Spiritual ecumenism, 1, 32–33
Spiritual Franciscans, 105
Stephen I, 12, 61
Stone, Burton W, 135
Suenens, Cardinal Leon-Joseph,
    39–40, 44, 47
Swiss Brethren, 127
Syllabus of Errors, 25
Symbols, 74–75

Tabbernee, William, 137
Tavard, George, 26
Tertullian, 63
Tetzel, Johann, 111
Theotokos, 66
Thirty-Nine Articles, 152–153
Tillard, Jean-Marie, 137, 153
Trent, Council of, 13, 17, 18,
    138–139
Troika, 153
Typoi, 10–11, 145–146, 179–180

Ubi Arcano Dei, 16
Unam Sanctam, 12, 21, 108
Uniatism, 86–89
    Uniate Church model, 144
Unitatis Redintegratio, 32, 48–50,
    76–77, 91, 97, 100–102, 115,
    146, 167, 188
United and Uniting Churches,
    181–182
Unity in diversity, 3–5, 7, 57–72
Utrecht, Declaration of, 176

Ut Unum Sint, 2, 32, 54, 95, 106, 160
Vatican I, 17, 18–19
Verona, Council of, 105
Via Media, 153
Victor I, 12
Volunteers of America, 169

Waldensians, 105–107
Waldo, Peter, 105
Wattson, Paul, 1, 199
Week of Prayer for Christian Unity, 1
Wesley, John and Charles, 160 ff
White, James and Ellen, 135
White, Mother Lurana, 199
Willebrands, Cardinal Jan, 10, 11, 36, 95, 145
William of Ockham, 103
Wittenburg, 111,
Wolsey, Thomas, 149,
Women, ministry of, 160, 186, 227
Worker-priest movement, 42–43
World Council of Churches (WCC), 49, 146, 187–189
World Missionary Conference, 43
Worms, Diet of, 112
Wyclif, John, 103–105

Yacob III, Patriarch, 70–71

Zizioulas, Metropolitan John, 81–82
Zwingli, Huldreich, 110, 119–120, 126–127

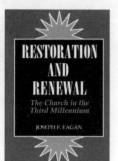